JOHN MACMURRAY

PETER LANG
New York • Washington, D.C./Baltimore • Bern
Frankfurt am Main • Berlin • Brussels • Vienna • Oxford

JOHN MACMURRAY
CRITICAL PERSPECTIVES

EDITED BY
DAVID FERGUSSON
AND NIGEL DOWER

PETER LANG
New York • Washington, D.C./Baltimore • Bern
Frankfurt am Main • Berlin • Brussels • Vienna • Oxford

Library of Congress Cataloging-in-Publication Data

John Macmurray: critical perspectives /
edited by David Fergusson and Nigel Dower.
p. cm.
Includes bibliographical references and index.
1. Macmurray, John, 1891–1976. I. Fergusson, David. II. Dower, Nigel.
B1647.M134 J64   192—dc21   00-049762
ISBN 0-8204-5264-5

Die Deutsche Bibliothek-CIP-Einheitsaufnahme

John Macmurray: critical perspectives /
ed. by David Fergusson and Nigel Dower.
–New York; Washington, D.C./Baltimore; Bern;
Frankfurt am Main; Berlin; Brussels; Vienna; Oxford: Lang.
ISBN 0-8204-5264-5

The paper in this book meets the guidelines for permanence and durability
of the Committee on Production Guidelines for Book Longevity
of the Council of Library Resources.

Printed in the United States of America

TABLE OF CONTENTS

PREFACE

John Macmurray (1891–1976) held chairs of philosophy in London and Edinburgh. Although largely outwith the fashions of professional British philosophy, his work received wide public recognition through his radio broadcasts of the 1930s, his numerous writings and the successive generations of students whose life and thought he influenced. Since his death, Macmurray's work has continued to receive critical attention both in North America and the UK. His key works have been re-issued by Faber, while he has returned to public prominence through Prime Minister Tony Blair's acknowledgement of his indebtedness to Macmurray's writings while a student in Oxford.

A multi-disciplinary conference on Macmurray's life and work was held at the University of Aberdeen in April, 1998 to gather together scholars from a range of fields, including philosophy, politics, psychology, education and theology. The present collection of essays contains an edited selection of the proceedings. Together these provide the most sustained scholarly reflection yet available on Macmurray's significance.

The editors wish to thank the conference speakers and participants, including many from overseas, who made the event so worthwhile and especially Esther McIntosh for her assistance with its organisation. We are also grateful to the Faculty of Arts and Divinity Research Committee at the University of Aberdeen, and the Scots Philosophical Club for their generous financial support of the project, and to Bronwen Currie at New College, University of Edinburgh, for her computing assistance.

David Fergusson and Nigel Dower

CHAPTER ONE

The Life and Thought of John Macmurray

Jack Costello SJ

I would like to offer two markers to track my course through this presentation.[1] First, I will make some linkages between Macmurray's life and thought but the main thrust of the essay is to present the life. In taking this tack, I hope to stimulate emotional knowledge of John Macmurray as much as intellectual understanding of his context and thought. Second, my essay will avoid intellectual analysis almost entirely. It will however, indulge in some interpretations. Analysis and deeper interpretation will emerge in subsequent essays in this volume.

Youth: Uniting Mind and Heart and Personal Mission

John Macmurray was born in Maxwelton in 1891, moved to Campelltown on Kintyre when he was five and then came to Aberdeen around the age of ten. Since the family lived in there for almost nine years, the city of Aberdeen has claims to being considered his hometown. I have chosen to step onto John Macmurray's life-path in its late Aberdeen period, but already, at that time, as we know from the Swarthmore Lecture[2] it is a life shaped by significant influences of which his father's traditional Scottish reverence for learning, referred to earlier, was only one. Religion defined the home life of the Macmurray family which was quickly moving by the years in Aberdeen to its full complement of five children. Both parents, James Macmurray and Mary Anna Grierson, had a deep Presbyterian faith expressed in family prayer and bible reading each day at home, and a stern, but not untypical, code for sabbath observance, including a ban on all play and laughter for the children. But, as Macmurray himself notes, these parents were not without feeling. Influenced by the evangelical fervour aroused in Britain by the preaching tours of Moody and Sankey some years before, they sought out a form of worship that combined sound theology and spiritual feeling to move the heart. They attended a Baptist Church at first, then moved to the Plymouth Brethren, and often, as a second service, attended the Gordon Mission in Justice Street on Sunday evenings.

It was in connection with the summer "Clout Mission" campaigns of the Gordon Mission throughout Aberdeenshire that John Macmurray, at the age of eighteen, began to assist and then to preach salvation in the evangelical manner to lost souls. As his parents had convinced him, the Gospel was a gift and it was meant to be given. But there was a great personal purpose behind his work at the Mission: John Macmurray, at the initiative of his father, was preparing himself to be a missionary in China. James had wished to be a missionary in China himself, and family difficulties requiring immediate financial care had made it impossible for him to realize this goal. He yearned for it for his eldest son. And indeed John was the stuff out of which missionaries were made—except for his health which, at that time of his life, was not strong. This evangelical and missionary fervour tested in the Clouty Kirk summer meetings was brought to his leadership with his fellow university students in Glasgow in the Student Volunteer Missionary Union.

John Macmurray kept a personal journal from the very end of 1908 until early 1913, and in it he catalogued the joys and anguish of this consuming religious view of his life. The journal begins by outlining a daily timetable that included religious exercises frequent enough to humble any monk. The daily entries reflect frequent self-disparagement as the young man strives for perfection and pinpoints mercilessly his least peccadillo.

Just six days into the new journal, he writes in a way that typifies his feelings and attitudes at this time in his seventeen year-old life, "How black the day's record seems when written on paper. And yet God has been in it more than for many a day past... Noted with care in Romans the expressions "Gospel of God," "Gospel of Christ," "My Gospel." God grant that I may sound the depths of that unfathomable sea of grace to the utmost extent of my small plummet." (Jan.2, 1909). The next day, a Sunday, he writes, "Enjoyed the services very much. The Lord was manifestly present among us. I believe some souls found Jesus tonight... O for a band of sincere young men to stand for God and God's truth in this day of declension and worldliness... O that God would enable me to speak out for Him there, to seek to woo and win some precious soul to Jesus' bleeding feet... O God, how far I have been from walking before thee and being perfect." He ends this entry, "I cannot say the day was lost but it has not the store of treasure hidden in it which it ought." (Jan.3, 1909). This is strong stuff. And in it, we can see the contours of the deeply generous and missionary sense he has of his life.

Meanwhile, in his studies at Glasgow University he was exercising an equally passionate interest in science even though he was enrolled in Latin and Greek classics. As he tells us in *Search for Reality in Religion,* it was in science that he was finding an intellectual method that opened up not only knowledge of the world but also a transformed knowledge of the doctrines of his Christianity. In applying scientific method to his reading of Paul's Letter to the Romans, he tells us that as traditional interpretations of Christian teachings collapsed around him—almost like a young Luther 400 years later—he was led to overthrow not his Christian religion but the conventional doctrines that claimed to express its meaning. His deeply-felt faith was unshakeable; its truth grounded in the practical love and faith of his parents. But even as faith in Christ remained a fixed and indubitable star in his firmament, it became clear to him that its formulations and interpretations can and must develop. From that point on he engaged in serious bible study from this fresh perspective. And he was driven to affirm a unity between science and religion that, for his lifetime, remained incontrovertible and only deepened.

Religious doctrine, as he wrote almost fifteen years later in an essay entitled "Maturity in Religion," must learn from scientific method by giving up any pretension to absolute, timeless formulations. Religious doctrines, like any human knowing, must submit to the same essential rules as science does. That is, it must do the following: display a humble attentiveness to its proper evidence, manifest an openness to revision of its formulations, exercise the need for collaboration (a variety of points of view on the issue), and practice the conviction that religious doctrines, like scientific formulations, if verifiable, are verified in the experimental method called human action. "By their fruits you shall know them" is, as the young Macmurray was discovering, a principle of verification—and falsification—of both religious doctrine and practice. In the 1930s and later, Macmurray gave Marx much credit for teaching him to understand the implications of Kant's assertion of the primacy on the practical in the areas of religion and ethics. However, I believe we can discern already from 1910–12, in the theological and religious transformations he was going through, a fertile seedbed for Macmurray's later articulations concerning the primacy of action over theory.

At Glasgow University, Macmurray's intellectual growth in both secular and biblical studies abounded. And by the time of the 1911 summer campaign with Mr. Smith's travelling mission, it came into inevitable and almost violent internal conflict with his evangelical preaching and the confident, external zeal required in its delivery. The rising conflict between the old methods and the new questions, the old answers and the new ones, was seriously accelerated by another momentous event in his life: during that summer he fell totally in love with Elizabeth Hyde Campbell, whom he called Hydie, the young woman who was eventually to become his wife.

He speaks in his journal of the growing strain and weariness that the mission puts on him. He notes that the positive response he received to his letter declaring his love for Hydie has "widened the breach between the old life and the new. A wider range of reading helped to bring to me a larger interest in life outside my narrow sphere." (Oct.14). His very respectable efforts at poetry become more frequent and more loving. At Torphins, while on mission, Browning's poetry becomes "his one passion." He notes, "I begin to feel as never before the strength and trend of the current of modern thought. Almost against my will, my dogmas and beliefs are being shaken and modified, the viewpoint is shifting..."

In May 1912, he records the family decision to move to London following the move there in 1911 by John's two sisters, Helen and Lilias. When school ended in June, he went to London for the first time in his life and was astounded by it. "I count it amongst the great experiences of my life. It has brought home to me how much bigger the world is than I had thought, and how much work there is to do in it." He complains, however, that ill-health attends him like a shadow. And, in fact, at the end of that summer, the doctors agree that John's health was not good enough for him to consider going to the inland mission in China. This was a decision he accepted with peace—and also with some relief since, although his faith in Christ remained fervent, he knew that the form of his religion and his approach to it were now moving in a direction that, as he put it, "quite unfitted me for a missionary's life."

The changes he felt happening in him during what he refers to as that fateful summer of 1912 can be felt in this entry: "London is wonderful, bewildering, fascinating. It seems to go on for ever, one great being, and yet always different: loving and hating, toiling and playing, serving God and the devil, breaking hearts, sealing loves, buying and selling merchandise and the souls of men; sinning, sinning, sinning, and yet all the while unconsciously winning nearer to the end of sin. Ah, London, London, devourer of the people, yet nurse of mighty men, thou mighty paradox, gateway at once to heaven and hell, I have eaten of thy lotus-buds, and I love thee to the forgetting of my home-land."

And yet it is fair to say his religious homeland is not so much forgotten as transformed. In a long reflection he writes poignantly, "I am convinced that no man can do a man's work unless he have a man's conviction in his heart about the central things. And a conviction is born of experience, not without pangs and travail. Would I be a man if I could set my life to defend the dogmas a man has created? But where is God? Why has he hidden himself?" he asks in anguish. He prays from deep in his heart, "Ah, Lord God, pity my feeble faith in thy Almightiness; the groping of my blind hands in the blaze of Thy Light of light. Give me eyes that I may see Thee. A heart that I may know Thee, a will that I may follow Thee. I am sore stricken, unless thou succour me..." And yet he concludes firmly, "the God who created needs, hungers, cries, in the human heart must needs fill them. To fear that faith cannot be found would be a denial of God... So thus far I know and believe. The noblest lives are linked with the highest beliefs. Faith is the social glue. When we cease to believe, we cease to live—either to man or God. Unbelief is spiritual death and intellectual death. It abolishes Love and enthrones suspicion—paralyses governments, religions, friendships, all societies of men. "We must believe or die." Thus faith is possible or life is impossible. It is my duty to find the faith which satisfies the need."

What an amazing statement from a 21 year-old, "It is my duty to find the faith which satisfies the need." The power of a simultaneous breakdown of older patterns and the outlines of a new synthesis that intimately unites the human and the divine were occurring, it seems, almost with every passing week. He speaks of "a certain undefinable shrinking from "piousness" and established forms." Despite his parents alarm and criticism, he sees the changes as somehow God's work in him. He feels he is being prepared for something else.

Because of all the changes—his love for Hydie, his developed respect for scientific method, and his shift towards more interest in and dedication to the world in which he finds himself—his sense of being a missionary remains strong—but its focus has shifted significantly. "[T]he time has come when I must begin to recognize my own life as under my own power, to be spent of my own free will upon others." As a result of declaring his love to Hydie and hearing of hers for him, he notes "there dawned upon me a new feeling of detachment, a new feeling of responsibility and a new feeling of strength... I now look on my fellow men as beings over whom I could exert an individual influence."

During his stay in London at Christmas that year, he met Rev. Richard Roberts, the pastor at Crouch Hill Presbyterian Church, and "learned from him about the foundation and purpose of the Swanwick Free Church Fellowship" which attracted him deeply. Its goals, as he put it, are "to rise in a positive faith, to cast off the burden of a negative religiousness and theology, to face the facts in fearless trust, to rediscover the will of God in our generation, above all to learn the secrets of (word effaced) experience and let them teach us the meaning of dogma."

At the same time as his religion becomes purified and more grounded in experience he is, precisely because of this change, growing in a critique of society's own entrapment by what he calls "prejudices and bonds of useless tradition." On Jan. 11, 1913, he observes almost prophetically—given that the start of the war is barely more than a year away, "Our whole civilization is overstrained and may smash up suddenly. The strain is apparent everywhere, and the attempts to repair matters are absurdly inadequate. What we need is a new life springing up from the very germs and bursting with its own vitality the dead seed-cloak of our old, effete, semi-pagan civilization. We are like square pins in round holes. The irksomeness of the forms which do not answer our needs, and the restraint of meaningless traditions makes the very truth of the past distasteful... I have continually to tear the fundamental morality of our society to pieces, even at the expense of wrecking my own prospects." He concludes, "it is just possible that the Swanwick fellowship may hold the first germs of the coming thing. For something is coming without a doubt."

And he ends his reflections on this period of huge and almost seismic transformation in himself saying, "Why should I complain, who have Hydie's arms and breast for consolation?" On Feb.16, his 22nd birthday, he continues this reflection. "My darling has made me anew, for God and man and herself... This year," he says, "has been the seedbed of my first true religious experience." He acknowledges that during the year earthly love almost took the place of his religious life, so deep and passionate did it become. By year-end, things have changed, but so too has his perspective on where he has come to. "There seems to be no distinction left between winning her and winning heaven. Nor is this a mere sick lover's exaggeration: it is a spiritual insight which has come of knowing that for a man to have learned to love fully and perfectly the woman of his choice is to have attained to the fulness of the measure of the stature of Christ. My love has grown to mean this by small degrees, and will spread out in greener, stronger life in the year ahead... I have not attained. Rather, I have caught an amazing view of the immensity of the height to be attained." He acknowledges his passion is tainted still with selfishness, but asks for "not less but more passion, only let it be under a still finer restraint... Give me also a scorn of all insincerity and a manliness that accepts its own responsibility: to temper all, a tenderness of sympathy which will take me out of myself. Why may I not be one who enters into the lives of others?" In reflecting on his most recent visit with Hydie, he notes "these days, like all other days with Hydie, leave me with a gulf between the present and the past. There is no power on earth for change equal to love... ." And, in his next to last entry in this journal – the only journal he ever kept in his life—he concludes, "The future is more intense than every before. I am not afraid. Let God decide what it shall be. My Hydie is with me... and there rises one fact, the eternal fact of *Christ.*"

Now why, in a presentation intended to touch on a philosopher's life of 85 years, would I choose to spend so much of it on the first 22 years— before he has taught a class or written a professional word? Quite simply, I find in these years the kernel of the man and of his philosophy both being formed at once. John Macmurray is the philosopher who emphasized that life in its fullest is a life of action, with other persons, in the world, and for the realization of world community. This action, he has already concluded can only be positive action and genuine action if it arises out of love. And this love can only be real and positive if it is grounded in the facts of our physical, emotional and relational existence.

I am suggesting that these three features of acting, feeling and thinking—and their integral relationship to one another in John Macmurray's later philosophy—have their roots formed and firmly intertwined in the young man's three-fold transformation during his university years: his intellectual conversion to the primacy of scientific method and its capacity to be fully reconciled with genuine faith, his falling in love with Hydie Campbell and the conversion in sensibility and perspective that being in love gave him with regard to the foundational place of love in personal judgment and action, and his transformed sense of the mission and his call as a missionary, wherein he saw that action was the heart of the matter, but it must be constructive action for the building of the world.

And at its heart, is his faith in Jesus who leads him in his thinking, feeling and acting. Jesus was the source and goal of his vision of a world community. Jesus was the fire of love by which this community could be realised. And Jesus was the gyroscope for discernment by which he formed his judgments and convictions about what it means for human beings to be real. In this sense, it is clear that in John Macmurray, the thought arises from and through the life imbued by his Christian faith. And the life is lived in a faithful striving to incarnate the inspiration underlying and within the thought. This can reasonably appear to be an exaggeration and gross simplification of Macmurray's philosophy—as though it might simply be an unfolding of a young man's noblest thoughts and aspirations. Of course it isn't so. But it is true to say that these were not tentative or passing convictions for John Macmurray. I am suggesting that the ideas and the passion expressed in these youthful reflections reveal the formation of the essential and unchanging contours of his sensibility, his thinking and his way of relating to others for the rest of his life. Not a small thing to catch it on the fly—and from his own hand and heart!

In the winter of 1912, Macmurray sat the examinations for the prestigious Snell Exhibition to Balliol at Oxford and won it—partly, he says, because of good luck and partly because his keenest challenger decided not to take the exam. After completing his Honours Classics work at Glasgow in September 1913, he went to Oxford immediately, having noted earlier that "both philosophy and history have been largely overlooked in my course of study until now, and are subjects which really interest me." (Jan.10, 1913 letter to Mr. Bailey). His Balliol tutor was A.D. Lindsay, a socially-oriented thinker who helped strengthen Macmurray's interests in seeing studies as preparation for life and service. At Balliol that year, Macmurray became friends with a brilliant, young South African named Jan Hofmeyr with whom he shared many ideas and his Christian faith. Together they hatched a plan to revitalise the SCM, and because of their style of thinking, both were soon looked on as heretics by their fellow Christians.

The War Years

When war broke out, Macmurray sought the advice of Richard Roberts on whether or not he ought to enlist. Roberts, a pacifist who was soon to be relieved of his position because of his views, advised against it. Macmurray compromised by not seeking a commission to an active regiment but enlisting in the Royal Army Medical Corps. The broad strokes of Macmurray's wartime involvements and his reflections on them for his work are traced in his Swarthmore Lecture and need not be repeated here. In 1915, after serving in France at medical centres at first at Merville, then Loos, and finally at the front, he reversed his decision and, in June 1916, accepted a commission in the Queen's Own Cameron Highlanders.

Early in 1917, he wrote his first known published piece of writing, a short reflection on a soldier's image of God in the midst of the carnage at the front. It was called "Trench Religion" and was published in 1919 in a book edited by Prof. David Cairns entitled *The Army and Religion*. In the summer of 1916, he returned to London for his first leave since arriving in France and, on October 9 in London, married Betty Campbell, his Hydie.

The most powerful story retained of his war years is arguably his own account of a sermon he gave in 1917 to a congregation of Christians in North London. In it he urged the congregation to distance themselves from a spirit of vengeance towards the Germans and to prepare themselves for the genuinely Christian work of reconciliation. After the sermon, he was rebuffed by all his listeners. Moved deeply by this experience which he perceived not as a personal rejection but a rejection of the Gospel, he turned his back on any institutional form of expressing his Christian faith. He continued to follow the way of Christ and to believe in and even to preach the Gospel when invited to churches, but he walked his journey until the year after his official retirement, outside any institutional affiliation. As he explained later when asked: I did it to ensure that I would have complete freedom to think my own thoughts and express my own views without being compromised and without having to worry about embarrassing any colleagues. He held to this choice until, late in the 1950s when, after his retirement from the University of Edinburgh, he and his wife Betty joined the Quakers the year after they had moved to Jordans. In this decision we see, in John Macmurray, a willingness—perhaps even a preference—to choose his own path and even to walk alone, a choice that colleagues later on cited in reference to his way of doing philosophy and to what some perceived as a certain withdrawal from academic collaboration. There were, as we know, other explanations for his relative solitude in philosophical circles during the 1930s, 40s and 50s in Britain.

In *Search for Reality in Religion*, Macmurray notes that during the First World War, with death occurring all around him, he lost his fear of death. In connection with this transformation, there is a story that he told only to his family and a few friends over the years. Before shipping out to France and while he was still in training at Sling near Salisbury, he had a vision. He was in a tent filled with men—smelly and half-drunk. Out of the darkness a shadowy figure approached him and said, "You will not be killed in this war. You will return to remake the world." As his wife Betty noted in her own diaries years later, this remained the most treasured prophecy of his life—to remake the world; so like the Hebrew phrase: *tikkun olam*, to mend or heal the world. Macmurray did survive the war, but barely. He was seriously wounded in the face and head by shrapnel during the last major German offensive on March 28, 1918 near Arras while trying to lead his company back to safety. For this gallant effort he won the Military Cross. And he observed ruefully thereafter that he was the only soldier he knew who was decorated for running away.

The Academic Career Begins

In 1919, John Macmurray returned to Balliol as the John Locke Scholar. It was during that year, in the face of philosophical squabbles among his colleagues, he resolved to read alternately the continental Rationalists and the British Empiricists. In this exercise he discovered a significant feature which guided his reading and interpreting of different philosophies in the future. Both camps, he noted, had diametrically opposed perceptions of reality, yet both employed a common underlying set of assumptions about the nature of reality; in this case, an acceptance that the universe and all the beings in it were able to be represented conceptually in atomistic terms. Both the Rationalists and the Empiricists, he concluded, were locked into a mechanical mode of representing reality. Once this key was found, he was able to locate further hidden premises in their propositions and positions. He also saw that these underlying assumptions are not simply logical conclusions but also emotion-laden convictions, convictions that were inextricably connected with the culture and social situation out of which the thinking of these philosophers arose. Although much refined in his thinking over subsequent years, this articulation of what he came to call "modes of apperception" and their history-determined context took its first, clear form for him at this time.

In September 1919, after completing his July examinations with distinction for the M.A. in *litterae humaniores*, Macmurray accepted a position as Lecturer in philosophy at Manchester University where he was undoubtedly exposed to Samuel Alexander's philosophy on the import of feeling on thinking—a viewpoint with which Macmurray had a growing agreement. At Manchester, he also met for the first time Irene Grant (his student at that time) and her husband Donald (an SCM officer who had been jailed in Scotland during the war for his pacifism), a couple with whom John was closely associated in the struggle against Fascism in the 1930s, and with whom he and Betty shared an intimate friendship for the rest of their lives. John continued his reading in various areas of philosophy, and the lecture notes that remain from these years reveal a detailed and nuanced reading of the Pre-Socratics and later Greek philosophy.

In March 1921, just a few months after William Temple was made Archbishop of Manchester, John accepted an invitation from his Oxford friend Jan Hofmeyr to become Professor of philosophy at Witwatersrand University in Johannesburg. Hofmeyr, a child genius, had at the age of 24, become Principal of the University. In Johannesburg, John quickly became involved in social issues, especially with those concerned with workers and with native blacks and their housing problems. He became involved also with a protest against the Transvaal government's decision to impose a poll tax which was fought and, to the surprise of the protesters, won. In one public speech, when feelings among his fellow-protesters were running high and a bit wild, Macmurray began his talk with rhetorical flourishes that roused the crowd to heights of feeling. Suddenly he stopped speaking. Silence fell. And he said, "You see, any fool can do that!" And he continued his speech in a quiet and measured tone, concentrating on facts rather than emotions. In contrast to this gentle delivery which characterised his professional style for the rest of his life, there is a delicious example of him consciously giving in with delight to rhetorical excess in an after-dinner speech about the excellence of Scottish universities to his fellow Scots at the local Caledonia Club in Johannesburg. It sparkles with the wit and humour for which Macmurray was well-known.

We still have from this period Macmurray's extensive lecture notes on Bosanquet's *Political Theory of the State* and reading notes on Gierke's *Medieval Forms*. Macmurray praises Bosanquet as being the best of English Hegelianism and especially for having a "grip on the full spiritual nature of social life and on its unity as an organised whole." His criticism of Bosanquet is his need to have the Ideal and the Actual realised in a concrete state. This leaves him, Macmurray concludes, fixed onto nationalism, and with nothing to hope for from medieval political philosophy since it is not based on nationalism. He also, in his course on the State, critiques what he calls "first look" theorists such as Bentham, Mill, Spencer and Marx as well as the sociologists Durkheim, Tarde and LeBon, and gives evidence of having read these authors with some thoroughness.

During their short 21-month stay in Johannesburg, John and Betty found time to take dancing lessons together, and time for John to take piano lessons—the beginning of what, if his wife's evidence can be trusted, was a totally undistinguished home career at the keyboard. As she complains to her diaries, he never learned to stop pounding the keys, and he never learned how to stop thinking through his moves from one note to the next when he played. He was, in her eyes—and ears—a philosopher playing at the piano. In the autumn of 1922, Macmurray was named as Jowett Lecturer and Classical Tutor at Balliol. The farewell stories that appeared in the Johannesburg *Star* and the *Rand Daily Mail* cite the wisdom, clarity of thought and expression, and the social concern and effectiveness of the departing Macmurray. In that time, there is evidence of only one publication by Macmurray: a short 1922 article solicited by Donald Grant for the publication *Vox Studentum* entitled "Personality," a portent of Macmurray's lifework to come.

Macmurray's Balliol career stretched from January 1923 to the summer of 1928 when he succeeded Dawes-Hicks in the position of Grote Professor of Mind and Logic at University College, London. During those five and a half years at Oxford, he did an immense amount of reading in modern European philosophy. In the summer of 1923, he gave the Jowett Lectures on "The Historical Approach to Modern Idealism" which, despite the sweep of his proposed syllabus, concentrated on Descartes and Spinoza. There are also notes from a course on Plato, Aristotle and Hellenism with some interesting ideas derived from his reading such as how the Near East (after Alexander) was the birthplace of ideas on deification of leaders (created to legitimise acting outside the constitution), on the Egyptian bureaucracy inherited by the Romans, on shared citizenship across cities or between two cities, on the place of the Jews in the Hellenistic era. There are many ideas here that help to explain his clear characterisations of the three main cultures (Hebrew, Greek and Roman) that, in his lifelong view, ground and define the culture of the west and the shape of Christendom. Here, in these Balliol years, we find his beginning articulations of the terms for true and false polities even as he is developing ideas that help him to distinguish in more contemporary terms between the mechanical, the organic and the personal.

Here, also, we find Macmurray doing concentrated reading and lecturing on Kant, German Romanticism and ethics. He shows in his progress through the German Romantics that he is both critical of and receptive to the widening of the meaning of faith and the place of feeling in their understanding of reason. On his way to Hegel, he studies Jacobi, Herder, Hamann, and Herbart and does some serious reading of Fichte and Schelling. Thereafter, he shows intense interest in Schopenhauer and Schleiermacher. Through this progress, he derives from the sensibility and searching of these thinkers the "mode of apperception" which he calls "organic" and which he describes as representing a progressive, dialectical development beyond the "mechanical" mode of thought which characterised the earlier stage of modern philosophy in Europe. One of the points that struck him in his reading of Jacobi resulted in the following observation by Macmurray: "In the certainty of existence, the 'I' and the 'Thou' are so immediately one that the onesideness of Idealism or Realism is out of the question." He goes on, "Jacobi is interested in the facts of consciousness. He is a modern. His standpoint is well called that of superior personality. The Absolute justification of moral individuality." And then he notes, "this would be perfect if it could escape subjectivism by accepting an objective revelation of God in a human personality." In this note, we can sense more than grasp intimations of his future focus on the personal.

In July 1925, he wrote to his friend Richard Roberts, now living in Canada, "I should state it thus: that if the world is to be comprehended, it must be in terms of personality." He finds in personality and its demand for integration and spontaneity, the terms for twentieth-century philosophy to incorporate yet go beyond mechanical and organic modes of thinking for conceiving of persons, the role of the State and of human society at its fullest—what he will later call community. What he wants of Christianity is that it be conceived of as at once personal in its content and practice, and scientific in its method of formulating doctrine. God, he states to Roberts, must be approached as "personal" since the personal is the fullest category we have—and yet God is infinitely beyond any meaning of "personal" that our experience provides. It was in wrestling with these questions that Macmurray came to his deep respect for the work of Thomas Aquinas, despite his reservations about the medieval manner of frequently philosophising from authority rather than depending on human experience and reason.

He continued his effort to master the western tradition. In his work on the Greeks, Macmurray dedicates himself to Plato and to an intensive study of the Stoics. He reads Kant and lectures on his ethics. In 1926, he wrote a popular article called 'The Influence of British Philosophy during these Forty Years' in which he speaks knowledgeably of the British Idealists Green, Bosanquet, Caird, Bradley, McTaggart, Ward, Baillie and Henry Jones, and concludes that Hegelianism, in defeating the mechanical conception of mind, succumbed in turn to an organic model of categorising being, a move to dialectical logic that was clearly more complex and truer to life than formal logic, and yet a logic incapable of understanding persons in their distinctiveness and in their constitution as persons through relationship with other persons.

Macmurray ends the article with a summary of his conviction concerning the need of twentieth-century philosophy to focus on the problem of "personality" as the critical requirement of philosophy in our time.

His explorations, since they focused on the most fundamental of issues, lead him in several directions at once: towards a reconstructed epistemology, metaphysics and philosophy of religion—all of which are broached from the perspective of personality in his essays 'Beyond Knowledge' and 'Objectivity in Religion' which appeared in Canon Streeter's 1927 collection entitled *Adventure: The Faith of Science and the Science of Faith.* The effort to conceive and formulate the nature of personality is by now, the heart of his philosophical inquiry.

Day by day, John had his classes, his colleagues—especially Charles Morris with whom he proposed and formally contracted with Macmillan to do a book that never saw the light of day—and his intense study. He was well-loved as a tutor by students as diverse as William Stuart Murrie, David Cairns, Richard Crossman, Alexis Kilroy Meynell, Hugh Gaitskell, Evan Durbin and the Canadian, Eugene Forsey, who was sent to him by Richard Roberts. As one of his students Dorothy Emmet remembers, he was found to be wild, insightful and, at times, entertaining as a lecturer. Student jokes arose around Oxford about both Morris and Macmurray that in their classes you were likely to hear not what Plato actually said but what these professors felt he ought to have said. In the same spirit, Macmurray laughed quietly at himself when, on one occasion, he held an audience spellbound for an hour on Leibniz only to say to a friend at the end of it that he knew nothing of Leibniz, that he had based his whole lecture on one sentence, "The monad does not have windows." One can believe there was some modesty even if a touch of truth in the story since, by 1926 he is lecturing on Leibniz, Spinoza and the British Empiricists for which some of the lecture notes still remain.

Meanwhile, at 5 Mansfield Avenue where they lived, John and Betty entertained, and in their socializing with A.D. Lindsay and his wife Rica among others tried, in a way that never got beyond straining, to enjoy life at Oxford. Betty—and John too in his own way—found Oxford society elitist, self-enclosed and extremely judgmental. But she was harder than he was on Oxford. She found Oxford condescending and suffocating in its narrowness. Betty was a feeler, an artist and, as she saw it, there was simply no place for her kind of person in the society of Oxford. When

John accepted the position in London in the summer of 1928 she couldn't wait to leave.

The London Years

John Macmurray went to University College, London, in September after declining invitations from two North American schools, Princeton University and an unidentified Canadian university, possibly Queen's, in Kingston. In a letter to Richard Roberts in January 1928, he noted that he felt he had to stay in England because "for thinking out the philosophy of Personality, which is my main job, it is better to be in the older civilisation than in the new one." Thus he set the parameters of his own context and professional direction for the coming years. But it was not to work out as he had hoped.

After moving into The Bolton Studios near King's Road, life began to overwhelm both John and Betty almost instantly. After months of ill-health, Betty had an exploratory operation and was found to have a tumour on or near her ovary. She then had a period of good health, but within six months of the operation Betty was again desperately ill due to peritonitis resulting from an ectopic pregnancy and a burst fallopian tube. This illness, and the consequent operation, ended their chances of ever having children, a loss they both felt very deeply.

Macmurray's work abounded. In his inaugural address entitled 'The Unity of Modern Problems' he traced out the history of western philosophy leading to his own analysis of the vital need for a philosophy of personality that includes but goes beyond the mechanical and organic categories of thought developed in earlier historical periods. This was followed quickly by an essay on 'The Principle of Personality in Experience.'

During this time, he was working on what was to be his first book called *The Western Tradition* in which he wanted to present his sweeping analysis of Western philosophical history that included his analysis of the Hebrew, Greek and Roman cultural forms, the role of Stoicism as an aberrant form in Christian morality, the rise of modern science as a systematic expression of human freedom and the progression through mechanical and organic thought forms to the contemporary need for a philosophical theory of personality to unite and advance this tradition. The book was too massive and unmanageable, and its contents—perhaps thanks to editorial advice—were finally published in a vastly revised form in three books: *Freedom in the Modern World, Interpreting the Universe* and *The Clue to History*. Meanwhile, as he notes in a letter to Richard Roberts, Macmurray was about to give five lectures at University College developing systematically the elements of his philosophy of personality. "I shall treat personality and the relation of persons in love as sacred and to be reverenced, and *nothing else.*" Unfortunately, these lectures have not been found, or even firmly identified by title.

The longstanding SCM connection continued and deepened for Macmurray. He published an essay 'What I Live By' in the *Student Movement* magazine, and achieved almost star-status at the SCM Quadrennial in Liverpool where he gave three presentations including his overwhelming keynote address entitled 'Ye Are My Friends' in which he presents the insight already expressed in his youthful journal that "friendship is the religious fact in human experience." As reports of the talk reveal, the effect Macmurray had on many was an experience not unlike that noted in the Scripture text: "This man speaks with authority, unlike the scribes and pharisees." This connection with SCM would flourish and also become more focused within a few years in his intimate association (along with Karl Polanyi) as court philosopher and father figure with the group of politically attuned SCM alumni/ae—The Auxiliary—led by Irene Grant, Kenneth Ingram and Kenneth Muir who, in their struggle against Fascism and their support for a Christianity that focused on forming community in this world, came to be called The Christian Left.

It is impossible to note all the involvements of Macmurray during these almost frantic 30s. A short litany will give the flavour if not all the facts or the quality of the relationships. At the University of London, including King's College, he had occasional to frequent contact with G.D.H. Cole, Professors J.B.S. Haldane and R.H. Tawney, Hugh Gaitskell, Harold Laski and many other socialist thinkers. Through J.H. Oldham, Joseph Needham, William Temple—the Archbishop of York, Rev. Eric Fenn, Joseph Coates, the SCM Christian Left and many others, he maintained and developed his explicitly Christian connections and projects—invariably with those Christian leaders seeking a transformed, Gospel-based social order. Through Kenneth Barnes' work at Bedales and later at Wennington schools, the Grith Fyrd Movement, the SCM summer camps, the Adelphi Movement and other agencies in later decades such as Newbattle Abbey, he commits himself to promoting new forms of education which are humanistic, participatory, based on a guiding notion of community, and directed to the transformation of both schooling and society.

In 1930, he begins a long and extremely influential relationship with the BBC by giving several series of talks on culture, religion, morality, education and the meaning of genuine personal living. This history of John Macmurray with the BBC has been well explored in an unpublished essay by Philip Hunt, Chair of the John Macmurray Fellowship in Britain.

He associates himself in a significant way through meetings, symposia, lectures and published articles with various non-religious movements seeking a new social order especially in the light of the new communist society in Russia and the rise of Fascism on the continent: among them, the New Britain and New Europe movements, the Adelphi, the Moot, the Peace Pledge Union and, later, the Commonwealth Movement. In that context, as well, he works to support the university placement of several (mainly Jewish) refugee scholars including Theodore Adorno and Karl Popper.

In the midst of all this professional activity, along with his wife, he enters into an exuberant exposure to the cultural life of London and to a critical yet deep affection for the work of D.H. Lawrence—especially as it called for a freeing of the "sensual" life. Their social life includes acquaintance with Sybil Thorndyke, Naomi Micheson, Herbert Read, T.S. Eliot, Patrick White—the Australian novelist, and painters Roy de Maistre, Francis Bacon, Martin Block, the playwright J.B. Priestley, and people who later figured large in the Labour Party. They entertain frequently and generously; and Richard Crossman was overheard to complain, "There's too much wine and drink at Macmurray parties."

It was on a Christmas visit to Donald and Irene Grant in Vienna in 1932 that John met Karl Polanyi and in their conversations was introduced to the early thought of Karl Marx. This is not the place to deal with the major influence Marx—or certainly Marx as interpreted by Karl Polanyi—had on Macmurray's thought. Within months of returning from Vienna, Macmurray gave himself over to a flurry of writing on Marxism, and the relationship of Marxism and Christianity. He produced three lectures which were published as a small book entitled *The Philosophy of*

Communism (1933). This writing was followed by three chapters in a book entitled *Marxism* (1934), edited by John Middleton Murry, an essay on 'Dialectical Materialism as a Philosophy' in *Aspects of Dialectical Materialism* (1934), and two chapters in a collaborative work called *Christianity and the Social Revolution* (1935) which he helped to plan and edit.

In 1935, Macmurray produced a provocative, even swashbuckling, book called *Creative Society* in which the influence of Marx became transparent in Macmurray's rethinking of the meaning of Christianity. It was in this book that Macmurray articulated most forcefully his view of the truly incarnate and anti-idealist nature of religion as lived and presented by Jesus. Real religion, he stated, is incarnate. It focuses on the Kingdom that is to be heralded and struggled for in this world, not in some after-world. The tendency to look to another world, a beyond, as the home of Christianity, he dubbed "false religion." Most Christian religion, he said, was infected by dualism; that is, by the destructive virus of Greek, other-worldly Idealism in its theology, and by Roman stoicism and materialism in its practice. Macmurray, leaned heavily on his view of Hebrew religion which he believed to be the authentic ground of Christianity. He attempted to think through the marks of "real religion" guided at once by the eschatological vision of the Kingdom taught by Jesus and by work to achieve equality, freedom and the building of community in this world. He believed these were the genuine, social signs that God's will was actually being done by us.

With Marx, he judged action to be of primary significance, and theory of significance only in terms of action. Again with Marx, he accepted the dialectical character of human development and the clear fact of enfleshment as our natural and spiritual condition. However, with equal forcefulness, he rejected Marx's fixation on economics and merely organic needs as the foundational meaning of this incarnate reality in history. He also rejected Marx's neuralgic rejection of religion, and with it, his refusal to place the self-transcending nature of personal relating at the heart of his anthropology. In *Creative Society*, Macmurray confirmed and even deepened the view of Marx's limitations that he noted at the end of his 1933 work on *The Philosophy of Communism*. He ended this book of his adulthood as he ended the journal of his adolescence: by critiquing almost viciously the hypocrisy of organised Christianity while holding firmly for the person of Jesus and expressing his conviction that at the heart of the Christian Gospel and its essentially Hebrew roots lay a far more true support of personhood and community than Marxism could ever offer.

It was on the basis of such convictions that Macmurray's presence in the work of the Christian Left in its resistance to the rise of Fascism was expressed. In an essay called 'A Provisional Basis for the Christian Left,' he wrote that: *the nature of our motives, convictions, methods of advocacy and forms of community must be primarily religious, not primarily political.* Responsible Christians cannot help but relate to the political dimensions of life since their work is to form community, and there is no community without a political dimension included in it. But their purposes and values in their political activity—even at their most forceful and prophetic—are to be determined by the imperatives of Gospel community—love, forgiveness, spontaneity in relating, the hope for reconciliation, respect for diversity, and a deep acceptance that the work is essentially God's, not their own. This is the ground of their freedom. He insisted repeatedly that these modes of acting must be alive and uncompromised in all the Christian Left's actions—their methods of challenging or resisting any agents and agencies as well as their critique of political theories that deny these essentially human realities. As he would put it much later in his Gifford Lectures, the political dimension in our social lives is a necessary and constitutive but subordinate dimension within full personal living in community. The full personal emphasis was needed. In the mid to late 30s, political policies and actions were critical in the face of the spread of Fascism. Politics was regularly being defined as the essential focus for analysis and resistance to Fascism and the National Government.

Irene Grant, the coordinator of the Christian Left, though deeply impressed by John Macmurray, was to her very roots a political animal. Correspondence between her and Macmurray in the summer of 1936, while Macmurray was lecturing in the United States and Canada, reveals John's efforts to invite her to this fuller perspective that he called "religious" in her activities and attitudes at the time—especially towards her more conservative opponents in the administration of the SCM. Macmurray himself was a proponent of the need to transform politics— few were more forceful or clear about the nature and evil of Fascism than he—but he never seems to have lost sight of the kind of transformation, under the impetus of Gospel faith, that was required; the kind that leads to genuine community of persons in free relations.

It was an interpretation of what it means to be truly "radical" for which there was only occasional recognition and meagre gratitude. Among his professional colleagues and occasional associates on the Left such as Haldane, Harold Laski, John Middleton Murry, John Strachey and others, his reluctance to embrace Marxism unreservedly and his radical Christian critique of its foundations were sometimes seen as strange and eccentric. On the other hand, others such as some administrators at the BBC, Max Plowman of the Peace Pledge Union, some of his Christian associates and philosophical colleagues, found his sympathy for Marx, for the Russian experiment, and for an eventual synthesis of the best of communism and Christianity altogether too sanguine and uncritical—even rash and dangerous.

It can be conjectured that this viewpoint figured at least somewhat in the early 1940s when Sir Stafford Cripps—who had been so impressed by *The Clue to History*—came, as Lord Privy Seal, to talk with Macmurray about his interest in making himself available for some war work. After the chat Cripps, who was hardly to be outflanked on the Left by Macmurray, must have determined that there was no work in the government for the philosophy professor. He suggested that Macmurray would do better for the nation by simply continuing with his work in teaching—despite the fact that most philosophy students had already left the universities and joined the war effort. This lack of invitation to serve directly in the battle against Fascism saddened Macmurray deeply. As a consequence, he did what he could through his wide relationships and with his own resources. He spent much of his time in the early 40s working on research for the Anglo-Soviet Public Relations Association. He headed its committee on 'Religion in Russia,' studied Russian, and gave occasional talks on the state of religious freedom in Russia at the time, and on the issues that were arising for both Russia and the West out of the situation there. He gave much time over a short period to the fledgling Common Wealth Movement. However, after a number of months, this relationship did not remain an active part of his work.

Macmurray's book *The Clue to History,* with its forceful assertion that the culture of Hebrew religion (as opposed to Greek and Roman culture) formed the authentic foundations of Christianity and western civilisation, was ready for publication and for broadcast on the BBC at the same time as *Creative Society,* perhaps even earlier. However, its content was considered too risky and provocative, and so was refused by John Reith of the BBC (in both 1934 and 1936) and refused for print by both Victor Gollancz and Faber. It had to wait three more years before it was published by SCM in 1938.

Meanwhile, Macmurray continued to give innumerable public lectures on all the themes raised in his BBC lectures and published as *Freedom in the Modern World,* themes such as education, the personal life, science and religion, art and religion and, the implications for a Christian doctrine and institution that respected legitimate human ways of knowing, feeling and acting. Several of these talks were drawn together in his 1935 book, *Reason and Emotion.*

Perhaps the most significant chapters of the book are the first three, in which Macmurray offers a reconstructed notion of reason that at once recovers much from Plato and Aristotle and goes beyond them to his own understanding of what he now calls "the personal life". Reason, he asserts here, is our capacity to act in terms of the other according to the nature of that other and not according to our own needs or prejudices. Being rational is most immediately and comprehensively reflected in our behaviour, in our full, personal interaction with one another, not in our thinking. Rational living is a way of behaving that is appropriate to the realities involved in the relationship and its contexts and, when it involves persons, results in building positive personal relations with all that implies by way of increased freedom, equality and mutuality. As a constitutive dimension of that fullness of behaviour, we find reason expressed in the form of feeling. Feeling constitutes the foundation of the process by which we invest a being or a relationship with value in our behaving. Feeling is unrelievably the root of our choosing and living by values (a direct rejection of the Stoics), and values are generated by a felt relationship to reality which is outside ourselves. Real (objective) as opposed to unreal (subjectively-induced) feelings are rational feelings, that is, ones which result in us feeling appropriately about the other, that is, feeling for the other according to the other's own nature and not primarily according to our subjective needs. They help to generate rational behaviour. And imbedded within feeling, at a third-remove from our full life of interaction with the world, is the rationality of intellect, whose role is to discriminate fact from illusion.

Macmurray concluded that appropriate feeling—which necessarily includes intelligence as a subordinate but constitutive part in it—is love. A further twist on his reconstruction of the meaning of rationality is his conviction that we can only know truly if we love truly. (Did this come somewhat from his interpretation of Plato's loving contemplation of the Forms as the ground for all authentic knowing?) This revolutionary inversion of the modern fixation on instrumental intellect as the exclusive legitimate form of being rational is expressed by Macmurray at the end of the first chapter. "The capacity to love objectively is the capacity which makes us persons. It is the ultimate source of our capacity to behave in terms of the object. It is the core of rationality."[3]

But it can be said—as it was suggested by Macmurray himself – that during those years at University College this is about as far as he got with his primary project as a philosopher. In 1939, soon after war was declared on September 3, University College moved to Aberystwyth, Wales. It moved back in September 1940, only to return to Aberystwyth again the next month to avoid more of the bombing that had destroyed part of the University—including Macmurray's office and many of his books and papers. In the summer of 1939, John and his wife Betty had moved to the Quaker village of Jordans in Buckinghamshire just north of London. They were quickly involved in efforts to house refugees flooding in from Germany and Austria, a duty which fell more heavily on Betty in the months before she rented out their new house in Jordans and joined John in Aberystwyth. Their lives for the next five years were, as for all others in Britain at the time, much disrupted, and the opportunity for John to do serious writing was not available. When he was not teaching, he gave himself to the study of Russian and to research on the condition of religion in Russia at the time.

Much later, in her diaries in the mid-1950s, Betty wrote with surprise and some shock the substance of a conversation she and John had just had together in which John said the 1930s were the least worthwhile and least productive time for him—whereas she, with all her involvement with her own painting and with other artists, had found it the best and most fruitful time of her life. This statement is significant. In it, Macmurray sees himself as having got deflected by events and choices from his specific philosophical vocation to help "remake the world." His primary mission, as he saw it, was to work out his philosophy of the personal. And despite all his writings and the refinements of his insights on the subject over the years between 1928 and 1944, apart from significant advances evident in his 1944 Upton Lectures on The Problem of Evil, it was not until his Gifford Lectures in the early 1950s that he actually put his philosophy of the personal into a comprehensive and tentatively systematic form.

In Betty's eyes, he had been the one in their marriage who had never lost sight of his purpose. In his own estimation, he had failed to bring his project to a timely expression—and perhaps thereby lost the opportunity to achieve even further refinements to it in his remaining years of strength. By the time he wrote his Giffords in the early 1950s, Macmurray was assailed by what he called, in a letter to Kenneth Barnes, an "allergy to writing." At times, it stopped him from writing even informal letters. What came so easily in the early 1930s—with the help of his trusty assistant Dr. Ephrosyne Sideropoul—was often stuck and locked by the 1950s. It is clear from family testimony, and her own diaries, that Betty should have got an Oscar for best-supporting actress in John's production of the Giffords. Without what she calls her coaxing and badgering, it is doubtful the lectures would ever have been completed. This revulsion for writing remained with Macmurray, off and on, for the rest of his life. It makes his considerable output in the 1950s and 60s, in several significant essays and in the two books *Religion, Art and Science* and *Search for Reality in Religion,* that much more remarkable. What is even more remarkable is the clarity and simplicity of expression in these writings, a quality that constantly suggests a soul deeply at peace with itself. This was not always so.

In April of 1944, just before University College returned to London from its four-year exile in Aberystwyth, Wales, and began to plan for its post-war expansion, Macmurray was informed that, due to the illness that had overcome A.E.Taylor the year before, the Chair in Moral Philosophy at Edinburgh University was open and was being offered to him. At Edinburgh, the discussion about a successor to the great Taylor had ended in a decision to bring in someone with an element of prophecy and spark, and Macmurray was their choice. Macmurray had little time to reflect before giving his response. When he finally decided, he stated simply in his letter to Provost Pye of University College that his main, but not exclusive, reason for accepting the post was in order to have the opportunity to write his philosophy of the personal which he felt could more likely be accomplished in Edinburgh than in fast-moving London where exciting challenges awaited every department in the University. By September, John and Betty had moved from London to temporary digs in Edinburgh, and later that autumn to 10 Bright's Crescent where they would live for 14 years until John's retirement from the University of Edinburgh in 1958.

The Edinburgh Years

Macmurray's first duty at Edinburgh was to build up the Department of Moral Philosophy and its course offerings as the university geared up to receive returning veterans. Over the next few years, A.R.C. Duncan and Errol Bedford came on as Lecturers, and the Assistants who came—and some went—included Peter Heath, Frederick Broadie, R.J.K. (King) Murray, Kenneth Rankin, Axel Stern, Howard Horsburgh and others. Aesthetics and then Social Philosophy, along with a second Ordinary course in Moral Philosophy, were added to the offerings.

On coming to Edinburgh, Macmurray had resolved to cut back on public talks and activities—which he did to some extent. Nevertheless, he continued to respond to invitations that explored or implemented what, in his mind, were fresh initiatives in education, religion and openness to world community. This led him to have a very active membership in the Inter-University Council for Higher Education in the Colonies that included lecture visits to Ghana, Nigeria, and a semester in Jamaica. He was a friend of George MacLeod and became a director and fundraiser for the new Iona Community. Along with the poet Edwin Muir and other colleagues, he played a major role in the birth of Newbattle Abbey College in the early 1950s, an effort to offer an education in the humanities to working people and union leaders. He was a long time board member of Wennington School, an experimental secondary school in Lancashire headed by his longtime friends Kenneth and Frances Barnes. He travelled to Canada in 1949 to deliver the lectures published under the title *The Conditions of Freedom*. He commented that these lectures were his first real effort to articulate principles for a social philosophy that took into account the limitations of the human, what Kant referred to as "the crooked timber of humanity."

Despite these enthusiastic endeavours, the spirit of these years in university life was much muted for Macmurray. As George Davie reports, at the first meeting he ever had with Macmurray, late in 1945, Macmurray declared, "Davie, the humanities are fighting for their life at Edinburgh, and they're losing the battle." The remedy in a nutshell, as Macmurray saw it, was "to conceive and teach each subject in terms of its place and function in the unitary life of contemporary civilisation." But, as the 1950s unfolded, he came to believe there was no will for a remedy because there was little perception of or feeling for the problem. The technological and functional fixation, in his view, was getting an irreversible stranglehold on the aims of higher education.

And this held true not only, or even especially, at Edinburgh. Analytic philosophy was sweeping England and it crossed over into Scotland without having to pass through any customs or immigration officers with a knowledge of the Scottish tradition in higher education. Even in his own department, Macmurray's approach to philosophy and to philosophical ideas as an expression of and exercise in personal and social formation was, in the eyes of some of his new, English-trained assistants, rather quaint and outmoded. What they perhaps could not easily explain is how the quiet-voiced professor was able to attract over 400 students every year to his Ordinary Class in Moral Philosophy—students who seemed rather convinced that philosophy should have something to do with living. Nevertheless, the split between the older and newer approaches was becoming larger, and one of the reasons Macmurray insisted on correcting all 400 examinations at the end of each term was that he could no longer trust that his assistants would review the papers within the spirit in which the course had been offered.

At the same time as he was entrancing most undergraduates and at least some of his university colleagues, Macmurray was receiving more mixed reviews from his graduate students. Although they—along with everyone else—found him unremittingly gracious and pleasant with them, some of his advanced students found their professor unwilling to engage in any discussion or debate over his ideas. As one described those classes, Macmurray spoke with consummate wisdom and a profound sense of peace and clarity. He appeared more as a religious prophet proclaiming eternal truth than a university teacher for whom the truth was something to be worked out with colleagues by approximations—which was, ironically, his own deepest conviction about how truth is achieved. The healthy dialectic he subscribed to in theory seemed to many of them sadly missing from his own practice in these seminars.

There is evidence to suggest, as I noted above, that some of his assistants also shared this view of the clearly great man. They felt somewhat abandoned or at least benignly neglected by him. The philosopher of the personal was, apparently, not always very solicitous in his recognition of his own colleagues. One can wonder if the conflict between the old and new approaches in philosophy joined with Macmurray's own temperament shaped an attitude verging on indifference that some felt in their dealings with Macmurray. By the end of his time at Edinburgh, as his wife notes in her diaries, Macmurray found himself intellectually somewhat more comfortable at New College among the theologians than with some of the members of the philosophy departments. But there were special interludes, as well. It was during the mid-1950s, when he served for two years as Dean of Arts and Sciences, that he made the acquaintance of Martin Buber, Carl Jung, Gabriel Marcel and the scientist Max Born, among many other luminaries—some of whom became personal friends.

During these years Macmurray was asked again to speak on the BBC, usually on religion and its meaning in society, and to give public lectures on topics as wide-ranging as the philosophy of government, the contemporary task of religion, mental heath and personal relationship, and the conditions of marriage today. Within academic circles, he presented clear and trenchant papers among which were 'The Abuse of Language in Logic,' 'Some Reflections on the Analysis of Language,' 'Language as Communication,' and the incisively titled 'Cogito Ergo Non Sum.' And, of course, there were the two volumes of the Gifford Lectures which, in some anguish and with great resistance, he prepared for delivery at Glasgow University in 1953 and 1954. On the occasion of the 1954 set of lectures, he received an honorary LL.D from Glasgow, his undergraduate university.

It was in the Giffords, now known in their published form as *The Self as Agent* and *Persons in Relation*, that Macmurray brought to fullest articulation his philosophy of the personal. Although there are areas in these lectures where he clearly advances his thought and refines his language and categories, the kernel of his position in the Giffords can be traced back to his earliest writings in the 1930s and, as I have proposed, to the formative experiences of his early 20s. In his book on the Gifford Lectures over their first 100 years, Neil Spurway observed that even considering the huge contributions of Samuel Alexander, Whitehead,

Dewey, Marcel and Michael Polanyi in their Gifford offerings, the series by John Macmurray was "arguably one of the most systematic Natural Theologies the benefaction has yet elicited." As systematic as he wished to be in his thinking, Macmurray himself always chose to refer to his project of "conceiving the logic and form of the personal" as a pioneering work and in no way a completed one.

In December 1954, Macmurray was named Dean of the Faculty of Arts at Edinburgh, a position he held from January 1955 to December 1957. It was a time when the university was growing and major decisions were being made in curriculum, faculty and the construction of new buildings, including the David Hume Tower which currently houses the Department of Philosophy. Despite his reputation for a certain monk-like detachment among some of his graduate students, Macmurray was judged by his colleagues to be a well-organised administrator with an unusual capacity to evoke creative discussion and exchange in the Faculty of Arts Committee meetings. Close to his heart as Dean was the new Department of Nursing which he strove to keep associated with the Arts rather than the Science faculty on the grounds that it is primarily persons that nurses attend to, not diseases, and healing requires above all a felt knowledge of the needs of the whole person. The job of Dean grew in its demands over those years, and some months before leaving it, Macmurray urged that it be reconceived as a full-time position.

Meanwhile, Betty does much work with the University Women's Club. She also continues to pass observations in her diary on events and people. In its pages, she bewails the lack of recognition given to John"' philosophy in academic circles. In one entry, she recalls with huge warmth, the arrival at the door, on his 80th birthday, of Norman Kemp Smith, a colleague and dear friend who, with a great smile, shyly announced: "Today I've become an octogeranium." She also notes, at another point, her surprise at the depth of loneliness John confesses to at times. This loneliness was increased dramatically years later in April, 1973 when his mother died at the age of 105. Yet it had dominated him for longer, and, in a letter to Reginald Sayers in the 1970s, he notes that it has been part of his life for years.

During these years, the Macmurrays had entertained generously and often at their home on Bright's Crescent. John had taken up gardening and did it with a methodical intent that challenged the famed regularity of Immanuel Kant. Every spring he used a tape measure to plan out his rose garden, and hand clippers to cut the errant blades of grass that escaped the mower. He weeded daisies with a missionary zeal and ethical intent. He kept lists on his hobby areas of geology and birding, he saved string in neat rolls and—to Betty's great dismay—took up the piano again but with no greater success. At one dinner he took out a tape measure and appealed to complex mathematical formulas to prepare a melon for cutting so that all five guests would be assured of a portion that was exactly the same size as the others. He became a dressmaker for his wife and carried this chore out with an exactness that drove the more easygoing Betty to distraction. She was required on many occasions to stand on the dining room table while he adjusted with exactness the hem of the dress currently under construction. Her diaries note the passing joys and sorrows, and one entry marks with chagrin the arrival of Frederick Broadie at the front door early on the morning of New Year's Day 1957 with the finished appendix he was preparing for John's book, *The Self as Agent,* and she frets at John's gentle incapacity, even after some hours, to see Broadie out the door.

Return to Jordans

John Macmurray said his goodbyes at the University of Edinburgh midway through 1958 even though his retirement officially took effect only at the end of that year. He and Betty moved from Edinburgh that summer back to the Quaker village of Jordans in Buckinghamshire where they had lived—when they were not in Aberystwyth—between 1939 and 1944. John immediately left for an exhausting three-month lecture tour of American colleges and universities during which he gave almost 90 lectures on his familiar religious, social and philosophical themes. During this extremely well-received tour, he wrote his wife every day and each letter was an affectionate expression of his yearning to be back with her to begin their retired life together in their new home.

In 1959, John Macmurray and his wife applied for and were accepted as members of the Quaker Community. This ended his long self-exile from membership in any organized Christian body. The Quakers offered the fullest welcome with the fewest demands. As John put it to Kenneth Barnes, there was no "need to sign on the bottom line" with regard to declaring his stance on traditional doctrines. Betty, as an artist, yearned for more expression of feeling and ritual in religion and she openly admitted that she became a Quaker more because it was the preferred religious home for John rather than for herself.

Because of his profound love for freedom in thought and action and his respect for diversity of cultural expression, Macmurray always saw himself as essentially a Protestant. It was his heritage, and the tradition where, finally, he felt he could most be himself. But because of his passion for an urgent and energetic building of world community, Macmurray showed a deep sympathy for positive elements in Roman Catholicism, especially after the Second Vatican Council. He saw its vast outreach, the centrality of the Eucharist in its sacramental system, its diversity of cultures, and its respect for the role of reason in religion in its theological tradition as huge pluses for advancing an effective form of world-wide community. In 1973, having read of the new initiatives of the Church in Latin America and seeing the first written expressions of Liberation Theology, he wrote to Kenneth Barnes saying that, in his view, "the Catholic Church is the vanguard of the revolution in our times." As a lover of freedom himself and a rejector of authoritarianism under any guise, he was well aware how this judgment about the Catholic Church might, for many people, simply not be credible.

The following years included much activity and some writing—and some significant difficulties with health for both Betty and himself. Just as *Persons in Relation* was being published, Macmurray accepted the invitation of his 1930s Christian Left friend, Kenneth Muir, to deliver the Forwood Lectures at Liverpool University which were published in 1961 under the title *Religion, Art and Science*. As his last major presentation of his thought, it is fair to say they represent more of a distillation and refinement than a significant advance on these topics after the Gifford Lectures. In 1964 he does a series of four Lenten talks on the theme 'To Save from Fear' and earns from his 97-year-old mother the trenchant query, "That's all very well, John, but where is God in all this?" As Betty acknowledged later, this firm admonition affected him deeply. At the same time, he is invited by his fellow Quakers to give the Swarthmore Lecture which gets published in 1965 as *Search for Reality in Religion*, a highly readable expression of his personal journey, his essential philosophy and his testimonial as a believing Christian. It is his last book, and is the most autobiographical he ever became.

In his correspondence, he reaches out to friends, former colleagues, students and general inquirers with his trademark care and graciousness. He is so disillusioned with the forms of politics and economics he sees in the West that he speaks in letters of wanting to start a "World Friendship Society" that would bypass the politicians and represent something fresh and vital to which governments would have to be accountable. He sees the partialness of his own accomplishments in philosophy and reminds an American doctoral student in a letter: "...I should never hope or desire that an honest student of philosophy should find nothing to reject in my results. That would be unnatural." He asserts the need for religion to incorporate everything good from the sciences and the arts. But even as he speaks of the arts as providing the aesthetic dimension of religion, his rejection of idealism remains fierce and so he continues to be suspicious of mysticism and says he has had no personal success with meditation. Despite his rich view of contemplation in art, he seems to have had no positive idea of contemplation in religion as a way, in faith-imbued imagination, of embracing the world in its full incarnate reality and not a way to flee or deny the pressures of nature and history and our full personal experience. His rather populist notion of mysticism is an idealist one that is not consistent with the rest of his philosophy. It cries out for modification at the deepest level according to his own best insights in the area of contemplation in art. And, in fact, it belies his own informal experiences witnessed to by family members, despite his harsh judgments about his efforts at "meditation."

The almost complete victories of technology and capitalism in the West and the reduction of education from learning as full personal formation in cultural life to the mere acquisition of discrete "skills" and "tools" for a work life affect him deeply. In 1968, he notes in his correspondence that he is attempting to write an essay entitled 'Education for a Stupid Society', but after writing 13 pages, it was left unfinished. He makes an effort to publish a collection of essays and talks on education that he did over several years, but the collection is rejected for publication first by Faber and then by the University of Edinburgh Press, and it remains in the Special Collection at the University of Edinburgh Library still unpublished. He resolves to write more, but finds he lacks the energy and will for it. His time is spent in domestic pursuits and gardening. And there, in his garden, beyond all efforts at theory or explanation, he enjoys the simple contemplation (at heart religious) that escaped him in the more formal exercises he called meditation. And the time also was passed, if testimonials can be trusted, in outrageously charming his neighbours who remember him to this day with great fondness.

The Final Years in Edinburgh

In early 1970, when he was 79 and Betty 77, they moved back to Edinburgh where they shared a house on Mansionhouse Road with their nephew, Duncan Campbell and his wife Jocelyn and their four children. The new home brings them to a city they love, and to their family and the children who give them new life. They are also closer to the medical care they both need with greater regularity. And, as far as health permits, they walk a lot.

Macmurray continues his correspondence to the degree, as he himself notes, he can get over his "fits of detesting pen and paper." In his letters, he offers occasional reflections on the world and his own journey through it. He notes to Kenneth Barnes his life-long struggle with pacifism at the time of both wars and his decision to be a combatant even in the Second World War, if that had been required. In the face of nuclear realities, perhaps, but even more from his deep consideration of the methods of Jesus and the heart of his message, he writes to the Canadian, Reginald Sayers in 1972 he is now a convinced pacifist. As he notes, "A violent revolution produces a violent society."

In 1971, he reluctantly gave permission to Reg Sayers to begin a John Macmurray Society in Toronto to study his thought. To a specific inquiry from Mr. Sayers concerning a person who had referred to John Macmurray as a communist, Macmurray wrote back forcefully, "In case there are other similar inquiries I had better let you have my own answer. I never have been a communist, nor ever thought of being one. I studied Marx and decided his major mistake was about the social meaning of religion. The fact that Jewish religion was not idealist destroys completely the Marxist notion that the belief in another world… is the core of all religion. After that, I turned to Christianity as revolutionary Judaism." This was a focus that he pursued in a lively fashion even to the last major public address he prepared. Macmurray put a great deal of reflection into a lecture for the Edinburgh Theological Club that he entitled "The Philosophy of Jesus." However, he acknowledges that he is "not very satisfied with the result." In this lecture, the outline of his pacifist view of Jesus is sketched. He writes, Jesus discovered that "a true community cannot be established by force... The only proper course is to live the true life of human community in the Roman Empire and to transform it from within." And yet as much as he longs to be a full disciple, Macmurray still does not rule out the possibility of people choosing, in some critical situations, for a non-pacifist path as a temporary measure. It is from this perspective of forming community that he analyses the mission of Jesus as an open method—the living of a love that brings justice, the overcoming of fear by trust, and the cure of the deeds of evil by forgiveness based in truth and in love. This is the only method by which the establishment of the Kingdom of God on earth can be realised, and there is no recipe for it. It is a mission to form true community, and the name of that community, as it pursues this mission, is the Church of Christ. As he writes to another correspondent, it is in this light that "I believe that a rediscovery of Christianity is due—even overdue." To other correspondents, he writes graciously of how pleased he is that his writings are being of some help to them.

He takes time to consider both his accomplishments as a philosopher and his limitations. On February 26, 1974, Macmurray responds to several questions put to him by Mr. Sayers, including one about Whitehead who he says "is a thinker I admire very much: I think of him as the last of the Evolutionary or Zoological Philosophers; and a great man, and of course I think of my own work as an effort—and even a successful effort—to go farther." But when he refers to the meetings of the young John Macmurray Society, he asks: "Is there anyone who can come and give a good, critical approach to [my thought]?" Even at the end, the conviction remained that he was only a pioneer.

An effort was made in 1975 by Kenneth Barnes to get Macmurray's name on Prime Minister Wilson's Honours List. For some reason not communicated to Barnes, the initiative failed.

The end for John Macmurray came quickly after some months of seriously failing health for both him and Betty. He died at home on June 21, 1976. His funeral service and cremation were at Mortonhall Crematorium in Edinburgh on June 25. As his wife noted in her diary: There was no music. The minister did not know John Macmurray so he gave a formal but not a personal statement. The interment of his ashes

took place in Jordans on July 31 in the cemetery adjoining the Friends
Meeting House after a memorial service. Readings on love as the heart of
the Christian message taken from Chapter 15 of the Gospel of John and
from the fourth chapter of the First Letter of John were given. Betty
Macmurray died in August 1982, and her remains lie in the same grave
alongside her husband's in the small and tranquil Quaker graveyard at
Jordans.

Among the testimonials offered in 1975 supporting the effort to have
John Macmurray knighted was one from Professor Tom Torrance who
described John Macmurray "as the quiet giant of modern philosophy, the
most original and creative of savants and social thinkers in the English
speaking world." Many among us today find this a judgment that is at
least worthy of serious examination.

NOTES

[1]   I would like to acknowledge the many people, especially Duncan and Jocelyn
        Campbell, who have provided me with much of the unpublished material contained
        in this essay.

[2]   *Search for Reality in Religion* (1965).

[3]   *Reason and Emotion* (1935), 15.

CHAPTER TWO

The Contours of Macmurray's Philosophy[1]

David Fergusson

Though idiosyncratic, John Macmurray may be considered one of the most influential Scottish philosophers of the twentieth century. He lived during a time when logical positivism and linguistic analysis were dominant trends, and when the interests of professional philosophers seemed increasingly remote to the concerns of contemporary culture. By contrast, Macmurray's work was characterised by a missionary zeal to provide for society a philosophical diagnosis of its condition.[2] He attempted throughout his work to establish rational connections between science, art, psychology, political theory and religion. It is this holistic impulse which makes Macmurray such a suggestive thinker to students of other disciplines. By the same token, it renders his work difficult to summarise and to assess. Nonetheless, some recurrent themes can be readily identified from a study of his major writings.

Christianity and Communism

Macmurray was one of the few philosophers in twentieth-century Britain to reveal an indebtedness to Marx. Like Christianity, Marxism is governed by a perception of the unity of theory and practice.[3] Through inverting Hegelian idealism, Marx had insisted that things are prior to ideas and that action is more primary than thought. The world inhabited by the philosopher was not a private intellectual theatre; it was a material and social world in which thought derived from action. The primary function of thought was to enable action to be become effective and right.[4]

In asserting the unity of theory and practice Macmurray supported a radical break with the dominant European tradition which had divorced thought from action. Every theory serves some form of action, he claimed, and it is in practice that all theories must be tested. The truth of judgment must serve and be tested by the rightness of action, since right action is more fundamental than true judgment.[5] In this respect, Macmurray appealed to the methods of natural science in which provisional hypotheses are constantly subjected to experimental test. "The scientific attitude and method is an effort to amend beliefs by accepting them as a basis for experiment."[6]

The scientist is constantly engaged in formulating provisional hypotheses which are subject to experimental confirmation. The search for religious knowledge pursues a similar route. The rejection of absolute certainty and the emphasis upon practical confirmation are stressed. Religious belief must always be subject to practical verification and a desire for dogmatic finality must be eschewed.

This perceived unity of theory and practice challenges any philosophy or theology which tends to separate thought and action. According to Macmurray, we see this occurring in a series of dualist splits which have characterised much Western thought. Whether it be a dualism between mind and body, the secular and the sacred, or the natural and the supernatural we find the same deep-rooted tendency to divorce the realm of thought from the realm of action. We distort our human situation if we isolate the life of the intellect from its rootedness in the embodied world. The philosopher who seeks escape and security in an ideal world of thought is committing the same error as the religious believer who forsakes this world through contemplation of the next.[7]

For Macmurray, human existence is essentially active. The human being is an agent who belongs to a physical and public world. Right action is action which is appropriate to the reality of this situation. In this sense Macmurray's philosophy is unashamedly realist. Thought must be determined by the nature of a reality which exists prior to and independently of the knowing mind. The task of thought is therefore to bring itself into conformity with this reality. "Reason is the capacity to behave in terms of the nature of the object."[8] For the human agent the reality to which he or she must seek to conform in thought and action is fundamentally personal. The agent is a person whose nature it is to become free through communion with other persons. To elucidate this claim Macmurray characterises the field of human action.

In the universe there are three types or categories of reality—material, organic and personal.[9] Corresponding to each is a type of freedom which might be described as "self-consistent behaviour." At the material level we deal with particles which behave mechanically. These particles manifest material freedom insofar as their behaviour is in accordance with the laws of nature. The definitive characteristics of such freedom are consistency and predictability. Organic behaviour is observable in the life-cycle of plants and animals. Here behaviour is determined by growth and change in response to stimuli from a material environment and by the tendency towards the reproduction of species. Organic freedom is realised where the processes of life are fulfilled. Moreover, one can perceive a single purpose of organic life in the development of a totality of inter-dependent life forms. This does not, however, exhaust the possibilities of freedom. A higher form of freedom is that which is appropriate to personal life. At the personal level, human beings can act freely and rationally in accordance with their nature as persons. The goal of personal life may be described as friendship or communion. Here free action is not for the sake of conformity to the laws of nature or the processes of organic life. Free action is realised in communion with other persons. Human identity is fulfilled therefore by living in, through and for others.

This analysis of personal life has important social and political implications which further Macmurray's rapprochement between Christianity and communism. Although personal freedom transcends material and organic life it nonetheless requires these as its field of action. The freedom that is possible for human beings can only be actualised within the physical and social world. This means that the way in which we relate to material and organic reality must serve and enhance the ends of personal life. The fullest expression of personal freedom must therefore involve an economic and social order in which all human activity is directed towards communion. Personal freedom cannot be created through state control but nonetheless the establishment of social and economic justice is a necessary condition for genuine human community. This requires a society based upon principles of co-operation rather than power, and it entails the breakdown of class structures.

> If social development is to be planned and controlled, the struggle for power must cease and social relations must, therefore, cease to be determined through the control and ownership of the means of production. In particular,

the division of society into a class which owns the means of production and a class which does not must disappear. The primary condition of a planned social development and, therefore, of the disappearance of economic determinism in the development of society is the realization of a society without social classes. And a classless society is a communist society. Communism, is therefore, the necessary basis of real freedom.[10]

However, there are aspects of his thought which distance Macmurray from communist orthodoxy. Marxist-Leninism, he argued, tends to ignore the importance of personal life and freedom by subordinating everything else to an organic conception of life. History is not an organic process which is subject to deterministic laws of development. The state cannot and should not seek to impose upon individuals conditions which will guarantee personal fulfilment. The freedom of personal life is here ignored with the dangerous totalitarian consequence that the significance of the individual may be lost sight of in the search for some wider social good. For Macmurray genuine community can only be created where human beings as individuals can realise their freedom in relationship with one another. In his later work, a distinction between community and society becomes more pronounced. A society is a functional entity in which individuals associate for the attainment of self-regarding ends. By contrast, in a community persons associate for the attainment of friendship or communion as an end in itself.[11] Although the organisation of society must promote the ends of community, the two are to be distinguished. There can be no creation of community through the reconfiguring of society by political means.

It has been argued, moreover, that the absence of many key Marxist tenets in Macmurray's thought calls into question his attempt to mediate between Christianity and communism. Elizabeth Lam has pointed out that in Macmurray there is little discussion of such essential Marxist ideas as the interpretation of history in terms of class conflict, the necessity for a revolutionary overthrow of the capitalist system by the proletariat, the sociological roots of knowledge, and the distinction between base and superstructure.[12] The absence of such doctrines in Macmurray's philosophy together with his criticism of Soviet communism might suggest that his own position was closer to that of the social democrat than the Marxist communist. Nonetheless, his philosophical and practical commitment to left-of-centre politics remained constant throughout his life.[13]

Macmurray was willing to concede that the Marxist criticism of religion had exposed the ways in which the Church often legitimated unjust regimes. Nonetheless, he is critical of the Marxist rejection of religion on the ground that religion can integrate the eternal and the temporal, the material and the spiritual, and the personal with the social. Religion, for Macmurray, supports and sustains the personal life.[14] It exercises a positive social role in enhancing just relationships between human beings, and in promoting the value of love. In this way it can transcend the merely organic social vision of communism. When we understand the function of religion in this holistic manner we shall recognise how central religion is to all human activity. Macmurray is here heavily influenced by his understanding of Hebrew religion, and he frequently appeals to the Hebraic tradition over against the Greek and Roman. For the Jewish consciousness, religion is not simply one compartment of life; it organizes and integrates the whole of personal, social and national life. It is commended by Macmurray for its lack of other-worldliness, its perception of the unity between individual and social action, and the connection it makes between national prosperity and righteousness.[15] The significance of Jesus lies in his transformation of Judaism from a national to a universal religion.

On the basis of his understanding of personal freedom Macmurray boldly claims that the ideals of Christianity transcend those of Buddhism and Islam. Buddhism seeks to overcome tension and enmity in human affairs through a personal fellowship which withdraws from this world, whereas Islam seeks to achieve social integrity through aggression and force. Christianity, by contrast, seeks to establish a universal fellowship between human beings on earth based on the principle of love rather than fear. While the history of Christianity represents a failure to fulfil this ideal, it remains valid as the teaching of Jesus.[16]

The proper function of religion is the celebration, promotion and anticipation of community amongst persons. It kindles love and overcomes the fear of death which threatens to destroy our personhood. Yet, while Macmurray has much to say about the role of religion in integrating and fostering the requirements of personal life, he has rather less to say about the concept of God. It is clear however that God is to be thought of as the infinite and eternal ground of personal life. As a physical object is an expression of matter, and an organism an expression of the processes of life, so analogously a human person is a manifestation of the divine, universal person who is the ultimate field of all action. In order to make sense of the uniqueness of personal life we have to assume that the ultimate reality is personal rather than material or organic.[17]

Macmurray's philosophical theology is given further shape by two negative considerations. First, he rejects any conception of God as set over against the world. A dialectical understanding of the God-world relation will inevitably set the supernatural in opposition to the natural, and this must give rise to a dualist religion. Here the human being becomes detached from this world through the presentation of another realm as the true home and destiny of human existence. Second, we should note Macmurray's low estimate of the role of doctrine in religion. The primary expression of religion is not in creeds, doctrines or dogmas but in action and communion.[18] A religious doctrine is to be assessed in terms of its usefulness in enhancing the personal life, and every religious statement must be subject to experimental confirmation. The activities of a religion are more primary than its beliefs.[19]

Reason and Emotion

The prophetic nature of Macmurray's philosophy emerges nowhere more clearly than in his claim that the crisis of twentieth-century culture has been generated by a split between the intellect and the emotions. The startling progress of science has been accompanied, he argues, by a crippling of the emotional life and a subsequent fragmentation of society. It is in emotional terms that we must attach values to actions and states of affairs, yet we are no longer certain of what our values really are.

In a state of moral confusion philosophy has a vital role to play. The philosopher has the task of diagnosing the causes of this malaise and of pointing towards its remedy. For Macmurray, the sickness lies in our emotional life. His prescription is not for a suppression of feelings and emotions in the interests of detached reason; this would only reinforce the dualism which is at the root of all our problems. Instead, Macmurray proposes a reordering of the emotional life in which we learn to co-ordinate our deepest feelings with the way the world is. This, he insists, is a rational and disciplined activity. Our emotions require to be educated, refined and made responsive not to our base inclinations but to the nature of reality. Where emotion becomes the expression of inappropriate desire or false perception it degenerates into sentiment. Insofar as our emotions are appropriate responses to that which to they refer they can be described as "right" or "wrong." In this respect we can speak of "emotional reason."[20] The development of our emotions is, according to Macmurray, often a hard and painful exercise, partly because it involves the need for much greater self-awareness. Being fully alive to things as they are can give us as much pain as pleasure. Emotional education must aim at what Blake called "the refinement of sensuality."[21]

This difficulty in ordering the emotional life can be seen clearly in human sexuality. Macmurray's discussion of the virtue of chastity is worth considering in this context.[22] He argues that the institutions of social life must be made subject to the ultimate goals of personal life. In this respect, marriage and the family do not exist as end in themselves and they are not to be idolised. Within marriage the personal goals of freedom and equality are sought yet traditionally these have been impeded by the economic and legal organisation of the marital relationship. Traditionally men have been allowed to develop their individuality through thinking, fighting, inventing and creating while women have held home and family together. This has led to a differentiation of function in which men have tended to represent the individual and the intellectual, and women the unitive and the loving. Macmurray notes (in 1935) that this differentiation is fading from western society and now a greater equality and mutuality between the sexes is required. Women are rightly seeking to realise their capacities as individuals and entering the world of literature and art, the professions, politics and industry. This radically new phenomenon in the history of civilization must be met with enthusiasm and courage.

In the past Christian morality has been too obsessed with externals. The conformity of behaviour to rules confining sex within the bonds of marriage is no guarantee of personal fulfilment. "To say that sex-relationships are moral because a man and a woman are married, immoral because they are not married, is to base morality upon something external."[23] This is to sever the link between sex and love, and we can see this separation most clearly in Victorian culture with its romantic sentimentalism and its dread of sex. The solution however is not to give free rein to our natural sexual desires. Mere sexual attraction is not a sufficient basis for a proper relationship between a woman and a man. It mistakes lust for love, and seeks enjoyment through rather than with another person. Our desires require to be disciplined and subordinated to the ends of personal life. When this happens we attain emotional sincerity and true chastity in our sexuality. Both the suppression and idolization of sex are dangerous.[24]

According to Macmurray, the activity of the artist is crucial for the proper expression of emotions. It is through art that we learn to value things in themselves, and to refine our sensibility. The artist creates and contemplates a work of art for its own sake, and not as an instrument for a higher purpose. The recapturing of a sense of beauty is crucial if our society is not to lose its freedom and sense of worth.[25] Aesthetic appreciation is not the expression of subjective taste but aims at an objective assessment of the work of art. We are aware of emotional objectivity in the common distinction we make between enjoying a good 'thriller' and enjoying one of the great classical novels. The work of the artist enables us to gain a clearer and purer perception of what is true and right. This is something that science by itself can never do. "So Darwin lamented in his old age that his mind had become a mere machine for grinding out general laws, and wished that he had read a poem a day."[26]

Yet art, he claims, has limitations which are only transcended through religion. The activity of the artist is essentially contemplative and solitary. The artist depicts life but *qua* artist does not participate in it actively. This passivity and solitariness of the artist together with the unreality of her creations can only be resolved by religion. Religion was historically the matrix out of which art and science arose and it continues to provide the unifying context in which these activities must be pursued.

Macmurray claims that there are two emotional attitudes which radically determine human life.[27] These are love and fear. Fear is a negative emotion which inhibits spontaneity and generates selfishness. The real antithesis of love is not hate but fear. Many false forms of religion are responses to the ultimate fear of death. True religion, by contrast, liberates us from false fears by enabling us to love life and other people. It does this not by promising some illusory escape from the harsh realities of our existence, but by teaching us to meet them without fear. This was a lesson that Macmurray had learned in the carnage of the Somme.

Real Christianity stands today, as it has always stood, for life against death, for spontaneity against formalism, for the spirit of adventure against the spirit of security, for faith against fear, for the living colourful multiplicity of difference against the monotony of the mechanical, whether it be the mechanization of the mind, which is dogmatism, or the mechanization of the emotions, which is conformity.[28]

The Primacy of the Personal

Macmurray's most significant philosophical work is found in his Glasgow Gifford Lectures which were published in two volumes under the collective title, *The Form of the Personal*. While the positions adopted here were not new they were defended in a more systematic manner than hitherto. His Giffords attempt to provide the necessary metaphysical underpinning for many of the moral, political, psychological and religious ideas advanced in earlier writings. His fundamental and provocative claim is that modern western philosophy has been ensnared by the adoption of a standpoint which is theoretical and egocentric. The self is treated as a pure, withdrawn subject looking out upon the world in relative detachment from other persons. The Cartesian approach to knowledge began by establishing the existence of the thinking self as the one indubitable fact upon which a system of knowledge was to be built. Thereafter, by demonstrating the existence of God and the veracity of sense experience, Descartes was able to establish the existence of the physical and social world to which the mind belonged in virtue of its close association with a body. The problems engendered by this approach are manifold. They include the dubious nature of the arguments used to establish the existence of God; the problem of the existence of other minds; the difficulty in demonstrating the independence of the spatio-temporal world; and the mysterious nature of the causal relationship between mind and body. The extent of these problems generated by the Cartesian method is seen by Macmurray as symptomatic of a deep-seated flaw. He argues that the problem with the theoretic and egocentric standpoint is that it distorts many of the beliefs and assumptions which are fundamental to the way in which we understand ourselves, the world and other persons. We need to return to first principles to expose the obfuscating tendencies of the Cartesian procedure.

A process of doubt, Macmurray argues, can only make sense against a background of positive belief. Moreover, to isolate mental activity as the distinctive feature of the self is immediately to exclude the possibility that action, the material world, and other persons are of definitive importance in understanding what it is to be human. Kant's unsuccessful attempt to begin with theoretical reason and then to introduce practical reason created a split in his conception of the self and the world. This convinced Macmurray that the practical standpoint had to be adopted as primary in philosophy.

Macmurray proposes that we substitute the "I do" for the "I think," and reflect from the standpoint of action. We should note that there is no hint of anti-intellectualism here since this proposal is itself highly complex and philosophical. Moreover, Macmurray does not wish to exclude the significance of the theoretical but only to reorient it. His procedure throughout the first volume (*The Self As Agent*) is to present something like a phenomenological description of the main categorial features of action. Through an analysis of the necessary features and implications of action Macmurray attempts to show how the agent is rooted in a communal and public world in which human identity is determined relationally and holistically.

He begins by arguing that action requires something to be acted upon. This implies the necessity of matter. To act upon matter, moreover, the agent must herself be material and hence embodied. Thus the material world together with the embodiedness of the agent are necessary features of action. Agency, however, cannot be reduced to mechanical or organic activity. It involves intention and choice not as mental events which precede and cause action, but as necessary aspects of action. The self can be agent only through being also subject, although it is equally true that the self is subject only because it is agent.[29] Thought and knowledge are therefore necessary aspects of action, yet these only become possible in and through activity. Knowledge informs action, and where it increases there is a subsequent increase in the range of possible activity.[30] The significance of Macmurray's subordination of knowledge to action is that all theoretical activity must be justified by reference to its practical implications. It is only in virtue of its reference to the practical that reflection can be capable of truth or falsity.[31]

The interaction with other agents is also a necessary condition of agency. It is through encountering resistance to action and being acted upon that the self becomes an agent. Here Macmurray focuses upon the significance of tactual perception (as opposed to the more passive visual perception favoured by other philosophers) through which the other person is encountered as one who resists my will. To understand the other I must attribute to her the form of activity I attribute to myself. Knowledge of what is involved in action must include a knowledge of other persons. All knowledge indeed arises out of personal participation in a social world.

In the second volume of the Gifford Lectures, *Persons in Relation*, we find Macmurray further developing the notion of what it means to be an agent. Here he moves from his metaphysic of the personal to its moral implications. The nature of the self is to be understood holistically. He argues that body and mind cannot be understood apart from one another, the self cannot be detached from the material world, and the individual exists only in dynamic relations with others. The human agent is therefore a person whose identity is bound up with the material and social world. I exist as an individual only in relation to other individuals, and rational action is action in which I treat the other as a person rather than an object at my disposal.[32]

In the second and third chapters of *Persons in Relation* Macmurray analyses the relationship between mother and child, and the growth of the child's self-consciousness within the matrix of the family. The child is born into an social environment that is dominated by the intentions of the mother in establishing regular patterns of feeding and sleeping. The child's progress does not consist in a rapid adaptation to the environment (as is the case with animals); instead, progress takes the form of the acquirement of skills such as discriminating colours and shapes, making sounds, and correlating sight and touch.[33] What we see emerging in the child is the development of a set of habitual skills which are consciously acquired and are not the result of sheer instinct. These skills, which are necessary conditions for action, enable the child to take his place as a member of a personal community. Moreover the development of skills requires the presence of a more mature person to provide direction and judgment in the learning process. The existence of two-way communication, particularly in the form of language, is thus crucial to the personal way of life. The role of communication is more constitutive of persons than it is of animals. Thus he claims in an oft-quoted passed.

[H]uman experience is, in principle, shared experience; human life, even in its most individual elements, is a common life; and human behaviour carries always, in its inherent structure, a reference to the personal Other. All this may

be summed up by saying that the unit of personal existence is not the
individual, but two persons in personal relation; and that we are persons not by
individual right, but in virtue of our relation to one another. The personal is
constituted by personal relatedness. The unity of the personal is not the "I",
but the "You and I".[34]

He goes on to distinguish three fundamental ways in which the other
person can be determined through action. (These three "forms of
apperception" are analogues of Kant's categories of the theoretical
understanding.) Macmurray identifies the three forms as contemplative,
pragmatic and communal. Corresponding to each of the three is a moral
code which will tend to be dominant in a social grouping. In other words,
the fundamental possibilities of human interaction are determined by
communal, contemplative and pragmatic ways of perceiving the world.

The contemplative mode is characterised typically by an egocentric
ethic which is marked by a dualism between the self and the world.[35]
Here the real world is the spiritual world into which the agent retreats.
The goal of life is knowledge and contemplation of the other world. In
order for the individual to realise this private ideal it is of course
necessary that the world around her be regulated in a particular way, and
this will tend to take the form of a functional social morality. Macmurray
finds the classical exposition of this moral code in Plato's *Republic*.

The pragmatic mode of apperception is manifested in an ethic which
subordinates the desires of the individual to the progress of society as a
whole. The emphasis upon technological achievement will tend to be
paramount in this outlook. Its origins lie in Stoicism and Roman law, and
it is expounded by Kant in his philosophy of obedience to the demands
of the categorical imperative.[36] Here the goal of life is not contemplation
but some organic purpose to which the individual must be subordinated,
and hence the prevailing moral code will be dominated by the rhetoric of
obedience and sacrifice.

By contrast, the communal mode of apperception is marked by a
heterocentric morality which gives a central place to the Golden Rule.
(Do unto others what you would have them do unto you.) This mode of
apperception is characteristic of the Hebraic tradition and is extended in
the teaching of Jesus. Human society is a unity of persons, and the goals
of personal life can be sought neither in retreat from society nor in
subordinating the interests of the individual to the group. A community
exists for the sake of friendship which is the final goal of all human

action. The organisation of society must therefore be based upon the principle of love rather than upon the principle of fear as it is in much political theory.

> The model of the family is to be realised in society at large. A community is a unity of persons as persons. It cannot be defined in functional terms, by relation to a common purpose. It is not organic in structure, and cannot be constituted or maintained by organization, but only by the motives which sustain the personal relations of its members. It is constituted and maintained by a mutual affection. This can only mean that each member of the group is in positive personal relation to each of the others taken severally. The structure of a community is the nexus or network of the active relations of friendship between all possible pairs of its members.[37]

Throughout the Gifford Lectures the models of the mother-child relation and the family are used to illustrate the nature of the personal. Yet it is clear from the closing chapters of *Persons in Relation* that Macmurray has not forgotten the social, economic and cosmic dimensions of personhood. The maintenance of justice in the regulation of economic life is a necessary though insufficient condition for the creation of personal relations in a community. Justice is a necessary component of every personal relation. The task of politics is to maintain, improve and adjust the indirect or economic relations of persons.[38] The State is to be seen as "a public utility" rather than some mystical, quasi-personal entity. It is a limited and fallible instrument of the personal and is not to be accorded a hallowed status.

In this context, Macmurray should be seen as an apostle of internationalism. The economic order is now an international order, he argues, and if it is to serve the goals of personal life it can do so only through co-operation and the establishment of international justice. The alternative is war and catastrophe. It is imperative therefore that human beings acknowledge their common humanity and make respect for personality the most fundamental law.

> The necessity of our time is the achievement of an effective world-order. This is not simply a desirable step forward in human progress. It is a necessity from which we cannot escape and in face of which we have no choice. We shall move from war to war, from catastrophe to catastrophe until somehow it is achieved. There is no effective alternative. The condition of freedom from now onwards is bound up with this. The effort to maintain the limited freedoms of our traditional, isolated communities, if we do no more than this,

is futile. They will continue to dwindle away, or to be violently suppressed, as
they are doing, unless we can universalize them. We have to establish freedom
for all men in a single world order, or lose our own.[39]

For the communal mode of apperception religion has a crucial role
to play. Its function is to create, sustain and enrich the community of
persons and to enable the bonds of friendship to transcend cultural,
national and racial differences. It does this through the idea of a personal
God who stands in the same relationship to each person, and who
therefore treats human persons as if they belonged to a single
community. Within this conception of religion, ritual is more important
than doctrine in promoting fellowship and community amongst persons.
In conceiving the world as one action we tend to conceive of God as the
creator who establishes the conditions for the attainment of personal
freedom. Macmurray concludes his Gifford Lectures with the warning
that this argument for the validity of religious belief does not promote
any particular system of religious belief.[40]

Macmurray is an ambitious writer paints on a broad canvas. He
relates to his social and political context, and he interacts with other
disciplines in a refreshing and sometimes inspirational way. In many
respects, he can be seen as embodying the Scottish tradition of 'the
democratic intellect'.[41] This may explain why his influence has tended to
be outside mainstream philosophy and within other disciplines. He is a
thinker whose work is suggestive of a variety of insights which can
usefully be appropriated by thinkers in other different fields. His
influence, moreover, has extended to an unusually wide range of
individuals who have gained recognition in a variety of fields of public
service. Macmurray, however, once remarked that even if he lived till the
age of his mother, who died at 105, he did not expect to see his work
accepted by a single trained philosopher.[42]

This comment however might need to be qualified in one important
respect. While Macmurray's work was not well received by fellow
philosophers during his own lifetime his critique of Cartesian patterns of
thought is now beginning to meet with widespread acceptance towards
the end of the twentieth-century. He might now be grouped along with
such distinguished names as Heidegger and Wittgenstein as one who
protested against the distortions caused by egocentric and theoretical
patterns of thought in philosophy. In particular he provides us with a rare
attempt to make philosophical sense of agency and relatedness as

intrinsic features of our humanity. If his work lacks the depth of Wittgenstein and Heidegger, it remains an excellent vantage point from which to release students from their ingrained Cartesian thought patterns.

At the very least, Macmurray's thought has the important function of exposing our habitual tendency to assume that there is a clear division between body and mind, self and world, individual and community, and private and social morality. In a series of sustained philosophical reflections, he provided insights that were subsequently to prove seminal for philosophers, theologians and social scientists. The need to arrive at some holistic conception of human life, society and the universe is impressed upon us as an urgent practical necessity. If this was true in Macmurray's lifetime it is true, *a fortiori*, in an age with greater nuclear, ecological, atomistic and global economic anxieties. Every way of life makes assumptions about what it means to be a person and the nature of the world and the societies in which we live, and Macmurray's philosophy does much to illuminate the connections between these.

NOTES

[1]   In this essay, I have drawn on material previously published in *John Macmurray* (Edinburgh: Handsel Press, 1992).

[2]   A.J. Ayer writes somewhat disparagingly of the way in which the missionary spirit infected Macmurray's philosophy. *More of My Life* (London: Collins, 1984), p.16. Macmurray himself disapproved of the appointment of Ayer to the Grote Chair he had held in London, remarking that he was merely clever and would have made a better professor of national football. *John Macmurray Newsletter*, Winter, 1980, 4.

[3]   *Creative Society* (1935).

[4]   *The Philosophy of Communism* (1933), 26ff.

[5]   *Freedom in the Modern World* (1932), 143.

[6]   'Beyond Knowledge,' *Adventure*, B.H. Streeter, J. Macmurray et al. (London: Macmillan, 1927), 35.

[7]   *Reason and Emotion* (1935), 227–228.

[8]   Ibid., 19.

[9]   *Freedom in the Modern World*, 175ff; *Interpreting the Universe* (1938), 206ff.

[10] *Philosophy of Communism*, 79–80.

[11] *Conditions of Freedom* (1950), 35f.

[12] Elizabeth P. Lam, 'Does Macmurray Understand Marx?', *Journal of Religion*, 20, (1940), 47–65.

[13] At a recent meeting of the John Macmurray Fellowship, a personal acquaintance of Macmurray indicated that, whenever his opinion was sought, he would always advise voting for the socialist (i.e. Labour) party in a British election.

[14]   *Creative Society*, 90ff.

[15]   59ff.

[16]   *Conditions of Freedom*, (1950), 91ff.

[17]   E.g. 'Objectivity in Religion', op. cit., 215.

[18]   Ibid. p.72. Macmurray's eventual decision to join the Society of Friends was
       influenced by the Society's lack of doctrinal rigidity. Cf. *Search for the Reality of
       Religion*, op. cit., 71.

[19]   E.g. *Search for the Reality of Religion*, 31.

[20]   *Reason and Emotion*, 26.

[21]   Ibid., 71.

[22]   Ibid., 117–144.

[23]   Ibid., 122.

[24]   It is not clear from Macmurray's deliverances on this subject whether he judged
       monogamy and fidelity to be features of 'emotional sincerity' in sexual behaviour.

[25]   *Freedom in the Modern World*, 218.

[26]   *Reason and Emotion*, op. cit., 164.

[27]   *Freedom in the Modern World*, 58ff.

[28]   Ibid., 66.

[29]   *The Self as Agent*, 100–103.

[30]   Ibid., 179.

[31]   Ibid., 183.

[32]   *Persons in Relation* (1961).

[33]   Ibid., 53.

[34]   Ibid., 60–61.

[35]   Ibid., 123ff.

[36]   Ibid., 125–6.

[37]   Ibid., 157–8.

[38]   Ibid., 188.

[39]   *Conditions of Freedom*, 99–100.

[40]   Ibid., 223.

[41]   Cf. George Davie, *The Democratic Intellect* (Edinburgh University Press, 1961).
       Macmurray's significance for Scottish culture is discussed by Craig Beveridge and
       Ronald Turnbull, *The Eclipse of Scottish Culture* (Edinburgh: Polygon, 1989), 96–
       99.

[42]   *The John Macmurray Society Newsletter*, 5.1 (1980), 4.

CHAPTER THREE

Macmurray and the Mind-Body Problem Revisited

Stanley Harrison

John Macmurray's antipathy toward the dualism of mind and matter was virtually life-long as well as central to his philosophical project.[1] Indeed, in many ways, his entire enterprise of rethinking the nature of persons and the interpersonal world just was a sustained attempt to help us get over deeply engrained habits of thinking which proceed along dualistic lines. At the core of this reconstructive effort was Macmurray's lifelong concern with religion, particularly his conviction that the alleged "subjective" or illusory character of religion was itself an error rooted in the false dualism of mind and matter. His goal was not to solve the problem of dualism (which he thought an impossible task as demonstrated by the development of modern philosophy) but to show how to resist the natural temptation to divide the human person into a mind and a body, thus not allowing the contrast between mind and matter to gain a foothold in one's thinking.[2]

Macmurray became convinced quite early in his philosophical life that there were no compelling reasons at all for speaking of oneself as "a mind," an immaterial entity, somehow mysteriously connected with a "material" object called "a body." But he makes an important distinction between the metaphysical dualism which divides reality exclusively into "minds" and "material" objects and the different dualism of "mind" and "body." The difference was due to the fact that normally when we are thinking about our minds and our bodies, "we are thinking of our bodies not as material objects but as animal organisms."[3] In other words, to think of one's body as a living organism was not to be considering it as a material object in the manner of a physicist; indeed, he argued, there was no legitimate way to think about one's organic nature in that strictly mechanist way. That Descartes did conceive his body in this way is of course well known, as is his characterization of all non-personal living things, plants and animals, in mechanistic terms, that is, as automata. This extreme conclusion, which so violates common belief, especially regarding animals, was an essential aspect of the radical nature of the metaphysical dualism of mind and matter.

Macmurray was convinced that "the idea of dualism only arises when we consider our own nature."[4] For him the natural classification of things suggested by common sense was a triad consisting of non-living things, living things, and persons. But, "it is only in reference to persons that the dualism arises at all, and persons form a relatively small class of objects in the world as we know it. That in itself suggests that the dualism is not really a metaphysical one but rather a personal one." [5] This meant that the relevant question or fact had to do with what it was about persons that might naturally suggest our having a dualistic nature. To determine this would put one in a better position to judge whether the inference to any rigid dualism of mind and body was justified. For Macmurray, the root of the dualistic suggestion was linked closely to our experience of being located in an *interpersonal* world, specifically in the fact that we eventually discovered "that our knowledge of ourselves is very different from our knowledge of other people like ourselves. I know myself from inside, as it were, while I know other people only from outside."[6] Each of us, he went on, also knows himself or herself from the outside but not as clearly as others know us in this way. This "double awareness," especially the experience of introspection, was the fact which, in Macmurray's view, most likely misled many into asserting the separate "entities" of mind and body. Our experience of the privacy of our thought was an aspect of our reflective consciousness easily misconstrued as a sign of the entitative nature of mind. But, he argued, asserting a metaphysical dualism of body and mind destroys the possibility of our knowing ourselves in the two ways we do. Since our double awareness is an incontrovertible fact, the mind-body dualism must be false.[7]

The history of modern philosophy, however, was for Macmurray the brilliant but tortured response to the lingering and deep seated problem of dualism. Macmurray's response to this historical outcome was to attempt to reestablish the unity of the human persons by having us learn to think from what he called "the standpoint of action." This meant working out some central implications of the Kantian insight that reason is primarily practical in order to overcome the standpoint of the "I think" which had dominated modern philosophy. Macmurray set out to show that "thinking," important as it is to human existence, was derivative from human action. His Gifford Lectures are his mature statement of the important first stages of this effort to develop a *theory* which would make plain what it meant to claim that action is primary, that is, that we must learn to think of essential nature through the category of our agency.[8] To do this successfully, he argued, would be at the same time to defend and to clarify the irreducible unity of the human person as an agent/knower already inextricably located within the unity of a dynamic processive interpersonal world. Ultimately, Macmurray argued for a comprehensive metaphysical unity involving the reality of a personal God continuously acting within history to achieve His divine intention.

Many have been impressed, and rightly so, by Macmurray's multi-faceted analysis and have found it immensely fruitful for thinking about a whole range of issues, especially in epistemology, ethics, culture (including science, art and religion), all linked to the metaphysical character of human persons and the interpersonal world. To read him closely is to learn a great deal about the paths taken in modern philosophy, ultimately in response to Cartesian dualism and especially the epistemological problems it engendered, some of which led into what Macmurray regarded as the cul-de-sacs of modern atheism, positivism and scientism. Still, despite his trenchant critiques of the metaphysical dualism of mind and matter and its derivative, mind-body dualism, and despite the undeniable value of the positive doctrine he articulates, this essay will argue that Macmurray's way of speaking about the constiuent factors of human nature and defending the unity of the human person is not complete.[9] The issue taken up here is whether Macmurray has provided an adequate account of persons as capable of reflective self-awareness, a mode of consciousness revealed perhaps most obviously and dramatically in our ability to use signs, for example in speech, to convey to other persons the meaning of our experience.

It seems likely that others readers of his Gifford lectures (or indeed of his other works) have been struck by the fact that Macmurray avoids altogether the language of "soul" and "spirit," or any appeal to a principle of *immateriality,* to explain either the general fact of human knowledge or the uniqueness of interpersonal relations. It is this which initially provoked this interrogation of the adequacy of Macmurray's account of the human person. Macmurray might have regarded such puzzlement as itself a sign of the dualistic habit of thinking that he wished to overcome. Nevertheless, the question asked here is essentially a simple one: Can he succeed in his account of the uniqueness of personal consciousness without invoking some strong principle of immateriality? Can he do justice to the reality of human persons without the category of "spirit"? And, if he cannot, has he escaped the mind-body dualism as cleanly and completely as he hoped? The argument here will be that he has not probed deeply enough into the nature of language or symbolization, that the uniqueness of human rationality as it is disclosed in our use of signs cannot be adequately accounted for without invoking a mode of consciousness which is best described as involving immaterial acts of awareness. This does not mean, however, a return to the metaphysical dualism of Descartes and his progeny. Macmurray was right to reject the "cogito" or any form of substance dualism as rendering human action utterly unintelligible and of destroying the basis for any viable form of intersubjective or interpersonal relations. Rather, the outcome here will be that Macmurray is much closer to the hylemorphic theory of Aristotle and, especially, to the medieval philosopher/ theologian Thomas Aquinas than he recognized.[10]

It seems altogether unlikely, however, that he would have welcomed any such suggestion given what he took to be the Aristotelian emphasis on the good life as primarily consisting in "theoretical" activity,[11] the primacy of which Macmurray sought to overcome with his own doctrine. Macmurray was obviously familiar with at least some of Aristotle's work.[12] There seems little reason, however, to believe that he ever read Aquinas. Indeed, his remarks relative to medieval philosophy are scant, negative and border on a stereotypical, if not cavalier, dismissal.[13] Be that as it may, one reason the hylemorphic view is of initial interest here is precisely because Aristotle originated it, at least partly, and Aquinas embraced and developed it, in response to the same error which Macmurray abhorred, namely, "the pagan dualism" of body and soul, a relative of the metaphysical dualism of mind and matter.[14] Such a dualism makes the *unity* of the human person spurious, an illusion, and defines the person as a soul-substance inexplicably conjoined to matter and somehow making it alive.

The appropriate context for understanding Macmurray's doctrine, however, is modern philosophy and his particular point of departure is Kant's "central and revolutionary conclusion that reason is primarily not cognitive, but practical."[15] Despite his brilliance, Kant failed, argues Macmurray, to salvage the essential unity of the human person. In the final analysis, Kant's appeal, for example, to the essentially inaccessible *noumenal* self as the hidden but necessary foundation of moral experience involves another incoherent dualism. Kant is unable "to think the unity of the same self in the theoretical and practical fields."[16] It was this unity which Macmurray set out to restore as a way of overcoming dualism once and forever. Kant's ultimate error was that, despite his claim that reason is primarily practical, nevertheless he had constructed his philosophy "on the presupposition that the theoretical is primary."[17] Despite his brilliant and history-making response to Cartesian rationalism and Humean skepticism, he too had unwittingly accepted the primacy of the "I think" as his frame of reference and it is this which finally leads to Kant's own profound skepticism concerning the possibility of metaphysical knowledge of reality. Macmurray summarizes his criticism in the following passage: "For thought is inherently private; and any philosophy which takes its stand on the primacy of thought, which defines the Self as the Thinker, is committed formally to an extreme logical individualism. It is necessarily egocentric."[18] Ultimately, this meant that Kant had no resource for thinking adequately about the inherent mutuality of personal existence which, for Macmurray, is the crucial empirical ground of religion. It was this failure that made it impossible, in Macmurray's view, for Kant to offer an adequate critique of religion.

The failure of the great German philosopher is the mistake which, in Macmurray's view, infects all "modern" philosophy.

[A]ny philosophy which takes the "Cogito" as its starting point and centre of reference institutes a formal dualism of theory and practice; and that... makes it formally impossible to give any account, and indeed to conceive the possibility of persons in relation, whether the relation be theoretical—as knowledge, or practical—as cooperation. For thought is essentially private. Formally, it is the contrary of action; excluding any causal operation upon the object which is known through its activity, that is to say, upon the Real.[19]

The inevitable result was an intractable dualism (indeed in principle a solipsism) fatal to any effort to think coherently the *unity* of experience. Descartes himself was not unaware of the serious dilemma his view involved, a deep conundrum about the very possibility of interaction between an unextended thinking thing (a mind/soul) and the extended thing (one's body). This dilemma is reflected in his own desperate speculations about the pineal gland as the point of contact between soul and body.[20] Macmurray sought to repair the problem by arguing that the unity of human experiences "is not a unity of knowledge but a unity of personal activities of which knowledge is only one."[21] To recover the irreducible unity which the battles of modern philosophy had fragmented meant starting over in a different place. That place was the primacy of action. Indeed it was the primacy of the interpersonal world.[22]

Now, an important feature of this interpersonal context and one which Macmurray acknowledges as necessary for recovering the primacy of *non-theoretical* personal knowledge is the replacement of the "I think" with the "I say." Macmurray's basic impatience with what he regarded as the tediousness and irrelevance of much of the linguistic philosophy which preoccupied so many of his contemporaries was mitigated to some extent by the fact that their heavy emphasis on language had helped restore its *public* character and, thus, the *primacy* of the interpersonal. To stress speech was simultaneously to stress the essentially *shared* nature of human experience. Persons were born to communicate, to enter into and sustain a *common* existence. With this shift in emphasis "thought becomes that aspect of speech which makes it intelligible—its logical structure. Speech is public. It is at once thought and action, …a unity of which 'mental' and 'physical' activity are distinguishable but inseparable aspects; …it establishes communication, and introduces the 'you' as the correlative of the 'I'; …the 'I say' makes the second person a logical necessity."[23] Thus, for Macmurray a definite positive effect of linguistic philosophy was to help everyone see clearly the central fact of personal *mutuality* and, by implication, the primacy of action.[24]

Few, if any, will disagree with Macmurray's emphasis on language as crucial for human existence. We are able to share experience with others just because we can mediate experiences *via* a common or shared system of signs. But what does not appear in his analysis, however, is adequate consideration of what some take to be the mystery of language nor, more generally, of the relation between intersubjectivity and our use of language or symbols. To be sure, Macmurray was fully aware that thought is inseparable from symbol-use, that speech is, as he says, "at once thought and action." Indeed, he devotes considerable time and space to a discussion of thought as symbolic activity arising out of our more fundamental life of action or "concrete activity."[25] Moreover, Macmurray also offers a provocative and perceptive discussion of the general process by which he believes words would have been developed. In his view, "words are reduced images which have become symbols."[26] The process he describes is one whereby, for example, through our native capacity for selectively attending to what we are experiencing, a child learns to associate a sound such as "crown" with the normal image/percept of the crown being worn such that the sound itself eventually becomes the substitute for the original referent. Thus, words are developed and through continued reduction of the sensory imagery, for example, dropping the sound itself out of consideration, silent thought is achieved. For Macmurray "the primary function of language is communication between persons" and the "use of language as a means of thought, which does not look beyond the expression of thought to its communication, is a secondary and derivative use of language."[27] Important as thought is to human existence, to the development, for example, of science or art or tool making, these are ultimately public activities located *within* the dynamic process of human cultures pursuing a life in common. Thought is something we do and has arisen within the context of our joint living; when our actions are stymied we are provoked into thinking; even private thinking should be understood ordinarily as a kind of temporary withdrawal from the immediate life of concrete action for the sake of a more efficacious return to practical activities.

There are other noteworthy features of Macmurray's analysis of the nature of symbolic interpretation. For example, he makes the distinction between words and ideas acknowledging an intimate relation between them, asserting for example that "over a wide field ideas and words have an *inner identity*"[28] (emphasis added). Throughout the discussion, however, the stress is on a functional interpretation ("A word is a sound used."[29]) and on the general process of *substituting* words for things, or words for ideas. He also notes that thought is richer than the words we employ, that language tends to "fossilize" what is being represented and that there is a form of human creativity at work in the effort to find new ways to adequately express the "meaning" of what we experience.[30]

Thus, Macmurray goes well beyond saying that speech is a public act crucial to constituting a shared public world requiring acts of awareness whereby the sensuous aspects of communication (the sounds heard, the gestures seen, the tactile motions felt, etc.); are transformed such that "meanings" are conveyed. But the degree to which he would acknowledge that an ordinary act of human communication involves something quite extraordinary is considerably less clear. Whether it involves a mode of consciousness which should be described as immaterial is what concerns us here.

The point is not that Macmurray did not have a fundamental appreciation for the remarkable fact of interpersonal communication. He obviously did and just as obviously made it central to his view of human persons. His theory of human persons as constituted by their relations proceeds from and always presupposes this phenomenon. Thus, for example, in his discussion of the mother-child relation he is very keen to point out that the infant/child is continually gaining direct experiential knowledge of the personal other (notably of the mother), a knowledge being mediated initially and, at first, vaguely by what the infant/child experiences of its mother through her actions and routines. This lived knowledge is pre-reflective, yet essentially continuous with and feeding into reflective awareness. A baby naturally communicates its pleasure and displeasure more effectively with its own developing gestures and vocal articulations. Likewise, in normal circumstances, the reflective parent normally interprets correctly the condition of the infant/child. As Macmurray notes, communication is prior to speech. If it weren't, the emergence of speech would be inexplicable.[31] Later, he argues very effectively that the child's first real cognition is a recognition of its mother, the one who has been experienced in her coming and going in a pattern of care-giving, the one whose sensed and felt persona has been retained by the imagining child, and whose reappearance normally confirms the inherent rationality of the world.

Macmurray's discussion of this, and more, in *Persons In Relation* is well-known to his readers and is indeed useful for thinking about how the world is being experienced by a newly emerging "self." At the same time, it seems important to ask: just what sort of knowledge does this infant/child have prior to its breakthrough into language? Macmurray, as noted above, clearly recognizes that an authentic interpersonal world would be impossible without speech in some form. Speech establishes communication and introduces mutuality. Language has emerged and developed because persons desire to communicate with each other. Furthermore, the reality of action itself presupposes a distinctive kind of interpretation or knowledge in order for it to be recognized as action? In other words, actions have to be taken *as signs* which signify or mediate something to their interpreters? Without this distinctive (i.e. symbolic) interpretation by the agent and/or other observers there would be no action as such. For action requires the presence of an informing intention. The agent must know what he or she is doing.[32] But human interpretation is quintessentially a matter of language. More specifically, it requires the reality of *naming*. While Macmurray acknowledges the importance of conventional signs, symbols or *names* for things, his treatment of reflective thought seems devoid of any particular concern for the ontological question as to the *type of consciousness* which makes symbolic or reflective activity possible. This is because his objective is to show, among other things, how the "theoretical" can be derived from the practical, and so how dualism can be overcome. He is much more concerned, in a Kantian-like way, with showing, for example, how the "structure" of our experience is determined by the function of attention, the role of memory, the primacy of intention over attention, et al. He briefly discusses what is traditionally called "abstraction" and "generalization" and explains these as a result of our power of selective attention. (We can isolate some feature of a thing, for example its color, or isolate the "material" world from the actual world. In each case, we "withdraw" from action.) The crucial point for Macmurray is that the whole process of thought is always relative to and so *derived from* our fuller concrete life of actions informed by intentions.[33] It is the primacy of the standpoint of action that concerns him.

One can appreciate Macmurray's essential strategy and yet press the additional question as to the type of consciousness whereby all of these activities are accomplished. The essential criticism here is that his analysis, penetrating and rewarding as it is, remains incomplete in an important way. Without an adequate consideration of this ontological issue, it is not obvious that he has escaped dualism as cleanly and definitively as he hoped. More than one question is involved here, but a central one is this: is it possible to understand the nature of sign-use or names without acknowledging *immaterial* acts of awareness as constituting their life? And, if not, what are the implications of this relative to the final response to the problem of our "dualistic" nature?

To throw these issues into clearer relief, it may help to consider a famous example, namely, the account given by Helen Keller of her own breakthrough into language in 1887 (when she was eight) in that dramatic moment when she suddenly realized that the tactile sensations being created in her hand by her teacher, Ms. Annie Sullivan, were in fact the name "water," that is, that those quick sensuous touches on the palm of her outstretched hand constituted a sign for the cool stuff that was gushing over her other hand.[34] By her own account this was a genuine breakthrough into the world of human meaning delivered only by way of her sudden insight into the reality of naming. The door that had kept her from authentic interpersonal communication had suddenly been unlocked. The key was the strange reality of names and it had literally been placed in her hand, yet only a unique act of awareness had turned that key and opened the door onto the fully personal world. Indeed it was a double discovery because with the insight into the name "water" was the implicit affirmation or judgment "This *is* water." Somehow the being of water could now be mediated by signs. Helen moved quickly to learn what other things were called, "teacher," "mother," "doll," et al. The deaf, speechless, blind child had broken through into the daylight of language and human understanding and she was thrilled. Now she could "see" what things were. At last she had emerged as a person who could share in the inexhaustible world of symbolic interpretations.

Now, surely, Percy is correct in drawing our attention to the strangeness of the copula "is" (and its cognates) since it is through our linking of signs to their referents by way of saying what things are that we establish ourselves as persons who can claim to know anything.[35] Further, there seems no gainsaying the fact that Helen's breakthrough, or that of any normal child, is achieved by interior acts of awareness which cannot be adequately understood by describing them merely as "energy exchanges," "neuronal firings," "synaptic closings," etc., although these factors are undoubtedly present and apparently necessary. But the meanings of these referents are available only through their names. Thus any attempted account of this phenomenon of naming in the reductionistic language of identity theory seems self-defeating because question-begging since every such account is itself just one more complex "is-saying" which *presupposes* the type of awareness (reflective consciousness) making possible and manifested by our symbolic expressions.[36] For both Macmurray and Percy our sign-use, our symbolizing activity, is the indispensable condition of reflective knowledge of anything. Indeed, it is the necessary and constitutive condition of *personal* consciousness. Furthermore, his stress on the irreducible privacy of thought indicates that he would not object to our stressing insight as an *interior* act of knowing. But, as noted, for Macmurray, the analysis does not seem to go beyond noting this along with the fact of "substituting" words, images or other symbolic entities for those realities we are seeking to refer to in some meaningful way. That reality is clarified by us through the media of signs standing for something else ("Helen, this is water.") he readily acknowledged. This is not to deny that our felt immediate experience always exceeds what we can symbolize, but without the actual interpretations how can we make the experiences actually meaningful? Personal consciousness seems preeminently constituted by the play of signs, by our continuous and creative linking of signs to one another and their referents. How then can one avoid asking about the precise nature *of the relation* between signs and signified?

Percy follows medieval philosophers in going beyond Macmurray by emphasizing that in the act of naming there is constituted an extraordinary relation between sign and referent, what some medieval philosophers referred to as an *intentional* relation of identity.[37] On this view, the symbol or name has the peculiar property of *containing* within itself, *in alio esse* (in another mode of existence) that which is being symbolized.[38] When what is being named is being conceived through the media of symbols or signs, it is not enough to say that the signs are being "substituted" for those features of reality are being named. Again, Macmurray would seem to agree that in some sense reality is known mediately through the signs which represent it, that is, through our symbolic interpretations. But what is the nature of this representative relation? For Percy, as for Aquinas and others, the relation between the name "water" and the actual water is a quasi-identity, an *intentional* identity of sign and signified achieved by the knower in a unique immaterial act of knowing. That sensory experiences, for example, the vocables, a series of odd sounds, or the marks on paper, or the movements in dance, etc., become the vehicles of representation is precisely what led medieval philosophers such as Aquinas to develop their views regarding the immateriality of our intellective power.

Does Macmurray fully appreciate the strangeness of this? Did he think there was anything mysterious about it or, for that matter, the intersubjective world? Once again, the issue is not that Macmurray failed to acknowledge the uniqueness of the intersubjective world as a dynamic reality within which each of comes to consciousness of ourselves as distinct individuals. On the contrary, that fact is central to his view. Percy and Macmurray (and Aquinas) are in full agreement about the uniqueness of interpersonal relations, especially in stressing their irreducibility to the organic or biological mode. But whereas Macmurray seems satisfied with having shown how the notion of the organic, of reaction to stimulus, is derived by abstraction from our idea of action and persons, Percy, like the medievals is not satisfied. He follows Thomas Aquinas and John of St. Thomas by drawing our attention to the mysterious intentional relation of knower and known, and the co-intentional relation of two knowers knowing the same thing (Ms. Sullivan and Helen Keller both recognizing, "Water is wonderful.") By way of the intentional relation there comes into existence a *communion* of knower and known, not merely a *substitution* of one thing for another. It may well be that this union is first mediated at the personal level by the unique feeling possible only to rational beings capable of that "acquaintance" which Macmurray says is personal knowledge.[39] But for Aquinas such insight involves an act in which the body has no share, in the sense that insight transcends physical energy, transcends electromagnetic oscillations in fashioning those signs by which all such realities are named and understood, including of course calling great classes of things "material objects," "bodies," "minds" or "persons," etc., thereby stabilizing experience (as Macmurray noted) and rendering it actually intelligible. But what is the status of those *objects of awareness* when we are talking about them, or privately thinking about them? It is not enough to say that speech makes the sharing of experience possible, true and important as this is. Macmurray, it seems, did not want to be drawn into the question of the type of consciousness whereby this sharing is constituted. But can one honestly avoid it? It is something of a paradox that the philosopher who spoke so eloquently and profoundly about the fundamental desire of persons for the community of friendship did not fully recognize the communal nature of human knowing, that is, the unity of knower and reality known achieved in the act of knowing.[40]

If knowing involves an intentional relation of identity and if the intersubjective or interpersonal relation itself depends continually upon the reality of immaterial modes of consciousness, then it seems that Macmurray should openly embrace the category of "immateriality"or "spirit" as integral to being a human person. Perhaps he thought that in order to achieve his project of working out the meaning and implications of the primacy of practical reason, to think from the standpoint of action, that he had to avoid altogether the vocabulary of "spirit" and "immateriality," that to engage in "soul" talk would inevitably entangle him in disputes which he needed to avoid in order to achieve his larger reconstructive task. If so, one can certainly sympathize with this intention. Yet it also seems possible, and perhaps equally likely, that Macmurray did not fully appreciate the mysterious character of human speech or symbolic activity, despite his keen analysis of modes of reflection (science, art, and religion), and even while he recognized the central importance of symbolising for personal consciousness and the interpersonal world. Had he done so, he might have been drawn into a serious consideration of the relevance of the hylemorphic view of the human person. What is more likely, however, is that he considered talk about soul as a remnant of a view which needed to be ignored and discarded, not revised.[41] But there remains the possibility that in overlooking the essentially mysterious character of the naming act, Macmurray has failed to clarify the unique metaphysical ground for the reality of persons and, thus, for the reality of religion.

Whatever the full story, the argument here has been that Macmurray's critique of dualism is not complete insofar as he restricts himself to the Cartesian (or Platonic) form of dualism. To recognize that there is a more sophisticated form of dualism after the manner of Aristotle and Aquinas is to be reminded that the mystery of human personality perhaps cannot be preserved without an explicit appeal to a principle of immateriality. Whether Macmurray would have been impressed by this claim, and how he would have responded to it, is difficult to discern. It may be that he would simply say that speaking of the human person as an incarnate spirit is simply an honorific way of stressing one's intrinsic worth.

NOTES

1   One of Macmurray's earliest essays, 'The Principle of Personality in Experience',
       published in 1928 in *The Proceedings of the Aristotelian Society*, Volume XXIX,
       316–330, when he is only in his mid-thirties, reveals quite clearly the essential
       connection he makes between modern atheism and modern dualism. In 'The
       Dualism of Mind and Matter', published in *Philosophy*, 1935, 264–268, Macmurray
       explores the error which lies "at the basis of all modern philosophy." (264)

2   'The Dualism of Mind and Matter', ibid., is devoted to exposing the various reasons
       which have been or might be advanced to justify the conclusion that "Reality divides
       without remainder into what is mental and what is material." (267) The essay is a
       masterful analysis, among other things, of the way in which the presupposition of
       dualism is already present in seemingly independent arguments for it. Nearly thirty
       years later he offers a fuller and still more penetrating critique of dualism when he
       presents his Gifford Lectures.

3   Ibid., 272.

4   Ibid., 269.

5   Ibid., 272.

6   Ibid., 270.

7   Ibid., 271–272 for the details of this argument.

8   Known under the general title of *The Form of the Personal*, the lectures (of 1953 and
       1954) exist as the two well known volumes, *The Self as Agent,* first published in
       1957, and *Persons In Relation,* first published in 1961. See p. 85 of the first volume
       for a concise statement of what Macmurray intends by asserting the primacy of "the
       standpoint of action."

9   Macmurray expected and welcomed vigorous objections to be raised in response to
       his analysis and his doctrines because he made no claim to presenting a completed
       philosophical system. The criticism offered in what follows is made in this spirit of
       trying to advance in a modest way the project he set in motion. See his comment, for
       example, in *The Self As Agent,* 203.

10   The doctrine known as hylemorphism is a subtle and difficult position which speaks
       to the essential unity of naturally occurring "substances" such as living things but
       argues that one must note the presence of two distinct but inseparable factors, matter
       and form, where matter is a principle of potentiality and form is the principle of
       actuality which determines a thing to be the kind of thing it is. Thus, for example, it
       was the "sensitive soul" of a dog, those powers of sensing, self-motion, learning,
       affectivity, etc., united with the nutritive, restorative and reproductive powers, which
       determined this creature to be an animal. What Aristotle termed the "sensitive soul"
       was the *form* of this substance, its substantial form, but was thus not itself a
       substance. The individual dog was the living substance. But the existential unity of
       these powers is what actually made Fido, for example, exist as a sensitive creature of
       flesh. For Aristotle, death was proof of the fact that one kind of thing, an animal,
       could become something altogether different. What had been the "body" of animal
       became something else, some other kind of material object. Strictly and truthfully
       speaking, a dead dog was no dog at all. There were not two kinds of dogs for
       Aristotle, dead ones and living ones. To be a dog meant that the thing could breath,

feel, run, bark, had a certain generic appearance, etc. Thus, to explain death one needed to acknowledge two distinct factors, matter and form. Since any material object already exists as the kind it is, Aristotle chose "form" (substantial form), thus retaining the language of his teacher Plato, as the principle of actuality or that which establishes the type of thing. Matter, taken in the most general sense, became the principle of potentiality or that which could be "informed" or exist as a certain kind and yet, as death showed, could lose its distinctive character or nature and become something else. It was the general fact of substantial change, literally a change of substance from one kind to another, which required the distinction between "matter" and "form." Aquinas follows Aristotle's analysis and develops his own highly nuanced doctrine of human intellective knowing as utterly transcending material or sensible conditions. To study the key ideas mentioned above, the reader is encouraged, for example, to consult Aquinas' *Summa Theologiae,* Part I, Questions 75–79, 84–87.

11 See, for example, *Persons In Relation,* 27.

12 Besides his early articles in the Proceedings of the Aristotelian Society, a fact which by itself suggests that he would have studied Aristotle, there are various references to Aristotle in other works, particularly in The Gifford Lectures. These, however, only reveal Macmurray's interest in Aristotle's generic definition of man as a rational animal and in his understanding of our social or political nature. One can presume that Macmurray was familiar with Aristotle's basic metaphysical notions, and thus his hylemorphism, but it evidently held no particular appeal for him.

13 See *Reason and Emotion,* 38, where Macmurray refers vaguely to "medieval dogmatism" in the context of discussing inherited views about educating or the emotions or disciplining the minds of children. "Medieval dogmatism said to the thinker. ...This is the truth. You must learn to think in such a way that you reach such and such conclusions." The point here is that unlike the informed appreciation one finds in Macmurray for Plato, Aristotle, Stoic philosophy and, of course, many of the moderns, the reader is hard pressed to find any working knowledge of medieval philosophers. In his appropriation of the history of philosophy, Macmurray seems to catapult from the Stoics directly to the post-medieval period.

14 "Behind the intellectual dualism of mind and matter lies the much older pagan dualism between body and soul and in particular the moral form of that dualism which looks upon the body as evil or the source of evil." Ibid., 131.

15 *The Self As Agent,* 63.

16 Ibid, 66.

17 Ibid, 67.

18 Ibid, 71.

19 Ibid, 73.

20 René Descartes presents his classic dualism in his *Meditations on First Philosophy.*

21 Ibid., 66.

22 The early chapters of *Persons In Relation,* especially Chs. 2–4, make especially clear each of us comes to self-awareness as we discover that we are already inextricably related to others whose actions have made the emergence our self-consciousness a reality.

23 *The Self As Agent,* 74.

24 See *Persons In Relation*, 12.

25 See *Interpreting the Universe*, (1933) where he directly takes up the question of 'Thought as Symbolic Interpretation.' (Ch. 2) There he develops his view that "Action…is primary and thought is secondary" and that "The activity of thought is…a substitute activity which in reflection takes the place of and 'represents' the concrete activity of immediate life." (39) Further, he notes that "ideas…are substitutes for the real thing with which concrete action deals." (40)

26 Ibid., 46.

27 Ibid., 46–47.

28 Ibid., 48. "Words, in the first place, are public symbols, while ideas are private symbols. They both serve the same function as substitutes in imagination for something in reality to which they refer." And, "…we are accustomed to use the images of words as our ideas, or, at least, as the main constituents of our world of ideas."

29 Ibid., 49. And, "A symbol is something used to represent something other than itself, and it is a symbol in virtue of this function." (50)

30 Macmurray's epistemological position stresses the importance of lived or "immediate experience" as that which is initially pre-reflective but itself grows and is influenced by our reflective development. Immediate experience is laden with or impregnated with implicit meanings and always exceeds even the best of our symbolic interpretations or expressions of it. There is always more to life than we can say or symbolize. See, for example, 'The Universe in Immediate Experience,' Ch. 1 of *Interpreting The Universe*.

31 Ibid., 60.

32 See for example his four propositions on pp. 100–104 of *The Self as Agent* for a fuller appreciation of how being an agent also means necessarily being a subject or thinker.

33 'Reflective Activity,' Ch. 8 of *The Self As Agent*, can be seen as a much extended development of his earlier discussion of symbolic interpretation in *Interpreting The Universe*.

34 The reader is referred here to the discussion of this episode as presented by Walker Percy in *The Message In The Bottle*, (New York: Farrar, Straus And Giroux, 1978), especially, pp. 34–45. Those already familiar with Percy's work will recognize my indebtedness to his way of dealing with what he regards as the mystery of language and the interpersonal world.

35 "What is the nature of the mysterious event in which one perceives that *this* (stuff) "is" water? What is the natural phenomenon signified by the simplest yet most opaque of all symbols, the little copula 'is'?" Ibid., 40. Percy is fond of referring to a person as an is-saying creature.

36 The terms sign and symbol are used interchangeably here.

37 This notion of an intentional relation between signs and signified and brought into existence by the knowing act of the knower is the heart of the matter here. Percy discusses this in various places. See, for example, 204ff., 229ff., 250ff. and 258ff.

38 In a footnote, Percy quotes John of St. Thomas: ."…What may be that element of the signified which is joined to the sign and present in it as distinct from the sign

itself? I answer: No other element than the very signified itself in another mode of consciousness." (*in alio esse*) ibid., 261.

[39] Macmurray is very definite in distinguishing this fundamental mode of knowledge he calls personal knowledge as not being knowledge that, or knowledge about, or even knowledge by acquaintance. Rather, he says, "it is acquaintance." This acquaintance is the basis of Macmurray's notion of immediate experience as the basis of knowledge. See Chapter 1, "The Universe In Immediate Experience," of *Interpreting The Universe*.

[40] For Aquinas, of course, who followed Aristotle in this, such activity was a key manifestation of the rational "soul," an aspect of which was the intellective power by which we form concepts, symbols, make judgements, reason, etc. Our rational soul was our "substantial form" making our material nature human.

[41] We recall his remark from *Reason and Emotion*. "Behind the intellectual dualism of mind and matter lies the much older pagan dualism between body and soul, and in particular the moral form of that dualism which looks upon the body as evil or the source of evil." (131) The irony is that Aquinas would have been his ally in the attempt to reinstate the intrinsic worth or goodness of human embodiment.

CHAPTER FOUR

Macmurray and Marx: The Philosophy of Practice and the Overcoming of Dualism

Andrew Collier

Macmurray was perhaps the first major British philosopher to be influenced by Marx, or even to read him at all thoroughly. His contribution to what has since come to be called the Christian-Marxist dialogue goes further and deeper than any other philosopher's: both in that what he learnt from Marx transformed his own religious world-view, and in that he incorporated Marx's ideas into that world-view in a more integral way than any other religious philosopher did. He tells how this happened in the autobiographical section of his Swarthmore Lecture *The Search for Reality in Religion* (1965). A conference on the question "What is Christianity?" probably in 1919, led him to "undertake a thorough study of the early writings of Karl Marx, with an eye to discovering, in particular, the historical relation between Marxism and the Christian tradition."[1]

The "early writings" cannot be those of 1844, since they were not published until the 1930s. Internal evidence suggests that they were the works of 1845, *The German Ideology* (including the long section on Stirner, which most scholars skip), and the *Theses on Feuerbach*.[2] Macmurray writes,

> I was wholly convinced by Marx that idealism is a dangerous illusion which must be rejected. But I was not convinced that religion is necessarily a form of idealism. In particular, the Hebrew religion, as it appears in the Old Testament, is not idealistic at all. On the other hand, a great deal of what passes for Christianity is undoubtedly idealist, and must either be cured of its idealism or rejected.[3]

He stresses the importance of this critique of idealism for his religious development, and defends the Hebrew heritage in Christianity against the Greek and Roman heritages. He suggests that "modern Communism might well be that half of Christianity which had been dropped by the Church in favour of an accommodation with Rome, coming back to assert itself against the part that had been retained."[4]

I shall first discuss Macmurray's development of Marx's critique of idealism, then give an account of Macmurray's dialectic of history which, like Marx's, has worldwide communism as its projected conclusion. I shall draw on Macmurray's books *The Philosophy of Communism* (1933), *Creative Society* (1935) and *The Clue to History* (1938), but the passages referred to in *The Search for Reality in Religion* are evidence enough that these are not, as is often claimed, themes that disappear in his later work; indeed, the critique of idealism underlies the personalist texts that are the core of his work.

The Critique of Idealism

> [Marx] is asserting that things are prior to ideas, and that action is primary and thought secondary in the nature of things.[5]

For Macmurray, these twin ideas encapsulate Marx's rejection of idealism. Whereas realism "makes the thing real and the idea the true or false appearance of the thing," idealism "asserts that the thing is the appearance of the idea." But this idealism arises because thought not practice is taken as the starting point. If we ignore practice, as those whose business is with ideas are wont to, it is hard to escape idealism, because of the following problem:

> How is it possible to test the truth of a thought by a thing? Even if you look at the thing to see if your thought about it is true, you are testing your thought not by the thing but by the visual appearance of the thing, and that itself is an idea, in some sense, because it is "in your mind." So runs the argument. And it is a very difficult argument to meet.[6]

> Now, this argument for idealism is only difficult to meet, indeed it only seems reasonable, provided we confine ourselves to a purely theoretical attitude. ... there is something else besides "the thing" which we contrast with thought, and that is action. ...the moment we begin to act we find ourselves in contact with things, not with ideas.[7]

It is at this point that we realize the reason for the Marxian rejection of idealism. To hold that reality is idea is to hold that thought is primary and action secondary.[8]

Modern philosophy, in other words, ends in idealism because it begins with "I think therefore I am" rather than "I act therefore the world is." So much is implicit in Marx's *Theses on Feuerbach*. But Marx does not work out this alternative philosophy, since his time is taken up with politics and economics. Macmurray does.

Along with Macmurray's Marxist case against idealism, there is his case against dualism, which in *The Clue to History* has become salient. Dualism may not deny the reality of things, but it does assert the autonomy of ideas, and the independence of theory from practice. But dualism is not a politically innocent philosophical mistake; it is linked in three ways with the division of society into working class and exploiting class. In the first place, oppression produces dualism because the oppressed can no longer connect the good they desire with the life they live, and so project it into another world; this is much like Marx's view of religion in the "opium of the people" passage[9]: the oppressed give themselves religion (or dualism) to ease the pain of oppression. In the paraphrase suggested by Graham Greene's Monsignor Quixote, it is "the poor man's valium." Secondly, dualism reflects the split between the classes in that theory become the prerogative of the oppressors and practice is denigrated as the work of the oppressed. The dualism of Plato and (to a degree) Aristotle express this sense of aristocratic superiority. And thirdly dualism, though a defective ideology of societies which bear in themselves the seed of their own destruction, is in a way a functional ideology for the oppressors since it deflects oppositional ideologies into distorted and ineffective forms. But to see how this works we must consider Macmurray's version of the dialectic of history.

The Dialectic of History

Macmurray gives his account of Marx's view of history in *The Philosophy of Communism*, and develops his own view in *The Clue to History*. In the former he accepts that all organic processes are dialectical, and that history hitherto has been, and currently is, an organic process. He regards Hegel as having discovered the nature of dialectic, and thinks Marx does also.[10] This is more questionable, but let it pass for now. He leaves it as an open question whether Marx regards all reality as organic and therefore dialectical, as the "dialectical materialists" of that time did, but anyway he denies that it is, as some is infra-organic (mechanical) and some supra-organic (personal). Most Marx scholars today would read Marx as closer to Macmurray than to "diamat" here. He has only one other reservation about the dialectic of history: when worldwide communism is achieved, he thinks, history will cease to be an organic process, because organic processes are processes of the adaptation of organism to environment, and under communism we will adapt the environment to ourselves.[11] Indeed, this is part of the reason why communism is necessary:

> Communism is... the necessary basis of real freedom. Marx was perfectly right in describing the new form of society as a human society. For it is the only possible form of social relationship in which human development ceases to be merely an organic process and becomes an activity of rational beings.[12]

Three things need to be said about this. (1) Both Marx and Macmurray recognise that in all human history, one way we adapt to the environment is by adapting it to us, but that we have hitherto done this in a blind and irrational way. (2) Both Marx and Macmurray recognise that communism would replace this blind power by conscious and rational collective planning. (3) Marx (implicitly) and Engels (explicitly) also recognise that even this collective control would be within limits set by nature which we ignore at our peril, and so would still be, in the last analysis, a form of adaptation to nature. If there is a real disagreement between Marx and Macmurray here, it can only be on this third point. But in that case ecological research has shown that Marx (or Engels) not Macmurray is right. However I am not sure that there is a real disagreement here, and if not then Macmurray seems to agree with Marx about history on all points, though he has some criticisms of current Comintern politics and philosophy, as well he might. The same goes for his most explicit contribution to Christian-Marxist dialogue *Creative Society*, where he attributes to Jesus "the main theoretical conceptions of Communism," namely "the unity of theory and practice, the dialectical nature of social development, the importance of class conflict, and the fundamental part played by economics in the social process"[13]—as well as, of course, the communist goal. On the communist goal itself, he leaves no doubt as to where he stands in *Creative Society.*[14] Christianity itself implies common ownership and production for need not for profit; freedom is maximised when equality is maximised; Christian sentiment and political democracy are both unreal unless combined with a communist economic order. Actually existing communism is criticised for undervaluing love relative to hunger out of the two main human impulses. This shows in three ways: it fails to recognise the extent to which class struggle depends on a sense of solidarity that derives from love; it fails to see that in the future communist society, when the hunger problem is solved, love would be supreme; and it is too ready to use violence as a means—though Macmurray admits that violence must sometimes be used, for example, in the Russian Revolution. With hindsight we can see, even from a purely Marxist standpoint, that there was a lot more than this wrong with Soviet Communism and the world Communist movement in 1935. And his idea that more co-operative international relations, particularly with the Soviet Union, were themselves a road to socialism, was certainly unrealistic. But one thing is clear: Macmurray cannot be co-opted for social democracy with a Christian face—let alone a social democracy which calls down the curse of all the Hebrew prophets upon itself by oppressing the fatherless. (e.g. Isaiah 10:1-4)

In these two books Macmurray is discussing communism and its relation to Christianity; in *The Clue to History* he is setting out his own version of a Christian view of history, without any detailed discussion of Marxist ideas. It is not a theory of history in Marx's sense—a set of laws governing the development of the various kinds of human society; rather, it is a grand narrative of history in the same sense as Kant's or Hegel's. In accordance with his personalist metaphysics, it is an account of history (or rather Judaeo-European history) as the realisation of an intention: initially, a divine intention for a united humankind with universal equality and freedom; from Jesus on, also a conscious human intention for the same thing. This intention is the unique expression of the true, God-given nature of humankind. As the will of God, it cannot be permanently frustrated. Three main concepts are used in explaining this saga:

(1) *Dualism and attempts to overcome it.* For Macmurray, virtually all errors are instances of dualism. This includes dualism of theory and practice and of things and ideas, but the salient dualisms are of sacred

and secular and of oppressor and oppressed. These are aspects of the
same thing—their separation is itself a dualist error. Hebrew society was
uniquely opposed to these dualisms, and hence the only religious society;
a religious society is contrasted with a society that has a religion, i.e. in
which sacred and secular are distinct. Dualism raises its head among the
Hebrews, but the jubilee law prevents class division from becoming
permanent, and the prophets denounce both dualisms. One might
instance Deutero-Isaiah's words:

> Hanging your head like a reed,
> lying down on sackcloth and ashes?
> Is that what you call fasting,
> a day acceptable to Yahweh?
>
> Is not this the sort of fast that pleases me
> —it is the Lord Yahweh who speaks—
> to break unjust fetters
> and undo the thongs of the yoke,
>
> to let the oppressed go free,
> and to break every yoke,
> to share your bread with the hungry,
> and shelter the homeless poor?[15]

Every renewal of the project of human emancipation seeks to overcome
these dualisms, but this intention is constantly deflected by being
compromised by such dualism. The history of Judaism, Christianity, the
Enlightenment and the modern world is the succession of such renewals
and deflections.

(2) *Self-negation.* Every dualism, every deflection of the divine
intention, is self-negating, and because it is so, serves the divine intention
willy nilly by its own self-destruction.

(3) *Progress.* The succession of renewals of this intention and their
deflections into new dualisms is not a mere succession but is progress.
"The level of freedom, equality and humanity which forms (medieval
society's) basis is of an immensely higher order than Rome ever
achieved."[16] Protestantism, the Enlightenment, and Socialism are all
further advances, though each is either corrupted or at least threatened by
new dualisms. "Christianity leads to liberalism, liberalism to ideal

socialism, ideal socialism to communism, as the fascist philosophers are accustomed nowadays to assert."[17] "Ideal" has a pejorative sense here; it refers to "socialist" parliamentary parties aiming at office "without any fusion of the political and economic fields," which consequently remain dualist and can only lead to an increase in the suppression of freedom.[18] Soviet Communism is not free from dualism in the form of an "ambiguous relation" between "the Soviet democratic organization of the whole people" and "the party dictatorship."[19] This might have been an accurate account of the situation under Lenin; by 1938 "dualism" had gone much further than that. He also discusses fascism which of course he rejects and regards as self-destructive, yet as having in a curious way captured the truth but reacted wrongly to it: Jewish consciousness will indeed create universal communism, which will destroy blood and race as the basis of civilization, destroy the beauties and heroisms of the struggle for power, deny the natural superiority of the white races, and of Germans in particular, and produce universal equality and brotherhood.[20] Only "the thought of the triumph of the Jewish consciousness fills me with joyous exhilaration, while it casts Hitler into the depths of despair."[21] The self-destruction of fascism, he thinks, will inevitably usher in the "socialist commonwealth of the world."[22]

This account of history is in many ways a dialectical one, despite Macmurray's rejection of organicism: progress through the self-destruction of successive dualisms. It has three obvious differences from Marx: Marx as an atheist did not think that there was a goal of history implicit it its beginning; he did not give conscious intention such a large part in the process as Macmurray; and he did not think that the communist outcome was strictly inevitable, since struggle could always end in "the common ruin of the contending classes."[23] Macmurray explicitly denies that history could end in the self-destruction of humankind.[24] His argument—that the negative is sustained by the positive and can therefore never destroy it—is peculiarly weak; a disease can destroy a body. The environmental crisis supports Marx rather than Macmurray on this point.

But the community of ideas between these two socialist thinkers is much more impressive than their differences, at both political and philosophical levels.

NOTES

[1] *Search for Reality in Religion,* 25.

[2] See Marx and Engels, *Collected Works*, Vol. 5 (London: Lawrence & Wishart, 1976).

[3] Ibid., 26.

[4] Ibid., 27.

[5] *The Philosophy of Communism*, 26.

[6] Ibid., 23.

[7] Ibid., 24.

[8] Ibid., 25.

[9] In 'Towards a Crique of Hegel's Philosophy of Right,' Marx & Engels, *Early Texts*, McLellan D. (ed.) (Oxford: Blackwell, 1971) 116.

[10] *The Philosophy of Communism*, 15–16.

[11] Ibid., 72ff.

[12] Ibid., 80.

[13] *Creative Society*, 91.

[14] See the chapter 'Christianity and Communism,' 142–169.

[15] Isaiah 58:5–6 (Jerusalem Bible).

[16] *The Clue to History*, 145.

[17] Ibid., 206.

[18] Ibid., 202–3.

[19] Ibid., 209.

[20] Ibid., 226–7.

[21] Ibid., 227.

[22] Ibid., 227.

[23] 'Communist Manifesto,' *The Revolutions of 1848*, 68.

[24] *The Clue to History*, 101.

CHAPTER FIVE

Proof of Sympathy: Scientific Evidence on the Personality of the Infant and Macmurray's 'Mother and Child'

Colwyn Trevarthen

> As a disposition to imitate is natural to mankind from their infancy, so they universally receive pleasure from imitation.
>
> Another important determination or sense of the soul we may call the sympathetic, different from all the external senses; by which, when we apprehend the state of others, our hearts naturally have a fellow-feeling with them. We see this principle strongly working in children, where there are fewer distant views of interest; so strongly sometimes, even in some not of the softest mould, at cruel executions to occasion fainting or sickness. This principle continues generally during all our lives.
>
> This sympathy seems to extend to all our affections and passions. They all seem naturally contagious.
>
> Francis Hutcheson, 1755, *A System of Moral Philosophy*, Volume I, Ch. 2.

The Infant and Scotland's Philosophers

In the eighteenth century, Francis Hutcheson, Professor of Moral Philosophy at Glasgow University, scandalised many in the church with the assertion that morality should be judged by the feelings of happiness it engenders in others. He held that sympathy and morality were innate principles in humankind, not dependent upon reason. Hutcheson's pupils Adam Smith and David Hume were influenced by this teaching and elaborated it, though in different ways. In *The Theory of Moral Sentiments* (1759) Smith expressed his thesis as follows:

Part I—Of the Propriety of Action; Section I—Of the Sense of Propriety
Chapter I—Of Sympathy
How selfish soever man may be supposed, there are evidently some principles
in his nature, which interest him in the fortune of others, and render their
happiness necessary to him, though he derives nothing from it except the
pleasure of seeing it.[1]

Sympathy… may… without much impropriety, be made use of to denote
our fellow-feeling with any passion whatever.[2]

A smiling face is, to every body that sees it, a cheerful object; as a
sorrowful countenance, on the other hand, is a melancholy one.[3]

Chapter II—Of the Pleasure of mutual Sympathy
But whatever may be the cause of sympathy, or however it may be excited,
nothing pleases us more than to observe in other men a fellow-feeling with all
the emotions in our own breast; nor are we ever so much shocked as by the
appearance to the contrary.[4]

With this psychological ability, attributed even to the unreasoning
infant, one human being can sense the movements of another, as if he or
she were their own person. One can pick up immediately, without
thinking or learning how, the other's impulses of intention, the direction
of their interests in experience, and their emotional feelings.

Smith further described his consciousness as inhabited by imaginary
other lives in addition to his own central self. Imagined others can take a
view of us, of our purposes and experience, that is different from what
we think we do and know—they can enter in dialogue with what we take
to be our own ideas, inside our thoughts. Thus, in a famous passage, he
portrayed the conscience as a spectator mind separate from the mind of
the self being observed, an 'impartial observer' who can direct
evaluations in appraisal of one's actions, taking a view on one's
innermost thoughts. He said:

Sentiments and Conduct, and of the Sense of Duty. Chapter I—Of the Part
III—Of the Foundation of our Judgements concerning our own Principle of
Self-approbation and of Self-disapprobation
We can never survey our own sentiments and motives, we can never form
any judgement concerning them; unless we remove ourselves, as it were, from
our own natural station, and endeavour to view them as at a certain distance
from us. But we can do this in no other way than by endeavouring to view
them with the eyes of other people, or as other people are likely to view them.[5]

When I endeavour to examine my own conduct, I divide myself, as it
were, into two persons. The first is the spectator… the second is the agent, the

person whom I properly call myself, and of whose conduct, under the character of the spectator, I was endeavouring to form an opinion.[6]

Smith described morality as the principle by which relations are given emotional value in terms of positive or negative sympathy. This is a very different view from the traditional belief that moral understanding can only come as a slow acquisition in the child of self-awareness, of that rational mastery of social rules, permissions and prohibitions that Freud called a super-ego, which is gained by processes such as identification and social learning—crude innate impulses coerced by training in how one should behave and by modelling of the actions and beliefs of exemplary individuals.

In the case John Macmurray made against individualism in the Gifford Lectures, he was not as sure as Smith of innate human powers. Nevertheless, he did argue, much against the prevailing view of his fellow philosophers, that a human being is not merely an intentional agent who generates and chooses experience by acting, but a person who lives, from birth, in relation to other persons. We expect to be able to communicate the actions, sensations and emotions of our lives, and to organise these lives in communities. Elaborate cooperation of various sorts, for various purposes, is taken for granted. Macmurray saw this cooperation as germinating in the intimate care with which a mother responds to her infant's helplessness and need for love. Thus he opened up a Christian perspective in moral philosophy.

It has been assumed, and argued with increasing vigour, by both the rational philosophies and the dominant empiricist and individualist psychology of the past three centuries that we can only be understood realistically as essentially separate embodied selves as rational individuals. We are said to live trapped in an acquired unity of experience that is cobbled together from the impressions of our diverse senses. We are born not only without intentions, but unable to influence the cognitions and intentions of others except by blind physical impingement on their sensations, or by instinctively or cunningly coercing them to act differently by subverting their motives of self-interest. Language is a learned code that gives us the only reliable bridge to the minds of others, and the only way to analyse our own thoughts. We never have a clear impression of the mental interior of others, except from their words. We have our emotions, and indeed instinctive affections, but what others feel has to be learned by comparing how they behave and speak with how we feel, behave and speak in situations we share with them. We have, indeed, to learn, according to these philosophers, the proper interpretation of our own passions and aversions in terms of arbitrary categories of emotion to which language gives names.

This is the central conception of what generally claims to be scientific psychology, now known as cognitive psychology.[7] I have called it the Subjective First position. It directs reason to conclude that we are born with minds as separate as our bodies, with everything in community to be learned. Observation of the expressive behaviours and responses of very young infants reveals that this last conclusion is incorrect.

The way an infant enters into communication with others' conscious states and purposes, discriminating dimensions and qualities of the motives behind them, proves that there really is an innate sympathy like that Hutcheson and Smith described. Infancy research now offers much solid scientific evidence for an alternative Intersubjective First position in the philosophy of mind. Normally, a baby's mutual responsiveness is so pleasurable and so natural to a willing and affectionately involved partner that its intricate regulations go un-noticed. It takes a great deal of refined physical investigation to measure its dynamic intricacy.

A Revolution in Infancy Research

The literature on the cognitive processes of infants is now very large. These processes are revealed in the ways infants show preferential orienting responses and learned discriminations, and by their developing competencies for engaging effectively with objects and events in the world.

At first, two or three decades ago, the interest of most developmental psychologists was kept with disciplined reason to analysis of the ways infants discriminate and categorise events described by the researchers in purely physical, objective terms. Stimuli of light, sound or touch, and objects of different simple geometric forms or in different kinds of motion, have been systematically presented for the infants, to invite them to choose with reference to the contrasts in inanimate dimensions of patterns or properties of objects, or in the kinematic regularities of changing events. Inevitably, given the strategy of research, the infants were found to be conceiving a physical reality in space and time with a kind of "naive physics."[8] At the same time a tradition of more naturalistic work, simply recording what infants do when they are alert and interested in every-day circumstances, has accumulated the data referred to above, which, by now, has convincingly demonstrated that infants have special awareness of the psychological motives behind the animate behaviours of human beings. They are especially attracted to events that distinguish a person who is displaying an affectionate interest in them, and a readiness for interaction and play, and these preferences are ruled by the principles of dynamic emotion.[9]

Infants have been found to have surprising preferences for musical dimensions of mothers' vocal play and for the rhythms and dynamic qualities of gestural games.[10] Infancy psychologists are leading a reappraisal of the natural foundations of music—its "biological" or evolutionary roots, distinct from its cultivated cultural varieties. Acoustic analysis of "game routines" and "baby songs" is, furthermore, leading to a different understanding of how linguistic narrative is generated, and to recognition of the pre-linguistic and para-linguistic psychology of human communication.[11]

By the end of the first year, a baby's discrimination of expressions of other persons' intentions and emotions is such that he or she is expert in joint awareness—eager to both co-operate in shared interests and tasks, and to "show off" as a performer conscious of the manner in which his or her actions are received by family and friends, ever the indulgent "audience".[12]

The data require us to credit infants with several psychological abilities. Indeed, the theory that "innate intersubjectivity" is the primary motive principle of infant learning and cognitive growth has gained wide acceptance—it cannot be dismissed as a romantic fantasy. All of which brings us to ask what role Macmurray's writings may have played in this recognition, and to a new interest in the similar insights of certain of his predecessors and contemporaries, notably Adam Smith, Martin Buber, Ronald Fairbairn and Donald Winnicott. In the course of what follows, we will also ask to what extent did Macmurray perceive the innate personal powers of the infant.

Macmurray's Philosophy Welcomed by Infancy Researchers

The Faber paperbacks of Macmurray's Gifford lectures, published in 1969 and 1970, were read with gratitude by a group of observers of infancy, all from outside mainstream psychology, who felt they had independently discovered innate human abilities of a kind that had escaped attention by the authorities of behavioural and cognitive development of children. *The Self as Agent* proposed that the human subject is active; first in movement, and thence perceptive and thinking—not first an immobile mind-being like Descartes' cogito who exists primarily through reflective processing of the body's sensed states. The second book, *Persons in Relation*, further concluded that human subjects are persons who are conscious of one another and who act in relation to one another. The new descriptions of infant intelligence were supportive of both these positions. First, hitherto unsuspected cognitive competencies of infants and emerging object awareness were shown to be the products of an active and discriminating engagement with the world, as Piaget had been saying for 40 years.[13] The second discovery was more profound and has led Piagetian cognitivism being turned on its head. [14]

Daniel Stern, a psychiatrist, Mary Catherine Bateson, an anthropologist and linguist, and Martin Richards and myself, ethologist and psycho-biologist, independently found evidence from films that young infants were proficient communicators with abilities for interpersonal awareness and communicative engagements that could not be explained by prevailing theories of how human cognitive development. Stern[15] described the playful interactions of a three-month-old twins. Bateson,[16] had analysed films of a 2–3 month old baby interacting with her mother and found that the behaviours took the pattern of an exchange of instantly perceived expressions of mutual interest. She called this "protoconversation," and identified it as the foundation for both language and "ritual healing practices." Richards and I, working with T. Berry Brazelton and Jerome Bruner at Harvard, had made films in which infants from one to six months were shown eagerly involved in face-to-face communication and in games in which each acknowledged the human person-ness of the other by expressions of interest and sympathetic mimesis. I called this evidence of "intersubjectivity," and claimed that it was the manifestation of an innate ability to relate to the expression of interest and feelings of another person.[17] Richards[18] was more interested than I was in the social modifications of infant impulses by the treatment received by others in society. I tried to comprehend the infant's intrinsic motives to know others, and to share experiences with them.[19]

By the end of the 1970s a 'movement' had begun—many developmentalists, especially those interested in the acquisition of language as a social activity, made observations of the special skills of infants for intermental life. Margaret Bullowa[20] edited a book that presents the decade's discoveries. This conveys well the new awareness of human communicative abilities, and how they precede and support the learning of speech. Other major contributors reported their findings in the proceedings of the Loch Lomond Conference edited by Schaffer.[21]

Soon the discovery, or rediscovery, of neonatal imitation gave a new energy to debates about the birth of consciousness.[22] Exploration of the steps to cooperative awareness before language made clear the distinction between the sympathetic expressive exchanges with mutual emotional regulation of "primary intersubjectivity," and the one-year-old's investigative mimicry motivated to facilitate learning, in "secondary intersubjectivity," of new "conventional" behaviours in dialogue with joint pragmatic awareness.[23] Further observation of the newborn's invocation and provocation of imitations and emotional sympathy, and developments in imitation, explained the motives of games in which a parent's "affect attunements" and rituals of pleasure and discovery strengthened affectionate bonds and supported the infant's early education[24] "Dynamic emotional narratives" and their transformation into conventional songs, melo-dramatic stories and games with and without objects gave the evidence needed to explain protolanguage forms.[25]

Did Macmurray Anticipate the Intersubjective Infant?

On looking closer into Macmurray's account of how the human mind manifests itself in infancy, we find much that does not measure up to what we now know about the part an infant can play in the Field of the Personal. Macmurray challenged the rational individualist orthodoxy, but did not go far enough. Certainly, his observation of infants was inadequate, even though the direction of his enquiry led to hypotheses about the "initial state" of a human person. True to his times and the powerful influences of Europe's philosophical convictions, he could not bring himself to grant psychological powers to newborn infants, only a potentiality for them. Indeed, he claimed that the special feature of the human organism was a lack of effective powers, to be born without instincts and entirely dependent upon a highly attuned and intelligent maternal care. He believed that an infant must learn to have purposes, and to be conscious of his or her intense relating with others. To this end a baby has a special receptivity, which constitutes some kind of appetite for human-ness.

Even though it is now generally granted that every newborn human mind carries a sensitive and expressive need for human company, it must be admitted that the nature and significance of this endowment is a matter that receives widely divergent interpretations and that generates controversy. It could be said that contemporary fascination with the mathematical world of artificial cognition, the emergent supposedly mental properties of hypothetical or implemented neural nets, the robotics of self-moving, problem-solving machines, and a growing interest in the genetic structure of languages, their evolution and the probability that their learning can be imitated by machines, all signal a resurgence of belief in the intrusion of mental events into biological matter by experience. Life in the society of more mature humans, with their cultural inheritance, programs the neural nets of the infant brain. The evidence for infant's motives, and their moral and imaginative power is still to be assimilated within the powerful new orthodoxy of cognitive science.

The nature of human selves and their relating—the creation in consciousness of imagined human presences and their purposes, thoughts and emotions; how these innate impulses to sympathise, act and know together in co-creative ways; what the process is that generates and directs the beliefs, institutions and customs of our communities and cultures—these questions still provoke denial and a confusion of reductive explanations. I think the issues may be clarified if we examine the foundational assumptions of Macmurray's philosophical enquiry, to see how they stand up to the evidence from three decades of discovery in infant psychology.

Macmurray's Infant Person

Lacking Instincts and Coordination

- The infant has no instincts; all purposive human behaviour is learned.
- The infant is uncoordinated, performing only random movements without even unconscious purposiveness, and possessing only essential physiological rhythms and a few reflexes.

An instinct is not alternative to learning, nor is it a fixed adaptive behaviour. It is a guiding principle, targeting what has to be learned. Innate behaviours, and all innate structures and processes of body-and-brain, have evolved as adaptive anticipatory strategies for life in a specific environment.

Newborn creatures learn instinctively. Newborn humans, and human foetuses, have unique orientations to experience that favour interpersonal relating.[26] Intrauterine learning of the prosodic features of the mother's voice identifies her.[27] Highly coordinated motor patterns of foetuses (observed by ultrasound in utero), or of premature newborns, could be called human instincts, in which case humans have more numerous and potentially more productive instincts than other species.[28] It is also true that these instincts have greater "plasticity," in the sense of prospects for development.

Movements of foetuses are already purposive, not un-coordinated or "random." First, they unite all body parts in one time and one body-centred space. Moreover, they show coherent patterns that are preparatory to actions that may not achieve controlled effects until after birth, sometimes many months after. These actions include: facial and gestural expressions adapted to "para-verbal" parts of conversation; vocalizations and lip-and-tongue movements anticipating speech; head and eye orientations of intelligent listening and looking; reaching with grasping; deliberate thumb-to-mouth placement for sucking; stepping as in walking, with coordinated upper limb movements; complex rotations of posture, etc. If air enters the lungs, a foetus can make expressively regulated cries.

Immediately after birth a baby can show well-coordinated orientation and tracking to audible and visible objects outside their bodies, including "pre-reaching" with hand and arm, and grasping to touch. They orient, gaze, smile, vocalise and gesture in effectively timed response to a person who seeks communication. Their expressive hand gestures are different from movements made as if to grasp an object. Newborns may react differentially to an attentive person's feelings and they recognise the mother's individuality. They communicate by imitated and complementary expressions in conversational exchanges. These "protoconversational" behaviours[29] are additional to more automatic, less well-coordinated responses to stimuli that serve in feeding, in soliciting protection, and in regulation of comfort and rest. However, even the vegetative or physiological "state" regulations of newborns are aided by psychological "mind-to-mind" effects—the benefits of mothering gained from warm body contact, olfactory stimulation and the fats and sugars of breast milk are augmented by the tones of affectionate maternal speech and by eye-to-eye contact with the mother.[30]

Orienting to see, hear and reach-and-grasp-for objects develops rapidly in the early weeks, but, with regard to their ultimate utilitarian purpose, these actions remain weak and ineffectual for several months. Rather do they function as rudimentary expressions of purposefulness, to which other persons can react with encouraging sympathetic expressions of "attunement," and the infant's orientations and gestures are immediately responsive to these expressions of sympathy.[31]

All early movements, including exploratory looking, listening and "pre-reaching," exhibit intrinsic rhythms, organised hierarchically to produce imbedded and cyclic sequences of repeated elements that give the impression of dynamic emotional narratives, in which the active subject passes through an orderly sequence of states of interest and excitement to calm resolution.[32] This anatomico-temporal organisation expresses the "intrinsic motive pulse" (IMP) of the infant's brain. "Time in the mind" [33] is not learned. It gives the newborn psychological powers of a time-bound intentionality and consciousness, and predisposition to narrative awareness and its communication that match the time elements that regulate adult consciousness and its conversational communication. The rhythms of infant expression are attractive to the matching impulses of adults. [34]

Foetuses and newborns show elements of the sympathetic musical sensibility that so characterises engagement in spontaneous play with affectionate companions in the early years of childhood. Mothers exhibit a complementary "communicative musicality" in their vocalisations, and in the ways their movements and touching respond to and stimulate the infant's lively body.[35]

Helpless and Totally Dependent

- The infant cannot respond to any stimulus to defend or maintain its existence; responses are biologically random. He or she remains totally helpless for a longer time than any animal. There is no innate adaptation to environment; all acts have to be guided by a caregiver, and all needs have to be provided.

True, infants cannot have an independent animal existence. They are helpless for longer than almost all other animals. But, many birds and mammals have a period of total dependency on the intelligent care of parents, and they cannot be said to be "persons in relation." Organic dependency is not the reason that infants are persons, and even newborn infants are not just waiting to be cared for. They may begin self-generated exploring and learning about the nearby environment within minutes of birth. Developing investigative curiosity is more persistent and systematic in the human infant than in young birds and other mammals, but investigative play is a feature of the behaviour of the young of all the more intelligent species. Its motivation is a powerful need. As with humans, frustration of this need leads to boredom and emotional illness in all intelligent, highly social species.[36]

In the case of infants, developments motivated by inquisitiveness do not, as Macmurray claims, appear to be initiated or directed by rational guidance from the mother, though they seek to benefit from adult assistance and are clearly aimed to the eventual mastery of a uniquely human cooperative awareness and joint interest in actions on objects. Infant's expressions of emotion when they experience success or failure in attempts to master objects or predict events, which are evident event in the early months – smiles of pleasure or pouts of disappointment – are manifestly adaptations for communication with a partner in joint enterprises and in the sharing of knowledge. Even "private" explorations have the potentiality to be shared at another time, or they can be shared "in imagination," with an "imaginary companion."

Piaget's theory of how the infant constructs an object concept by accumulating evidence generated by acting on objects, and his demonstrations, persuaded psychologists to see the earliest signs of epistemological motivation.[37] But Piaget totally disregarded the potential of infantile behaviour for protoconversational intersubjectivity and cooperation in consciousness. Macmurray exaggerates the infant's dependence on motivation and intelligence of the mother.

Random in Activity, with Separate Modalities of Sense But Seeking Direction and Form

- Intentionality co-ordinates the initially random behaviour of the infant and increases consciousness. The first movements are not automatisms because there is a continuous progress to controlled activity, acquiring direction and form.
- Perceiving is acquired by a hierarchical and systematic learning—first separate skills for each modality, then combinations as accumulated habits.

"Intermodal representation" of reality at a superior "subject-centred" level far beyond the impressions in a single sense, is present from birth. This "equivalence of modalities" is obvious, for example, in the ability of infants less than an hour old to reproduce the seen expression of another person by a movement of part of the infant's own body that he or she cannot see, as in an imitated tongue protrusion or smile. However, this is not the most obvious sign that a newborn has an integrated consciousness that unites input from all modalities. The infant's curiosity about events in the nearby world is one in which sights, sounds and touch experience are equivalent foci of interest, equivalent goals for satisfaction.[38]

The newborn's non-automatic will-to-act-within-experience employs the whole body and all its senses in one time-space frame referred to the body. This motivation, which is built in the brain of the human embryo months before birth, is ready at birth to detect objects remote from the body, and can orient the body and its parts to objects, provided they are nearby and sufficiently stable and distinct. In this frame phenomenal (but not rational) "concepts" are generated. These concepts in body-related brain space are, moreover, inherently rhythmic in brain time, as their motives are.[39]

Experiments to measure the ability of infants to perceive and discriminate, which depend on the willingness of even newborns to display preferences and aversions in selective orienting and "problem solving," show that properties of objects—their visible spatial location, motion, size, form, pattern or texture and colour, or their audible location, rhythm, pitch, loudness and many other acoustic qualities, and comparable tangible aspects of location, configuration and substance— can be discriminated by neural mechanisms already formed at birth. Learning new categories of object or event proceeds rapidly, especially sensitive to recurrent events, and those that are contingent upon the baby's actions. But, the retentive matrix of the brain has many initial "constraints," or preferences and aversions, that give an adaptive direction to discrimination of the features of natural objects and their "habitual" extension in time and space.

As Macmurray says, we must accept the existence from the start of the process of a deliberate intentionality. Intentionality, does not come as a sudden miraculous intrusion.

Awareness of "object permanence" and of causal relations in time between objects and events that are interacting does not show conspicuous developments until the last months of the first year.[40] Nevertheless, cognitive developments, proceeding step-by-step and changing at predictable ages indicate that the baby has intrinsic rational powers, the development of which does not depend totally on the rational interpretations and foresight of adults.

Indeed, provided that essential organismic needs are met, what the infant requires is joyful, intuitive, irrational emotional support of affectionate company, in companionship.[41] Companions share rationality, they do not instil it.

Dependent on Others' Minds, and a Rational Tradition

- The baby cannot think or act, but depends on the thought and action of others. Rationality is present only germinally, in the appeal to the other for rational assistance.

- The infant is adapted to complete dependence on adult rational foresight. This dependence is uniquely human. A relative independence is gained in development by 'appropriating the techniques of a rational tradition'.

Human parenting is an intuitive behaviour, which may be, but does not have to be, rationally thought about. [42] Infants depend upon its authentic, intuitive and sympathetic motives, as well as upon its intelligent, well-informed and culturally transmitted skill. Moreover, even newborns show a kind of rational or conscious purpose in their reactions to persons.

Logical exploration of events and objects develops from the infant's selective curiosity and investigative and re-investigative activity, probing the limits of consciousness. Coordination and selectivity of investigations increases greatly in the first 6 months, as muscular body support, receptor organs and brain systems mature, and neural networks benefit from selective refinement and tuning. However, self-centred, fact-governed problem-solving is not the only motive for logical or propositional thought. The principle, most primitive, and most productive factor in the development of logical thought is the inherent conversational, or proposition-making and proposition-receiving, mimetic duality of the human mind.[43]

Preferences and discriminations of activity guided by awareness how evidence of natural categorical distinctions in perception; e.g., as with the fundamental rhythms of conversation and music, colours are seen by infants as a palette of different contrasting kinds, matching the perceptual categories of adults, excepting those with some kind of genetic colour-blindness. Such categorical awareness, and the emotions associated with sharing the results of experience, appear to underlay the fundamental sense of beauty.[44]

Imitations of eye opening and eyebrow movements, mouth and tongue movements, hand opening, finger movements, head movements and vocalizations appearing within minutes of birth attest the adaptation of the infant to learn by interaction with the specific bodily form, and rhythmic patterning, of expressions of partners in conversational, as well as tactile, play. Moreover, newborns can repeat an imitated reaction, apparently to provoke a sympathetic reaction from the partner,[45] or, possibly, to test the partner's identity as a familiar companion.[46] This means that the infant has a dyadic "conceptualisation" of the "self-with-other," or a competence for having states of relation between "self" and the "other." Bråten calls this the representation of the "virtual other" in the human mind.

To explain the imitative ability of a newborn, we have to postulate a supplementary body mirroring mechanism that identifies the correspondence, or engagement, between another person's body and that body the infant "feels" and "uses" within him or herself as a unified, or integral, resource for acting. Infants imitate other persons expressions to engage in reciprocal communication—their reproductions of expressions are signals inviting, or "provoking," an imitative reply, or some emotional expression of interpersonal feelings.

Emotional expressions can be mirrored by very young infants with immediate sensitivity. The infant's expressions are appropriate indices, qualifying the fate of the encounter, and they powerfully affect adult partners. The coordination of infants' perception and movement for emotional regulations in intersubjective encounters with conversational partners is precocious. It has many features peculiar to humans.

After nine months, strategic behavioural operations of object-seeking and combinative manipulation of objects indicate the development of new cognitive and executive schemes for object use.[47] Infants progressively gain new powers of memory through infancy, and from the end of the first year exhibit awareness that is directed in a continuity of experiences over past, present and future.[48]

All of these developments in active cognition are, in normal development, accumulated in equilibrium with impulses to share and negotiate purposes with other persons. Disturbance of the genetic regulation of this dynamic equilibrium at a critical point in mental growth can lead to the cognitive and intersubjective abnormality of autism, which manifests itself unambiguously in the second or third year after birth, as toddler masters mimetic understanding of social conventions and prepares to learn language.[49] The development of autism, in contrast to the normal process, proves that the human child has innate motives for cultural learning and for assimilation of a "rational tradition."[50]

Feels Only Comfort and Discomfort But Associates Satisfaction of Needs (Motives) with (Intentional) Human Care

- The infant is adapted to express satisfaction or dissatisfaction with his own condition. There is, at first, only a capacity for the feelings of comfort and discomfort. The mother interprets his cry, and his expression of satisfaction is associated with human care and physical contact; this need is therefore not biological but personal.
- The infant has need for a 'conscious personal relation' with mother. The infant is a person, that is with activities motivated by intention; the intentions are the mother's, the motives are the infant's. All the infant's activities in maintaining his existence are shared and cooperative.

Yes, an infant is adapted to protection and care of a person who will act with a mother's devotion. The gentleness, responsiveness, joyfulness of this care determines the psychological maturation of the infant's motives, awareness and learning. The infant certainly has identifiable human needs for human company that no animal possesses. However, it would be an error to imply that no animals have psychological needs in their period of initial dependency on maternal care. The early experiences of gentle care benefit the infant's growing brain through its internal chemical regulation. This is also the case with rats and monkeys in which the emotional quality of mothering has demonstrable hormonally mediated effects in brain growth.

Infants are not long satisfied only with nurturance and comfort. Nor are infants expressions of distress, displeasure or pain merely automatically counter-balanced by a smile of satisfaction when the bodily problem is resolved. Babies benefit from communicative responses of their parents, or of siblings and peers. They seek playful encounters.[51] The intrinsic regulation of brain maturation is stimulated by the joy of play, now recognised to be essential for the healthy development of an infant's self in all its psychological complexity.[52]

A happy mother feels her baby to be a rewarding companion because the emotions and enthusiasms that the baby expresses are a sensitive reflection of the mother's own needs for personal relatedness, and for joy.[53] It is the natural emotional dynamics of the baby, expressed in body movement, not just receptivity to care and physiological regulation of "state", which makes this possible.[54] Emotionally unwell mothers, notably those suffering from post-natal depression, may have serious problems meeting their infants' emotional needs, which can lead to a vicious circle of disturbing communications and further emotional disturbance.[55]

Has Undiscriminated Feelings of Need—Must Acquire Emotions of Delight in Company and Fear of Being Alone

- The infant's primitive and undiscriminated feelings of need for care differentiate into emotions of relating to the mother as a person; delight in communication is associated with fear of being alone. Soon the infant cries just because he or she feels alone.

Human life is regulated by a palate of emotions with opponent values that determine how individuals will approach or avoid one another; how they will develop their relationships and mutual understanding, and how they will assert and apprehend expressed impulses of motive and emotion. Infants show many emotions, and these control and are in control of their contacts and relationships with persons from birth.[56] Early expressions, and their sensitivities, go far beyond "primitive and undiscriminated feeling of need for care."

The detached and rational philosophical argument that a newborn infant has no knowledge and can therefore attribute no feeling to a cause, even within the body, has engendered the pernicious, immoral belief in some medical practice that a newborn can feel no pain, that all the baby can do is give reflex signals of discomfort or need. There is abundant physiological and behavioural evidence that foetuses do feel pain and may suffer serious shock from it. Modern practices in intensive care of newborns control avoidable suffering and consequent medical risk.[57]

Many of the infant's emotions, even at birth, have little to do with eliciting or confirming the reception of care for vital functions or bodily comfort. For example, in a good, happy relationship, and in moments of wakeful interest, the mother can count on her two-month-old infant to provide more than just a smile of satisfaction for services received, or for comfortable contact with her body and its movements. Even premature newborns smile to a human voice and in response to affectionate human mirroring of expressive gestures. This is beautifully shown in the film of Saskia van Rees described below.[58]

We conclude that the personal relationship between infant and mother is much more equitable or shared than Macmurray describes.

Wants Consciousness to Respond to Stimuli But Has No Intentions, Imagination or Knowledge

- The infant has no intentions or knowledge of his or her own, only motives of consciousness. Motives are feelings that select movements in response to stimuli. They generate distinguishable behaviours with a conscious component.
- Knowledge depends on the basic skill of imagination coordinating visual and auditory images to which tactual feelings later become coordinated
- A child gains skills of personal maturity, an animal those of biological maturity and all the child's skills are acquired; he or she learns how to learn.

We can accept that the infant must begin with no worldly knowledge and therefore without "explicit" intentions. Nevertheless, the definition of motives as 'feelings' that direct movements to the "ex-periences" of stimuli (not "in response to stimuli"), and that learn how stimuli afford useful consequences seems adequate to justify the conclusion that there is consciousness behind the infant's activity.

Admitting that infants' movements are motivated to pick up experiences in this way, we distinguish a number of distinct motives that are present at birth and that are rapidly elaborated in a predictable sequence of differentiations and reintegrations thereafter, all the way to verbally embellished rationality.[59] The contents of a particular consciousness depend, as Macmurray argues, on the motives that lead to that kind of experience being selected and elaborated. Immediate consciousness of persons and their feelings has priority in infancy.

The account of awareness built up by association between initially separate senses and actions of body parts does not fit what one observes of the initial coordination of infants' perceptions and movements.

However, it is certainly the case that the categories and plots of a baby's imagination, specifically adapted to know or describe a particular artificial world with particular companions who have their own habits and understanding of meanings, must be learned. The baby is also developing an extended consciousness, gaining powers to connect experiences and to live with the flow of familiar, meaningful events in time.[60] Human consciousness, that is, consciousness of knowledge, seeks to be shared with other persons—it has what Margaret Donaldson calls "human sense."[61]

Imagines Phantasies, and Displays Them to Others And Learns by Being Taught

- The development of phantasy, the play of the imagination, is not governed by logic (i.e. by practical reference to an object), but by feeling; it is not present in animals except in the lowest form. In play the infant does not just *exercise* skill, but *displays* it.
- The infant's play is not merely an exercise, but a display of skill. He or she does not merely learn, as animals do, by instinct helped out by trial and error; the infant is taught. The acquirement of skills is an education.

In spite of their absolute need for care—perhaps taking advantage of this dependency—infants enter into imaginative, experimental play very early. The selective imitation by newborns of exaggerated, unusual, expressive actions (such as tongue protrusion, exaggerated mouth opening, conspicuous hand and finger movements, blinking) may be regarded as playful—part of an instinct to pick up by mimicry peculiar traits, or "customs," in familiar others' behaviours.[62] Play with infants, involving what Vasudevi Reddy calls "other awareness," has subtle emotional regulations and moral implications from early days.[63] It has epistemological value as well.

Games of feeling strengthen affections within habitual routines of companionship. Humorous teasing tests the capacity of both parent and infant to predict the others actions and feelings, coordinating their intentions and interests, identifying their habits. Recognition of the individuality of companions by their indexical expressive features is increased by the negotiation of habitual rituals and signs, including rhythmic/prosodic games that become 'narratives of feeling' in the 'theatre of play'.[64] Gentle, benign teasing has a motivating function in intersubjective play. Shigeru Nakano shows that play with infants involves positive emotions of "incident affinity"—a delight in shared risk and combat with trickery. Favourite, laughter-eliciting games are always dramatic.

Intentions in infants' games with objects may lead them to participate with a parent's playful presentation of a toy.[65] Explorations of objects and experiences of surroundings add familiar objects and situations to the shared sources of pleasure. The peculiar feature of human play in infancy, intensified in the toddler and preschool periods, is the use of symbolic imagination to enrich transactions and the pursuit of plans with playmates. Toddlers' capacity for imitative pretence is used to make cooperative games with peers[66] or with imaginary friends. A one-year-old will try to act like another person who is using an object in a special way, as an ornament for the body, as a tool, as part of a construction, and so on. This kind of imitation and the imagination does not occur in the apes. It is a human mimetic and socio-dramatic 'instinct' that generates cultural learning—of rituals, language, roles and artefacts of all kinds.[67]

Has to Be Taught Beauty and Morality, in Education

- The child does not learn aesthetic or moral judgements but is taught, in education, which is a cooperative process dependent on imaginative foresight with intended form. The distinction between good and bad or right and wrong is evaluated by a tutor, and the child is educated to submit to reason.

Moral aspects of interpersonal relationships originate in the mixed dynamic emotions that regulate habitual relations of trust and good fellowship, and, implicit in the emotional reactions that even very young infants have with other persons,[68] they form the fundamental motivation for educational practices in which the child's motivation for learning with others is fully recognised.[69]

Complex emotional behaviours, indicative of shame, shyness, jealousy, etc. can be observed in infants less than six months of age. The subtle emotional responses of infants to the attentions and actions of others, with discrimination of persons familiar and liked from those unfamiliar and disliked, means that moral feelings originate much earlier than is often claimed. The same may be said for fundamental aesthetic reactions, which assist persons to agreement in their experiences and creations. Infants soon show pleasure in satisfying effects of their actions, and dismay at unexpected and confusing effects. They show pleasure in sharing beauty, as this is defined by Turner, who defines beauty as the opposite of something that inspires shame.[70]

Genesis of feelings of what is good or right is not simply a matter of submitting impulses of self-satisfaction to judgements of goodness and badness or rightness and wrongness imposed by the authority of elders' reason. This has the important implication that inculcation of rules of fairness or justice by lessons or by example should be carried out in a way that treats the child as an interested party, with feelings and capable of negotiating the realisation of a principle, and soon capable of working out arguments of principle, affectionately and co-operatively, with a peer. The Moravian educator Comenius appreciated this nearly four centuries ago. In his words:

> When they [children of the same age] talk or play together, they sharpen each other more effectually; for the one does not surpass the other in depth of invention, and there is among them no assumption of superiority of the one over the other, only love, candour, free questionings and answers....My aim is to show, although this is not generally attended to, that the roots of all sciences and arts in every instance arise as early as in the tender age, and that on these foundations it is neither impossible nor difficult for the whole superstructure to be laid; provided always that we act reasonably as with a reasonable creature.[71]

The foundations for this "reasonableness" show themselves very early in human development. Infants, even as young as two months, show shyness or coyness when a partner pays too close attention.[72] By six months reactions to strangers are complex blends of fear and bold attempts to "make friends" by offering play.[73]

Repeatedly insensitive treatment of infants causes them to become resistant and uncooperative, anxiously protesting or withdrawn. An infant is also capable of strident self-assertion with a caregiver, and interactions with siblings can be jealous or combative.

Such subtleties of interpersonal response do not encourage belief that all moral judgements are taught, or, indeed, that moral reactions, about fairness or justice are essentially rational judgements.[74] On the other hand, arbitrary, rule-governed customs and manners of ethical action can be avidly taken up as models by infants and toddlers, who are certainly motivated to learn by example. Imitation is a key motivate at stages of development when new levels of relationship are being negotiated by infants or toddlers. It is a motivated activity, regulated by interpersonal feelings, including those of love and admiration, or anger, disgust and fear.

As Comenius made so clear in his far-sighted writings, effective, moral and cooperative education is founded on belief in the child's fundamental reasonableness—on his or her natural interest in becoming an active member of a "community of learners."[75]

Has Personal Skills of Communicating Before Language

• Long before the child is taught to speak he or she is able to communicate, meaningfully and intentionally, and understands what is said to him or her before being able to respond in words. This identifies the infant as a person and not an animal.

Infants have no comprehension of word meanings, but can communicate their thoughts, interests and changing interpersonal attitudes with precision and discrimination in intricately controlled exchanges with their partners expressions of dynamic psychological states. By one year an infant can pick up joint orientations to objects and events that thereby become shared topics.[76] These facts lead to a radical reappraisal of what it is that language contributes in mental life and stimulate a revision of the rationalist or cognitivist theory of language, its structures and of how they are acquired. It becomes less attractive to postulate an innate mechanism solely devoted to language acquisition. At first the child is interested in communication, not language.[77]

Infants are, as we have said, naturally musical beings. They feel, hear and respond to the rhythms and melody of their mother's playful movements and vocalizations. In protoconversation a two-month-old shows precise sense of timing and melody in interaction with the intuitive rhythms and prosodic variations of a parent's "motherese."[78] By four months the baby engages attentively with action songs, making movements and sounds that exquisitely fit with the beat and prosody of the partner's expression. Mothers rock babies and sing softly to lull a them to sleep, but they also "attune" expressions of interest and excitement to the infant's more lively motives[79], and offer their own joy in lively dancing, chanting and singing, and their infants happily join in.

Music psychologists find cross-cultural universals in mother's songs, as well as prosodic differences that lead the infant into the conventional expression of the "mother tongue." New research is discovering the original motives of human beings for inter-synchrony by means of poetic and musical forms of expression. These are basic for the child's acquisition of speech and other codified ways of acting and meaning. The semantic definition of terms and cohesive grammatical functions of language arise out of the dynamic motive processes that generate foci of interest and intersubjective coordination of motives. These are controlled in interactions with other persons by non-verbal processes of expression and imitation in infancy. Mary Catherine Bateson identified and named the activity "protoconversation." She realised that "infant semiosis" depends upon the ritual of intersubjectivity that is evident in communicative behaviour soon after birth. Merlin Donald[80] has presented a persuasive theory that human collective mentality evolved by two steps. *Homo erectus* used sympathetic body awareness and mimetic narrative display to convey thoughts, interests, purposes and feelings. This lead to the evolution of language in homo sapiens. Preverbal infants and toddlers, under two years of age, show remarkable powers of imitation and representation of interests and roles by mimesis. It is called imaginative play, or meta-representation.[81]

Conclusions: The Field of Companionship in Cultural Life

Debt to Immediate Predecessors, and to Scottish Philosophy

Macmurray's Gifford lectures were undoubtedly influenced by the new understanding of human relations, and the sources of consciousness of these relations, that had been gained by the 'Object Relations' school of psychoanalysts. In the preceding two decades, Klein[82] and Fairbairn[83] had broken away from Freud's conception of the original state of the mind in infancy. The knowing infant subject was seen by the Objects Relations Theory as a more motivated being with greater internal complexity of feelings and images. Fairbairn claimed that the baby had a separate ego from birth, ready from the start to engage with an external "reality." Guntrip and Winnicott were developing this new concept of personal relations, the latter greatly enriching the idea of what a child creatively contributes to attainment of a place in the human world and a grasp of its meaning.[84] Bowlby[85] transformed Object Relations Theory with his observations on the emotional effects of separation and loss of maternal care, and his Darwinian theory of the infant's innate drive for proximity and emotional attachment to a devoted and dependable maternal figure has led to an approach that still dominates research in emotional development in the US.[86] In London, Bowlby's followers at the Tavistock have brought greater human sympathy to work with children distressed by experiences of broken or disordered attachments, or by congenital disorders of psychological development, such as autism.[87]

In the USA, Mahler, responding to difficulties in treating childhood emotional disorders, had turned to the study of normal infant development.[88] Harry Stack Sullivan[89] developed his interpersonal psychiatry that gave a more balanced attention to the emotional representations in both patient and therapist. Mahler's work was later to inspire a radical reappraisal of infant feelings and selfhood by Daniel Stern.[90]

The mid-twentieth century also saw Wittgenstein, drawing on the anguish and confusion of his own life, moved to reject a positivistic analysis of the logical underpinnings of language that he had worked on with Russell, in favour of a philosophy of mind that seeks to explain the fundamental nature of consciousness and voluntariness. He undertook an exploration of expressive symbolic "forms of life" that he said make "language games" dependent on the whole activity of human communication of "pictures in the mind."[91] Whitehead's Gifford Lectures, in the early 1920s, had defined human organisms as makers of actions directed toward objects, and makers of concepts of those objects.

He re-animated the Heraclitian understanding of "process" as creator of structure, and described the unification of the many elements throughout nature in a "community."[92] In a very different direction, Piaget's demonstrations of the active adaptation of the infant mind to objects and what could be done with them was building a logical cybernetic theory of an infant's self-activated consciousness. But Piaget was not interested, except incidentally, in actions directed toward persons.[93] The infant he discovered is a rational individual—a cognitive isolate seeking realistic representations of the objects of acquisitive and manipulative actions.

A giant in Macmurray's past whose analysis of the philosophical and theological significance of personal relations was Martin Buber.[94] Buber's poetic account of empathy and wisdom must have inspired Macmurray's theory of the personal. Buber proclaimed that the human self can, at any time, be in dialogue with others, or with an "other." His "I-Thou" or "I-You" relation signified a ready acceptance and reception of the moral worth in the "other," quite different from an pragmatic I-It relation with a thing to be simply sensed and used.

The communitarian trend that emerged so clearly in Macmurray's philosophy, threatened to bring disembodied "Cartesian" thought into an unsympathetic scrutiny. It is perhaps for this reason that his ideas have been repeatedly pushed to the periphery of established British philosophical debate, so preoccupied with arguments about what, and how, words mean, in spite of the potentially greater validity of the different approach that psychology could have taken. Mainstream Anglo-Saxon psychology, while seeking to distance itself from mere philosophical speculation, in effect has connived in a rationalistic "single head" approach, with important effects in the philosophy of education.[95] For most of this century our psychological researchers have been principally occupied with psychophysics, psychometrics, learning and human performance of single subjects—not directly with motivation, voluntary action, emotions in human relationships.

Looking further back in time, we see that Macmurray's theory of personal powers draws on a tradition of Scottish philosophy that came to brilliant maturity in the 18th century. Macmurray was educated at Glasgow University, where the Scottish Enlightenment began, before he took up a scholarship to Oxford. In Glasgow, Frances Hutcheson (1694–1746); Thomas Reid (1710–1796); David Hume (1711–1776) and Adam Smith (1723–1790) had examined the sources of will and perception that reside in natural feelings and concepts, and in common use of language. As we have seen, Smith, not only a path finding economic theorist, developed Hutcheson's theory of human "sympathy." This historical connection is so important that we shall have to re-examine its implications in a summing up of what Macmurray is claiming for the mental life of the personal, and especially for its initial state in the infant.

Macmurray Is Distant from His Infant Subject

Notwithstanding the growing realisation of the complexity of infant mind work, Macmurray, like Freud, projects from a philosophical interpretation of motives and problems of adult life back to a conception of infant consciousness. Freud was attempting to explain confused and defensive emotional states and distorted consciousness of adults suffering from anxiety or psychiatric illness. Macmurray was building a justification for his philosophy of the moral foundations of the modern state in a defence of the essential human need for rational freedom.[96] He appears to derive his description of infants largely from the accounts of others, or from common sense. In both cases, what is described as infant awareness and emotion is based more on deep inarticulate adult introspections and longings; and on a remote, rather male, observation of infants' weakness, need for maternal care and reactions in distress. Neither Freud nor Macmurray is primarily concerned with an unprejudiced discovery of what infants' motives are like—how they function in development in the infant stage itself, or how they develop into the beliefs and actions of a toddler who, though barely speaking, is part of society and aware of many of its meanings. Neither shows evidence of systematic examination of how infant's actually behave and think their way into and out of situations. Finally, the relationship inferred between and infant and the mother owes little or nothing to how a mother herself experiences interactions with her infant.

Freud revolutionised thinking about unconscious drives and fantasies, which may, indeed, be related to the partly-formed motives and conscious states of infants. Macmurray insists on the primacy of personal relations and the fundamental personalisation of experiences, which again should bear a substantial relationship to the communications of infancy when responses to persons are so compelling. Nevertheless, it is risky to infer infantile mental life either from pathological states of adults, or from adults' intuitive or rational and verbally articulate beliefs.

The findings of contemporary psychology of infants, benefiting from 25 years of intensive experimentation on infant's perceptions and preferences, from microanalyses of audio-visual recordings of infant activity in communication with a freely responding mother, and from a fresh hypothesis about inner causes of psychological life, does not accord well with the descriptions of either of these authors, even though there are a number of points in which recent evidence does support Freud's theory of unconscious motives and the effects of early learning, and it obviously accords with Macmurray's thesis of the primacy of the personal in human social affairs. We have to sort out the inconsistencies. To do so must have importance for understanding of the adult condition and its problems, as has been effectively argued by feminist psychologists concerned with the one-sided view an individualist patriarchal culture has imposed on moral aspects of human relationships and their development.[97]

A Larger Scientific View of the Human Spirit in Infancy

With the new insight from micro-analyses of infants' activities in precise communicative interaction with their partners, psycho-biologists are led to accept that fundamental motive processes in the brain by which the body is made to move as a coherent agent and by which the different modalities of awareness are assimilated in a single space-time field of consciousness, are functioning even before birth.[98] The human brain endows a newborn with an active consciousness that can find immediate resonance with the rhythmic impulses and forms of expressive movement in other human beings when they are encountered by the infant for the first time. The newborn human mental vitality detects and seeks to converse with the corresponding vitality of any person who is willing to attend to and react contingently with the infants efforts at sympathetic communication. In close sympathetic engagements with others, a wide range of human expressions are sensitively perceived by the infant.

Modern research has shown evidence of a rich and receptive human spirit in the newborn infant, with other-sensing moral sentiments and a capacity to both seek and offer companionship to a sympathetic adult who derives pleasure from interacting with the infant's expressions of vitality and affection.[99] The baby could even be said to possess an immortal soul, in the sense that this special human vitality comes afresh in every human life the same, wholly independent of the experience of living, but "expectant" for it.

The infant's humanity, like all impulses in living beings, is both a creative principle and a need. Its uniqueness is in the nature of the need. As Macmurray points out, the helplessness of the infant anticipates a sympathetic and intelligent human environment. This helplessness is not, however, just a negative state, a lack of instincts. It is evident, from careful experiments in controlled situations, that perturbation or rupture of spontaneous human contact and exchange of sympathy will cause a young infant to show expressions of deception or unhappiness, as if sad and fearful because left alone, abandoned.[100] This "depression" of the spirit, of vitality in communication, of shame mixed with panic or anger, can recover and turn to happy conviviality if the partner re-establishes reciprocal, contingent engagement. In the same way, a mother suffering from depression, to the extent that she cannot freely and spontaneously express love for her infant and cannot appreciate the infant's offers of communication—a mother who, unable to sympathise, is being either withdrawn and unresponsive, or intrusive and manipulative—will cause the young infant, under three months, to avoid her eyes, and to express depression and irritation in vocal, facial and gestural expressions.[101] The baby of a depressed mother may carry this depressed mood over to reactions with other human partners when they seek communication, depressing them. Alternatively, anguished love can make intolerable demands, and even an infant can feel an impulse to withdraw from insistent, intrusive manifestations of affection.

Alone and anxious sadness or angry rejection are evidently possible from the moment of birth. It is increasingly recognised by the medical profession that a prematurely born infant, while kept alive in the ingenious technology of intensive care, can show signs of suffering physiological decline and autonomic dysregulation if isolated from human contact or treated insensitively, and such a baby will benefit both psychologically and physiologically from close and affectionate care.[102]

As a wonderful example, the aforementioned film by the Netherlands psychologist and documentary film-maker Saskia van Rees shows a two month premature baby making appreciative reactions to the tender and instantly responsive attentions of the father. He is mirroring the looking, face expressions, smiles, vocalisations and hand gestures of his daughter while she is 'kangarooing' under his shirt against his chest. The two enter into a precisely contrived duet, exchanging expressive signals in a regular rhythm, with compatible and mutually responsive phrasing.

Another beautiful document by this perceptive observer shows the lively satisfaction that a baby born just a few minutes previously can show when surrounded by the contact with the mother's body, or with her hands while immersed in the water of a warm bath, listening to the music of cheerful, animated female speech.[103] The baby listens as if in a forest full of birds. The joyful vocalisations of a quartet of women—the mother, a friend and two midwives—are reacting with the infant person in the most natural way. Every movement or expression of the newborn is reflected with musical 'attunement' by the ladies. The instantaneous sympathy of the adults is patently obvious in these imitations, as is the infant's reflecting awareness.

Thus, modern naturalistic research has brought proof that infants are born as human beings who express personal powers of consciousness. Macmurray's view of human nature has been confirmed and extended. Much more is implied by what psychologists have seen and documented. Their researches give support to a rich common-sense understanding of the "personal powers" born in humans and developing rapidly in the young child. Our assessment of Macmurray's theory of the infant's mind to the mother's care and teaching opens the way to an examination what this psychology implies, morally and politically.

A Closer Look at the Evidence

It is necessary to emphasise that the most recent observations of neonatal sociability, although they accord well with developments later in children on the way to mastery of the culture's language and logical rationality, do, nevertheless, pose a paradox.

Why is it that the newborn, who orients so strongly to a human voice and who replies to an affectionate touch and the sight of a parent's face with a smile, gestures and coos, also makes sustained efforts to imitate peculiar actions—exaggerated tongue protrusion or blinking, a wide open mouth, a sustained finger extension, all movements that have been presented to the infant with intentional emphasis by an adult "experimenter"? These hardly seem likely candidates for any essential innate repertoire of expressions to regulate intimate interpersonal relationships and the emotions excited in them.

Perhaps this explains why so many very conscientious developmental psychologists have felt they had to look for evidence to 'disprove' neonatal imitation. Why does the baby not only imitate a peculiar act but then fixate intently on the adult before repeating the strange gesture in a way that invites the adult to repeat the performance, as Emese Nagy has demonstrated?[104] Apparently, unlikely as it may seem, a young human is motivated to observe, learn and use completely arbitrary body movements made as specially marked mannerisms or signs.

And this is but the beginning of a mimetic curiosity for other persons' social habits that grows rapidly. By six months the baby has learned rituals of play—routines of teasing games, with prescribed sequences of body movement, and chants or songs in which patterns of vowels and rhymes signal phrases and resolution of the narrative impulse attract the baby to synchronise and harmonise with them in choruses. The baby is also now vocalising in imitation of distinctive speech sounds of the "mother tongue," and making facial expressions and gestures of the hands to match those older playmates use to mark their utterances with dramatic emphasis and dance-like grace. He or she is beginning to be recognised by family members as a talented performer of simple ritual signs and displays, and the bold infant displays delighted pride in all such accomplishments, or a converse shame when they are not recognised and admired in good fellowship. Then comes what Tomasello calls the "miracle" of nine months,[105] when the infant deliberately orients to what another person is intending to do, joining in attention to focus on the meaning of their interest in utilitarian objects, following the aim and sequence of their actions to divine and share their exploratory or constructive purpose, and perhaps imitating the intentions implied by what they try to do.[106]

This development of companionship and pride in knowing and doing, plus curiosity about what it is that others pretend[107], is recognisable as a necessary series of steps towards the child's understanding the arbitrary symbolism of words. It also makes the technical uses and appropriate form of cultural objects transparent in the child's consciousness. Cultural learning is well underway months before words are imitated and used to label the invented objects and actions of pragmatic social intercourse. It is motivated to enrich the creativity and share-ability of the child's actions and interests.

I believe that the complex instincts for culture that infants and toddlers demonstrate require us to reappraise both the moral and political aspects of social life beyond the family. If even infants are moved to notice and want to join the cooperative awareness of the world that we know as the historically created culture, then they have a sense of propriety—of what is right and proper, what is honest and dishonest, what is helpful and what is malicious. They have more "responsibility" for their actions and understanding than can be assumed by any theory that social beliefs and laws can only be acquired after long practice with invented language and reasons. Above all, these motives of infants show that meaning is not a statistical accretion of impressions in an "overconnected neural net," or a structure of learned linguistic categories, but an actively sought consciousness of what can be known and done by a "Me" in a community, These mimetic and exhibitionist motives are source of the emotions of pride and shame that regulate self-consciousness

Cooperative understanding in any society is generated and maintained co-operatively through companionship, with dedicated and immediate interest in the awareness, intentions and feelings of other human beings. It follows that even the most elaborated and sophisticated legal or religious codes of conduct and belief, and the rules and procedures for all commercial, artistic, scientific or technical creations in adult societies retain their links with the moral foundations that a one-year-old can sense in his or her attempts to take hold of meanings and to display this knowledge for the appreciation of others. Beyond monetary or consummatory advantage, they are ideas in a collective imagination with value because they have been, or could be, shared.

The politics of individualism, encouraging competition for privileges, wealth, comfort and pleasures denies the pride of sharing generously with others, and the gains in health and vitality of thought that come from comradeship in life's work. On the other hand Marxist notions of the supreme importance of work itself, and the right of all to an equal share in what is produced focuses on the material object of collective activity, and not sufficiently on the motives of sympathy and discovery that give that object interest and meaning. They led, by a bitter and relentless logic, to the absurd Cultural Revolution in China.

Motives to Learn Communal Ways and the Meaning of Things: To Win a Place in the Social World

What does it mean that infants can contribute so much of themselves to a personal relation with the mother, or with anyone else sufficiently receptive to their motives and feelings? What difference can it make to Macmurray's philosophy that he, with Freud, Winnicott and many others, has underestimated the infant's psychology in certain respects? What does this conclusion imply for the ideas of Macmurray about society and its morality education and politics? And for Winnicott's equating of the relationship-teasing playfulness of children with the creation of culture?

Our account of the impulses and responses that animate the earliest experiences of a human being indicates that there is a crucial positive motive force in human life, which is missing from Macmurray's account. It comprises the motive for shared interest in meaning, focusing not only on the other person, but also on the reality they might share, and the creations they might make together. In Macmurray's negative motives may become part of a positive creation of joint understanding; concerned with both contemplative and pragmatic things, with beliefs, aesthetics and scientific technology. It can perhaps explain the goals of romantic humanism and the forces that generate both good and bad art, and also Hobbes' competitive individualism and a defensive appeal of laws of right and wrong to regulate behaviour in society.

Such a powerful motivation to share the creation and use of meaning with loyal and trusted companions must also open the way for mistrusting enmity; for bigotry, rivalry and tyranny, for exploitation and conflict of interests. But, the essential value of companionship and respect for shared experience as part of the human spirit of life cannot be gainsaid. Without it no belief in or awareness of meaning would be possible, and there would be nothing sacred either. Religious faith proclaims in a higher purpose, a supra-rational moral authority—it attempts to create a consciousness that gives sacredness to each person's impulse to find an elevating meaning to relationships and to all experiences of living in this world, joyful or bitter as these may be, and their searching for comfort in a community that accepts solidarity of belief.

The scientific intellectuals, gurus of an information-hungry culture, who wish to do away with religion entirely, would do away with any comprehension of virtue or morality in life, and thereby do away with the sense of companionship and community. The populations they believe in are the conflicting societies of individuals driven by information to the senses, and by a reflex desire to survive, physically and physiologically—a drive to achieve reproductive success at minimum "expense." It is the old notion of an economy of materials and rationalised facts, given realism by inappropriate reductive use of physical evidence. It suits the strong, the privileged and the self-satisfied in their success.

For me, a psychologist and biologist, other-consciousness sympathy is a fact of human nature. My research on the human responses of infants from the moment of birth has proved that there is an innate readiness for human companionship, a need and a skill for exchange of motive states. This gives rise to an immediate moral relating, in which the infant and his or her companion show concern for one another. They exchange emotions that give value to their feelings and the way they sense one another. I have described some typical experiences of this work, and the consequences of some problematic situations that can be called experiments. However, most of the understanding we have of infants' abilities for responding humanly to human presences do not come from any contrived test of behaviours or responses. They come from careful description of the spontaneously motivated occasions of living. In the past thirty years such observing has revolutionised our scientific awareness of the human spirit and its sympathies.

Can A Modern State Be Governed According to Macmurray's Principles, and with Regard for Motives of Companionship?

Tony Blair, Britain's Prime Minister, admires John Macmurray's philosophy, and claims to have learned from it. In his foreword to a

recent collection of Macmurray's writings on self and society, Mr. Blair
says Macmurray writes better and with more relevance than hallowed
philosophical texts—that his programme is broader in scope. It is modern
because Macmurray has confronted what Mr. Blair calls, "the critical
question of the 21st century: the relationship between individual and
society." Macmurray's philosophy increases an understanding of the
world and our ability to change it. Blair continues, with familiar rhetoric,
"Now the task is to construct a new settlement for individual and society
today. We have reached the limits of a narrow selfish individualism; but
have learnt the mistakes that collective power can make." The role of
government for today is, he believes, clarified by Macmurray's view of
the individual in society. By rooting his vision in the personal world and
in intention, Macmurray rejects simple determinism. "The personal is not
submerged in the social or organic." It is matter of human spirituality.
Macmurray, for whom spirituality was based in this world, has
influenced "a whole generation of Christian philosophers."

Can we hope that in the practice of his high responsibility Mr. Blair,
with his cabinet, will keep a clear and comprehensive vision of the
sympathetic nature of persons in relation—of what they feel they need of
one another? Above all, can we hope that he, and they, will recognise
the need of every human citizen—of any age, backround or ability—for
pride of place that reflects others' respect for him or her, and for that
pride? When a government approaches matters of law and order
("combating" crime and drugs); supporting the aged and socially
dependent (responding to a ten-fold increase in pensioners); social
welfare ("fighting" abuses of the system, creating jobs); health care
(cutting waiting lists, administering health more efficiently, dismissing
incompetent doctors or nurses, buying more beds, training nurses);
education (deciding what teachers and education authorities should do,
raising literacy and numeracy); the economy (setting interest rates,
stabilising supply against demand), will they count on the deep need of
every individual to have self-respect, to do the helpful thing? Will they
remember that all persons—toddlers to old-age pensioners, convicted
criminals in prison, critically ill, the unemployed, the drug dependent, the
cold and poorly nourished, as well as all of us with paid jobs and families
to care for—want a self-confidence that releases a natural and
pleasurable generosity of spirit in self and others? Those are the key
questions. This confidence is not a product of logic or instruction; it does

not require coercion, nor does it demand money, except as a cipher. It can be weakened or turned into hatred by alienation, shame and humiliation, or by incitement to revenge.

NOTES

[1] *The Theory of Moral Sentiments*, DD Raphael & A.L. Macfie, (eds.) (Oxford: Clarendon, 1976), 9.

[2] Ibid., 10.

[3] Ibid., 11.

[4] Ibid., 13.

[5] Ibid., 110.

[6] Ibid., 113.

[7] I have called this the "Subjective First position." 'Intersubjectivity', *The MIT Encyclopedia of Cognitive Sciences*, Rob Wilson & Frank Keil (eds.) (Cambridge, MA: MIT Press, 1999), 413–416.

[8] E. Spelke, 'The Origins of Physical Knowledge', *Thought Without Language*, L Weiskrantz (ed.) (Oxford: Clarendon, 1988).

[9] M. Legerstee, 'A review of the animate-inanimate distinction in infancy: Implications for models of social and cognitive knowing', *Early Development and Parenting*, 1, (1992), 57–67. Colwyn Trevarthen, 'The self born in intersubjectivity: The Psychology of an infant communicating', U Neisser, (ed.), *The Perceived Self: Ecological and Interpersonal Sources of the Self-Knowledge* (New York: Cambridge University Press, 1993), 121–173.

[10] S. E. Trehub, L. J. Trainor & A. M. Unyk, 'Musical Prototypes in developmental perspective', *Psychomusicology*, 10.2 (1991), 31–45.

[11] C. Trevarthen, T. Kokkinaki, & G. A. Fiamenghi,Jr., 'What infants' imitations communicate: With mothers, with fathers and with peers,' J. Nadel & G. Butterworth (eds.) *Imitation in infancy* (Cambridge: Cambridge University Press, forthcoming).

[12] M. Tomasello, 'On the interpersonal origins of the self-concept', U Neisser, (ed.), *The Perceived Self: Ecological and Interpersonal Sources of the Self-Knowledge* (New York: Cambridge University Press, 1993), 174–184.

[13] J. Piaget, (1954) *The Construction of Reality in the Child* (New York: Basic Books, 1954), *Play, Dreams and Imitation in Childhood* (London: Routledge & Kegan Paul, 1962).

[14] J. Shotter, *Images of Man in Psychological Research* (London: Methuen, 1975).

[15] D.N. Stern, 'A micro-analysis of mother-infant interaction: Behviours regulating social contact between a mother and her three-and-a-half-month-old twin.' *Journal of American Academy of Child Psychiatry,* 10, (1971), 501–517.

[16] M.C. Bateson, ' "The epigenesis of conversational interaction": a personal account of research and development', in M. Bullowa (ed.), *Before Speech: The Beginnings of Human Communication* (London: Cambridge University Press, 1979), 63–77.

[17] C. Trevarthen, 'Conversations with a two-month-old', *New Scientist,* 2 May 1979, 230–235; 'Communication and cooperation in early infancy. A description of primary intersubjectivity' In M. Bullowa (ed.), ibid., 321–347.

[18] M.P.M. Richards (ed.), *The Integration of a Child into a Social World* (London: Cambridge University Press, 1974).

[19] C. Trevarthen, 'The concept and foundations of infant intersubjectivity', S. Bråten (ed.), *Intersubjective Communication and Emotion in Early Ontogeny.* (Cambridge: Cambridge University Press, 1999) 15–46.

[20] M. Bullowa (ed.), *Before Speech: The Beginning of Human Communication* (London: Cambridge University Press, 1979).

[21] H.R. Schaffer, *Studies in Mother-Infant Interaction: The Loch Lomond Symposium* (London: Academic Press, 1977).

[22] E.g. A.N. Meltzoff & M.K. Moore, 'Imitation of facial and manual gestures by human neonates', *Science,* 198, (1977), 75–78.

[23] C. Trevarthen, L. Murray, & P. Hubley, 'Psychology of infants' in J. Davis & J. Dobbing (eds.). *Scientific Foundations of Clinical Paediatrics* (London: W Heinemann Medical Books, 1981), (2nd edition), 235–250.

[24] E.g. M. Heimann, M. & J. Schaller, 'Imitative reactions among 14–21day-old infants', *Infant Mental Health Journal,* 6(1), (1985) 31–39.

[25] E.g. N. Ratner, & J. S. Bruner, 'Games, social exchange and the acquisition of language'*Journal of Child Language,* 5, (1978), 391-400.

[26] J-P. Lecanuet, W. P. Fifer, N. A. Krasnegor, & W. P. Smotherman, (eds.), *Fetal Development: A Psychobiological Perspective* (Hillsdale, NJ: Erlbaum, 1995); C. Trevarthen, 'Foetal and neonatal psychology: Intrinsic motives and learning behaviour' in F. Cockburn (ed.), *Advances in Perinatal Medicine.,* (Proceedings of the XVth European Congress of Perinatal Medicine, Glasgow, 10– 13 September, 1996) (New York/Carnforth, Lancs., UK: Parthenon, 1997), 282–291.

[27] E.g. A. J. De Casper, & W. P. Fifer, 'Of human bonding: Newborns prefer their mother's voices', *Science,* 208 (1980), 1174–1176.

[28] P. G. Hepper, 'The behavior of the fetus as an indicator of neural functioning' in J. P. Lecanuet, W. P. Fifer, N. A. Krasnegor & W. P. Smotherman (eds.) *Fetal Development: A Psychobiological Perspective.* (Hillsdale NJ: Erlbaum, 1995), 405–417.

[29] M. C. Bateson, ' "The epigenesis of conversational interaction": a personal account of research and development', op. cit., C. Trevarthen, 'Foetal and neonatal psychology: Intrinsic motives and learning behaviour', op. cit.

[30] D. Zeifman, S. Delaney, & E. Blass, (1996). 'Sweet taste, looking, and calm in 2– and 4–week-old infants: The eyes have it.' *Developmental Psychology,* 32, (1996), 1090–1099.

[31] C. Trevarthen, 'The nature of motives for human consciousness', *Psychology: The Journal of the Hellenic Psychological Society* (Special Issue: 'The Place of Psychology in Contemporary Sciences', Part 2. Guest Editor, T. Velli), 4.3 (1998), 187–221.

[32] C. Trevarthen, T. Kokkinaki, & G. A. Fiamenghi,Jr., 'What infants' imitations communicate: With mothers, with fathers and with peers', op. cit.

33 E. Pöppel, & M. Wittmann, 'Time in the mind', in R. A. Wilson & F. Keil (General Editors) *The MIT Encyclopedia of the Cognitive Sciences.*(Cambridge: MIT Pess, forthcoming).

34 E.g. B. Beebe, J. Jaffe, S. Feldstein, K. Mays, & D. Alson, 'Inter-personal timing: The application of an adult dialogue model to mother-infant vocal and kinesic interactions', in F. M Field & N. Fox (eds.), *Social Perception in Infants* (Norwood, NJ: Ablex, 1985), 249–268.

35 S. Malloch, 'Mothers and infants, and communicative musicality', *Musicae Scientiae* (forthcoming).

36 F. Wemelsfelder, 'The concept of animal boredom and its relationship to stereotyped behaviour', in A. B. Lawrence & J. Rushen (eds.), *Stereotypic Animal Behaviour* (Wallingford, Oxon: CAB International, 1993), 65–95.

37 J. Piaget, *The Construction of Reality in the Child*, op. cit..

38 C. Trevarthen, 'The nature of motives for human consciousness', op. cit..

39 C. Trevarthen et al., 'What infants' imitations communicate: With mothers, with fathers and with peers', op. cit..

40 J. Piaget, *The Construction of Reality in the Child*, op. cit.; E. Spelke, 'The origins of physical knowledge' in L. Weiskrantz (ed.), *Thought Without Language* (Oxford: Clarendon Press, 1988).

41 E.g. V. Reddy, 'Playing with others' expectations; Teasing and 'mucking about' in the first year.', in A. Whiten (ed.), *Natural Theories of Mind* (Oxford: Blackwell, 1991), 143–158.

42 H. Papousek & M. Papousek, 'Intuitive Parenting: A dialectic counterpart to the infant's integrative competenc', in J. D. Osofsky, *Handbook of Infant Development* (Second Edition, New York: Wiley, 1987).

43 S. Bråten, (1992) 'The virtual other in infant's minds and social feelings', in A. H. Wold (ed.), *The Dialogical Alternative* (Festschrift for Ragnar Rommetveit) (Oslo/Oxford: Scandanavian University Press/Oxford University Press, 1992), 77–97; C Trevarthen, 'Intersubjectivity', op. cit.

44 F. Turner, *Beauty: The Value of Values* (Charlottesville: University Press of Virginia, 1991).

45 E. Nagy, & P. Molnár, '*Homo imitans* or *Homo provocans?*' Abstract, *International Journaly of Psychophysiology*, 18.2 (1994), 128.

46 A. N. Meltzoff & M.K. Moore, 'Imitation, memory and representation of persons', *Infant Behaviour & Development,* 17 (1994), 83–99.

47 A. Diamond, 'The development of the ability to use recall to guide action, as indicated by infants' performance on A-not B.', *Child Development*, 56, (1985), 868-883.

48 C. Rovee-Collier, & P. Gerhardstein, 'The development of infant memory,'N. Cowan, (ed.), The Development of memory in childhood (Sussex: Psychology Press, 1997).

49 R.P. Hobson, 'On the origins of self and the case of autism', *Development and Psychopathology*, 2 (1990), 163–181.

50 C. Trevarthen, 'An infant's motives for speaking and thinking in the culture,' A. H. Wold, (ed.), *The Dialogical Alternative* op. cit.

51   S. Nakano & Y. Kanaya, 'The effects of mothers' teasing: Do Japanese infants read their mothers' play intention in teasing?', *Early Development & Parenting*, 2.1, (1993), 7–17.

52   A. N. Schore, *Affect Regulation and the Origina of the Self: The Neurobiology of Emotional Devlopment* (Hillsdale, NJ: Erlbaum, 1994).

53   D. N. Stern, 'Joy and satisfaction in infancy,' R. A. Glick & S. Bone (eds.), *Pleasure beyond the pleasure principle* (Newhaven, CT: Yale University Press, 1990), 13–25.

54   C. Trevarthen, L. Murray, L & P. Hubley, (1981) 'Psychology of infants' in J. Davis & J. Dobbing (eds.), *Scientific Foundations of Clinical Paediatrics*. (London: W. Heinemann Medical Books, 2nd edition, 1981), 235–250.

55   T. Field, 'Infants of Depressed Mothers', *Development and Psychopathology*, 4, (1992), 49–66; E. Z. Tronick, & M. K. Weinberg, (1997) 'Depressed mothers and infants: Failure to form dyadic states of consciousness', L. Murray, & P. J. Cooper (eds.), *Postpartum Depression and Child Development* (New York: Guilford Press, 1997), 54–81.

56   C. Trevarthen, 'Emotions in infancy: Regulators of contacts and relationships with persons', in K. Scherer & P. Ekman (eds.), *Approaches to Emotion*. (Hillsdale, NJ: Erlbaum, 1984), 129–157.

57   H. Als, 'The preterm infant: A model for the study of fetal brain expectation', in J-P. Lecanuet, W. P. Fifer, N. A. Krasnegor, & W.P. Smotherman, (eds.) *Fetal development: A psychobiological perspective* (Hillsdale, NJ/ Hove,UK: Erlbaum, 1995), 439–471.

58   S. van Rees, S. & R. de Leeuw, *Born Too Early: The Kangaroo Method with Premature Babies*. Video by Stichting Lichaamstaal, Scheyvenhofweg 12, 6093 PR, Heythuysen, The Netherlands, 1987. For an acoustic analysis of an episode of vocal exchange from this video see C. Trevarthen. T. Kokkinaki, & G. A. Fiamenghi Jr., 'What infants' imitations communicate: With mothers, with fathers and with peers', in J. Nadel & G. Butterworth (eds.), *Imitation in infancy* (Cambridge: Cambridge University Press, forthcoming).

59   C. Trevarthen, 'The concept and foundations of infant intersubjectivity'. op. cit.

60   D. N. Stern, 'The role of feelings for an interpersonal self' in U. Neisser (ed.), *The Perceived Self: Ecological and Interpersonal Sources of the Self-Knowledge* (New York: Cambridge University Press, 1993), 205–215.

61   M. Donaldson, *Children's Minds* (Glasgow: Fontana/Collins, 1978).

62   G. Kugiumutzakis, 'Intersubjective vocal imitation in early mother-infant interaction', in J. Nadel & L. Camaioni (eds.) *New Perspectives in Early Communicative Development* (London: Routledge, 1993), 23–47.

63   V. Reddy, D. Hay, L. Murray, & C. Trevarthen, 'Communication in infancy: Mutual regulation of affect and attention', in G. Brenner, A. Slater & G. Butterworth (eds.) *Infant Development: Recent Advances* (Hove, East Sussex: Psychology Press, 1997), 247–274.

64   D. N. Stern, 'The role of feelings for an interpersonal self,' U. Neisser (ed.), *The Perceived Self: Ecological and Interpersonal Sources of the Self-Knowledge* (New York: Cambridge University Press, 1993), 205–215.

65 C. Trevarthen, C. & P. Hubley, 'Secondary intersubjectivity: confidence confiding and acts of meaning in the first year,' A. Lock (ed.), *Action: Gesture and Symbol: the Emergence of Language* (London, Academic Press, 1978), 183–229.

66 J. Nadel, & A. Pezé, 'Immediate imitation as a basis for primary communication in toddlers and autistic children,' J. Nadel & L. Camioni (eds.), *New Perspectives in Early Communicative Development* (London: Routledge, 1993).

67 M. Donald, M. *Origins of the Modern Mind* (Cambridge & London: Harvard University Press, 1991).

68 C. Trevarthen, 'Mother and baby—seeing artfully eye to eye' in R. Gregory, J. Harris, D. Rose & P. Heard (eds.), *The Artful Eye* (Oxford: Oxford University Press, forthcoming), 157–200.

69 J. S. Bruner, *The Culture of Education* (Cambridge, MA.: Harvard University Press, 1996).

70 F. Turner, *Beauty: The Value of Values*, op. cit.

71 John Amos Comenius (1592-1671), *The School of Infancy*. translated by D. Benham. London, 1858. Quotation from R. H. Quick, *Essays on Educational Reformers* (London: Longmans, Green & Co., 1910).

72 V. Reddy, 'Shy expressions in two-month-olds', paper presented at the Annual Conference of the Developmental Section of the British Psychological Society, Oxford, September 1996.

73 C. Trevarthen, 'Signs before speech', in T.A. Sebeok & J. Umiker-Sebeok (eds.), *The Semiotic Web, 1989.* (Berlin, New York, Amsterdam: Mouton de Gruyter, 1990), 689–755.

74 C. Gilligan, *In a Different Voice: Psychological Theory and Women's Development* (Cambridge, MA: Harvard University Press, 1982).

75 J. S. Bruner, *The Culture of Education*, op. cit.

76 E.g. R. Bakeman, & L. B. Adamson, L. B. 'Coordinating attention to people and objects in mother-infant and peer-infant interaction', *Child Development*, 55 (1984), 1278–1289.

77 J. S. Bruner, *Child's Talk: Learning to Use Language* (New York: W. W. Norton & Co, 1983).

78 B. Beebe, J. Jaffe, S. Feldstein, K. Mays, & D. Alson, 'Inter-personal timing: The application of an adult dialogue model to mother-infant vocal and kinesic interactions', in F. M Field & N. Fox (eds.), *Social Perception in Infants* (Norwood, NJ: Ablex, 1985), 249–268; C. Trevarthan et al., 'What infants' imitations communicate: With mothers, with fathers and with peers', op. cit.

79 D. N. Stern, 'The role of feelings for an interpersonal self', op. cit.

80 M. Donald, *Origins of the Modern Mind* (Cambridge & London: Harvard University Press, 1991).

81 A. M. Leslie, 'Pretence and representation: the origins of "theory of mind,"' *Psychological Review*, 94 (1987), 412–426.

82 M. Klein, P. Heinmann, S. Isaacs, J. Riviere, *Developments in Psychoanalysis* (London: Hogarth, 1952).

[83] W. R. D. Fairbairn, *An Object Relations Theory of the Personality* New York: Basic Books, 1954); J. S. Grotstein, & D. B. Rinsley, *Fairbairn and the Origins of Object Relations* (London/New York: The Guilford Press, 1994).

[84] D. W. Winnicott, *Playing and Reality* (London: Tavistock, 1958); M. Davis, & D. Wallbridge, *Boundry and Space: An Introduction to the Work of D. W. Winnicott* (New York: Brunner/Mazel & London: H, Karnac Books Ltd, 1990); R. A. Hodgkin, 'Making space for meaning', *Oxford Review of Education*, 23(3), (1997): 385–399.

[85] J. Bowlby, 'The nature of the child's tie to his mother', *International Journal of Psychoanalysis*, 39, (1958), 1–23.

[86] L. A. Sroufe, *Emotional Development: The Organisation of Emotional Life in the Early Years* (Cambridge: Cambridge University Press, 1996).

[87] A. Alvarez, *Live Company: Psychoanalytic Therapy with Autistic, Borderline, Deprived and Abused Children.* (London: Tavistock/Routledge, 1992).

[88] M S. Mahler, F. Pine, & A. Bergman, *The Psychological Birth of the Human Infant* (New York: Basic Books, 1975).

[89] H. S. Sullivan, *The Interpersonal Theory of Psychiatry* (New York: Norton, 1953).

[90] D. N. Stern, *The Interpersonal World of the Infant: A View from Psychoanalysis and Development Psychology*, op. cit.

[91] A. Kenny, *Wittgenstein* (London: Penguin Books, 1993).

[92] A. N. Whitehead, *Process and Reality: An Essay in Cosmology* (Cambridge: Macmillan University Press, 1929).

[93] J. Piaget, *The Construction of Reality in the Child* (New York: Basic Books, 1954); *Play, Dreams and Imitation in Childhood* (London: Routledge & Kegan Paul , 1962).

[94] M. Buber, *I and thou* (translated by R. G. Smith) (Edinburgh: T. & T. Clark, 1937).

[95] J. S. Bruner, *The Culture of Education* (Cambridge, MA.: Harvard University Press, 1996).

[96] E.g. J. De Rivera, 'Love, fear and justice: Transforming selves for the new world' *Social Justice Research*, 3.4, (1989), 387–426.

[97] J. Benjamin, *The Bonds of Love: Psychoanalysis, Feminism, and the Problems of Domination* (New York: Pantheon, 1988).

[98] J-P. Lecanuet et al., *Fetal Development: A Psychobiological Perspective*, op. cit.

[99] C. Trevarthen, 'Brain Science and the Human Spirit', op. cit.

[100] L. Murray, & C. Trevarthen, 'Emotional regulation of interactions between two-month-olds and their mothers', T. Field & N. Fox (eds.), *Social Perception in Infants* (Norwood, N.J., Ablex, 1985).

[101] L. Murray, 'The impact of postnatal depression on infant development' *Journal of Child Psychology & Psychiatry*, 33.3 (1992), 543–561.

[102] H. Als, 'The preterm infant: A model for the study of fetal brain expectation', op. cit.

[103] S. van Rees, & H. Biemans, *Floortje* Video by Stichting Lichaamstaal, Scheyvenhofweg 12, 6093 PR, Heythuysen, The Netherlands, 1984.

[104] E. Nagy, & P. Molnár, P. *Homo imitans* or *Homo provocans?*, op. cit.

[105] M. Tomasello, 'On the interpersonal origins of the self-concept', in U. Neisser (ed.), *The Perceived Self: Ecological and Interpersonal Sources of the Self-Knowledge* (New York: Cambridge University Press, 1993). 174–184.

[106] A. N. Meltzoff, 'The roots of social and cognitive development: models of man's original nature,' T.M. Field & N.A. Fox (eds.), *Social Perception in Infant* (Norwood, N.J., Ablex, 1995), 1–30.

[107] J. Nadel, & A. Pezé, 'Immediate imitation as a basis for primary communication in toddlers and autistic children,' J. Nadel & L. Camioni (eds.), *New Perspectives in Early Communicative Development* (London: Routledge, 1993).

CHAPTER SIX

Personal and Impersonal Relationships

Robin Downie

In this essay I have three aims: to examine Macmurray's distinction between personal and impersonal relationships; to examine his view of the possibility of a science of human beings; and to consider whether his idea of personal relationships and the attitudes involved can be extended beyond human beings, and if so how this might affect the concept of community.

The central thesis in Macmurray's *Persons in Relation* is that "Persons are… constituted by their mutual relation to one another."[1] or that "The unit of the personal is not the 'I' but the 'You and I'."[2] He allows however that there can be impersonal relationships between persons.

> But within this relation, which constitutes my existence, I can isolate myself from you in intention, so that my relation to you becomes impersonal. In this event, I treat you as object, refusing the personal relationship. This is always possible because the form of the personal involves its own negation. Impersonality is the negative aspect of the personal; since only a person can behave impersonally, just as only a subject can think objectively.[3]

Macmurray holds that it follows from this distinction between personal and impersonal relationships that there can be a science of persons thought of impersonally as objects, but there can be no scientific knowledge of persons as persons. There can indeed be knowledge of persons, but it is personal knowledge, which is not scientific knowledge.

> [A]ny objective or impersonal knowledge of the human, any science of man, whether psychological or sociological, involves a negation of the personal relation of the 'I' and the 'You', and so of the relation which constitutes them persons. Formally, such knowledge is knowledge of the 'You', that is, of the

other person; but not of the other person in personal relation to the knower, but as object in the world. I can know another person as a person only by entering into personal relation with him.[4]

What does Macmurray mean by a personal relationship? He explains it in terms of a contrast between two kinds of attitude. Attitudes are "intentional," or in other words they are constituted by what we consider to be appropriate to their objects. A personal attitude is therefore constituted by what we regard as appropriately directed at persons. Seeing a person in this way puts me in a personal relationship. But an impersonal relationship with a person is also possible. Macmurray gives the example of a teacher of psychology.

> Let us suppose that a teacher of psychology is visited by a pupil who wishes to consult him about the progress of his work. The interview begins as a simple personal conversation between them, and the teacher's attitude to the pupil is a normal personal attitude. As it proceeds, however, it becomes evident that something is wrong with the pupil. He is in an abnormal state of mind, and the psychologist recognizes clear symptoms of hysteria. At once the attitude of the teacher changes. He becomes a professional psychologist, observing and dealing with a classifiable case of mental disorder. From his side the relation has changed from a personal to an impersonal one; he adopts an objective attitude, and the pupil takes on the character of an object to be studied, with the purpose of determining the causation of his behaviour.[5]

He goes on to say that he could have illustrated the impersonal relationship or attitude by reference to an employer, an examiner or a judge, but "even these would be rather special examples of what is, in fact, one of the commonest features of our everyday experience."[6] The conclusion is that "our relation to another person may be either personal or impersonal."[7]

Macmurray is saying something interesting and important here, but I believe that there is both an oversimplification and a confusion in his position. I shall begin with the oversimplification. Let us consider whether it is true to say that a relationship between persons is wholly constituted by the attitude with which these persons view each other.

We can use the word "relationship" in two ways: to stand for the bond which links two or more people, or to stand for the attitudes which bonded people have to each other. As examples of the first sense of relationship we might mention kinship, marriage, business association, or teacher-pupil. As examples of the second we might mention fear, pride, respect, envy, contempt etc. Thus someone, seeing an adult and a child together, might ask what is the relationship between them, and receive an answer in terms of the first sense of relationship: "teacher and pupil," or "father and son" etc. Or he might ask, "What sort of relationship do Jones and his son have?" and receive an answer in terms of the second sense of relationship: "Jones loves his son, but his son can't stand him."

The two senses of relationship, or preferably, the two aspects of any relationship, are connected in various complex ways. For example, if the situation is a business transaction, where the bond is economic, then the attitude of the parties would not characteristically be one of affection or friendship. There are of course no logical impediments to such an attitude developing out of the business transaction, and indeed it is material for romantic comedy when the attitude in the relationship is inappropriate for the bond.

Macmurray's oversimplification here is that he concentrates entirely on the attitudinal aspects of the concept of a relationship, stressing its intentionality. There are two aspects to this oversimplification, which are highlighted by attention to the "bond." The first is that there is a plurality of possible types of human relationship. For example, there are bonds of friendship, kinship, citizenship, and neighbourliness. Again, people can be linked as doctor-patient, teacher-pupil, minister-parishioner, host-guest, and many, many others. In sticking to the more abstract "personal relationship" Macmurray fails to see the variety of bonds which are possible in the relationships we can have with each other. The second aspect of the oversimplification is the normative character of human relationships. The bonds are constituted by different sets of rules which bind on both parties in the relationship. There is more to a relationship than its intentionality; relationships have duties and responsibilities.

If we stress the "bond" aspect of human relationships we might indeed be led to question whether in the end there is such a thing as a purely personal relationship—a relationship of persons as such. It can be argued that what Macmurray is calling a "personal relationship" is just a convenient generic term for the multiplicity of the specific bonds which lock us into the myriad of roles which constitute society. Or, to put it another way, it is arguable that our relationships to each other are those of the multiplicity of the social roles through which we act. Now, as shall see, there is a sense in which Macmurray might not disagree with that claim. But he might prefer to put the point differently, by saying that every personal relationship has its impersonal or (in his terminology) its "negative" aspect. Certainly, we shall need to examine the relationship between being a person and having a role. But before doing so let us look at the personal attitude which, for Macmurray, is what primarily constitutes a personal relationship.

As has been said, Macmurray stresses the "intentional" nature of attitudes and relationships. What does that mean? The most important point about an attitude for our purposes may be brought out if we say that an attitude is two-sided. In the first place, it must be an attitude of something, where "something" is always a disposition of some sort, such as hope, fear, distrust, forbearance, or the like. In the second place, attitudes must be to something; it is conceptually impossible for an attitude to lack an object. It will be possible to describe this object in various ways, but for any particular attitude there will be one description under which the object of the attitude must by definition fall. For example, an attitude cannot logically be one of hope unless it is to an object which is believed to be in some sense a good to the hoper. The connection between hope and an imagined good is thus a necessary one, and we might go as far as to say that a person could not understand the meaning of "hope" unless he knew what it was to imagine a good, and to imagine a good is to lay the foundation for acquiring the concept of hope. A similar analysis applies to all attitudes; they can be identified by means of the characteristics which their object is believed to possess, and thus a belief is at the root of all attitudes. The object under the description which is implied by the attitude-name may be called the formal object of that attitude. For example, the formal object of hope is an imagined good which, it is believed, may come about, and the formal object of fear is a believed danger, and so on.

What is the formal object of the personal attitude? The answer is that it is a person thought of in a special way, or under a special description. Macmurray stresses that what is important about persons is that they can be agents. Note that this of course is not any neutral biological point but is already an evaluative one. Moreover, for all that the theme of agency pervades his Gifford Lectures, it becomes clear that there are other qualities of persons which he also values. Thus, the agency is carried out in a community of equal, free, self-realizing agents.[8] Or, as he also puts it: "A community is for the sake of friendship and presupposes love. But it is only in friendship that persons are free in relation..."[9] The attitude which constitutes Macmurray's idea of a personal relationship clearly has affinities with Aristotle's conception of a society of friends, with Kant's idea of a kingdom of self-legislating ends-in-themselves, and with Christian "agape."

It is now easy to understand why the psychology tutor's attitude to his apparently neurotic student ceases to be a personal attitude. It is because the formal object of the psychologist's attitude is not a person in Macmurray's normative sense, but a human being exhibiting certain symptoms open to causal explanation in terms of the laws of psychology. This is reasonably called by Macmurray an "impersonal" attitude. But Macmurray takes a step in the wrong direction—this is the confusion referred to earlier—when he suggests[10] that this "impersonal" attitude can be generalised and is present as the "negative" element in the multiplicity of our everyday role relationships of employer-employee, teacher-pupil etc. For our role relationships are not in the same sense "impersonal," although in a quite different sense they may be so described. Role relationships of teacher-pupil, husband-wife, are impersonal to the extent that they are partly constituted by socially sanctioned norms or duties and responsibilities; but the psychologist's relationship is "impersonal" in that he views his patients or clients as causally determined systems. He studies his clients as a scientist studies the behaviour of a deterministic system, as a botanist might study a plant. Now there may be disorders of the mind which give rise to causally determined behaviour which can be studied by a psychologist, but Macmurray goes wrong, I believe, when he suggests that causal factors of this kind are components of all personal action. Of course, it is true that all personal action has causal components. For example, personal action could not take place without events in the brain and nervous system, and meaningful speech requires the occurrence of causally determined sound waves.[11] But the causal components here are necessary but not sufficient conditions of action or meaningfulness. In the case of obsessional or psycho-pathic behaviour, on the other hand, the causal conditions are sufficient. Macmurray suggests that there is no antinomy between freedom and determinism with respect to action. This is true if we think of the causality of action in terms of causally necessary conditions, but if we say—and the psychology example suggests this—that there are sufficient causal conditions in the standard cases of personal action, then the antinomy has not been solved.

The more important issue for a philosophy of the personal concerns the other sense of the term "impersonal"—the sense in which we act in everyday life as teachers, parents, passengers, patients, citizens, and so on. How are impersonal attitudes in this sense related to personal ones (in Macmurray's terminology), or, in my own, how is acting in a role related to acting as a person? Macmurray is ambiguous here. He suggests that all our personal relationships have an impersonal or "negative" aspect.[12] But, as we have seen, this could mean either that there are causally necessary conditions of action (which I do not dispute) or that in addition to acting as persons we are also at the same time acting, say, as an examiner or a parent. Rather than try to work out what exactly Macmurray may mean I shall pose the question in my own terminology and ask what is the relationship between acting as a peson and acting "impersonally" in the sense of acting in a role, where "role" refers to socially sanctioned norms of behaviour.

It might first be suggested that the relationship is one of identity, in the sense that acting as a person just is acting as an X, Y or Z, where these name social roles. If this thesis were valid, then it would be possible to have a complete explanation of human behaviour in terms of one or more social sciences. For there can be detailed objective descriptions of the roles which people have in society.

This account, however, omits to mention one essential aspect of every action—the choice requirement. People can choose to accept or reject their roles. Moreover, while playing the role of doctor, teacher, father, trade unionist or the like, a person can be detached from his roles, or can laugh at himself in them. This suggests that there is an important personal dimension to action which is not caught by the concept of a social role. In other words, to understand an action it is important to know how the person himself sees the action, or more generally, what is his attitude to the role. And understanding of this kind does not come from applying any social science to action. Macmurray, I believe, would agree with this.

It might be argued that "person" itself is a role-concept, and that therefore what I am calling the "personal" dimension to action can still be explained in terms of the social sciences which deal with the concept of a role. Now there is a great deal to be said for the view that "person" is itself a role-concept. Consider, for example, the history of the term "person." Historians of ideas tell us that the term "person" is derived from the Latin "persona," which was originally a mask through which came the sound of an actor's voice. The term is then extended to mean a role in a drama, or "dramatis persona," and from there it easily comes to mean a social role. It is in this sense that the term "persona" is used in Roman Law, where it stands for someone as a subject of rights. In other words, the history of the word suggests that "person" is an institutional notion. And we find in Stoic ideas that the notion of "person" takes on a deeper metaphysical meaning as it deepens in social significance. The Stoic idea of all men as citizens of a single City of God combines the ideas of the supreme metaphysical value of the person with the social idea of the person as a bearer of rights and duties. Hence, in view of its history, it might seem natural to regard "person" as itself a role-concept. But to say all this is not to say that "person" simply names yet another role. If "person" is a role-concept it is not in the same category as other roles; it cannot be since it cannot be chosen. Thus, it is not that Mr X is a committee member, a teacher, a husband, and a person. The connection between personality and roles is different. To bring this out consider the Greek idea of an "ergon". The Greeks saw the significance of a craftsman as lying in his function, and his virtue in being a good craftsman. For each craft or art there was said to be an end, and the craft was designed to further the end. This idea was extended by Aristotle to apply to man as such. He was thought to have an "ergon" or function and a particular virtue. This line of thinking suggests that there is a role or function of man as such. But there may be a category mistake involved here. It is harmless enough to speak of the "ergon" or function or role of a person if by that is meant such things as that persons develop in characteristic ways, carry out some activities better than others, and so on. In short, it is harmless to speak of the role of a person as such if by that is meant only that "person" is evaluative and a different concept from that of "human being." But if it means that a given individual human being is an X, Y, Z, and a person (where "person" is put in the same list as the other roles) then the concept of a person is distorted and the concept of a role is trivialized. The point of introducing the concept of social roles is to stress the often neglected social or impersonal side to morality, to provide a means of conceptualizing the "what-you-have-got-to-do-as-a-such-and-such." But if the concept of "person" is itself analyzed in this way there is nothing left to contrast with the impersonal side to morality. It is therefore important to keep a concept of personality irreducible to that of a social role.

The answer to the question of the relationship between being a person and acting in a role, then, is that persons necessarily act in roles, or that all actions have a social dimension. In Macmurray's terminology this means that a purely personal relationship is impossible—all relationships have an impersonal aspect—and a purely impersonal relationship of persons is equally impossible. As he says himself, the master may value personal qualities in his slave, such as honesty.[13] Nevertheless, it is unclear to me how far Macmurray would agree with the view I am putting forward about the nature of a person. Certainly he says that all personal relationships have their impersonal aspect, but it will be remembered that he is generalising this from the psychology example, in which the impersonal aspect must be interpreted in terms of causal conditions. But to say that all personal relationships have an impersonal aspect in the sense that they have necessary causal conditions is different from saying that they have a necessary social or role aspect— that a purely personal relationship is impossible. Whereas I am not denying the former thesis—which is obviously true—I am asserting the latter, and Macmurray might well disagree with it because it entails a view of the self with which he might disagree.

The foregoing will become clearer when I have discussed my second question: Can there be both "personal knowledge" and scientific knowledge of personal action? Certainly, there can be scientific knowledge of the impersonal aspects of personal action, what I have called the "social role" aspects, for there are social sciences which investigate the multiplicity of the roles which constitute the fabric of any society. Note, however, that I differ from Macmurray in that I hold that these sciences are not causal but descriptive. Macmurray wishes to insist that science is necessarily causal in its assumptions.[14] I shall not begin a detailed dispute in this context, but be content for the moment in calling my social sciences "social studies," or the natural history of society. The more important question here is whether there can be a science, in any sense, of the personal aspects of action in its normal as distinct from its pathological manifestations.

Macmurray is quite clear that there cannot be; personal knowledge for him is non-scientific. This, of course, must be the case if we assume, as he does, that science must proceed by looking for causes, for he holds that personal action is free and non-causal. But if we do not make the assumption that science is necessarily causal we are left with the question of whether there can be a scientific, or at least a systematic and generalisable, study of the personal. For example, let us imagine that we are trying to understand the actions of Miss X who is a nurse. It is clear from the previous section that we can make a start by understanding the actions of Miss X in terms of nursing sociology. But it might be said that nursing sociology does not tell us what it is for Miss X to be a nurse, how she, as a person, sees her role. This is the irreducibly personal dimension to the complex "Miss-X-as-a-nurse," and this irreducibly personal dimension does not admit of scientific understanding, whether causal or non-causal.

Yet some social scientists or psychologists might dispute this claim. They might maintain that their studies can give us scientific or systematic knowledge of this personal dimension. For example, we can refer here to the concept of "verstehen," deployed in some social sciences. It is not entirely clear to me what is meant by the term, but it has become the received expression for the kind of understanding of action we aim at when we try to put ourselves on the inside of actions and capture their meaning. Theorists of nursing, social work and counselling sometimes use the (equally unclear) term "empathy" in attempting to describe the process of understanding an action from the inside.

There are two difficulties with this. The first is that it is doubtful whether we can really substantiate the claims made by some members of the caring and pastoral professions, that they can enter into or empathise with the feelings of others, and that they can even offer professional training for this. Every normal human being can do this to a limited extent and no doubt some people are better at it than others, but there is really no evidence that some professions can do it better than the average person, or that training improves what we have by nature. This is an important practical consideration, but for present theoretical purposes the more important difficulty with the ideas of "verstehen" or "empathy" is whether they are properly called scientific, in even a wide sense. Scientific understanding is a matter of fitting events into a pattern and of tracing systematic connections. Moreover, scientific understanding is concerned with things in their generality, with the common or universal properties of things or events. And the same is true of the understanding which the social sciences give of action. They are concerned with what a soldier, a dentist, or golfer might do, or they are concerned with "people in stress situations," or the "one parent family." Understanding of this sort, however important, is not the same as that involved when we suddenly see, or slowly come to realize, what it is for a specific, named individual, now standing in front of us, to be a soldier, or to be in a specific situation of stress. Understanding of the latter sort is concerned with actions in their particularity, with the uniqueness of situations. We might put the point differently by saying that whereas science, including social science, gives us horizontal understanding we must in concrete situations supplement this by what we could call vertical understanding, the sort of understanding which comes from insight into a personal history. Sometimes the terms "narrative understanding" or "narrative truth" are used here.

The reason why there cannot be scientific understanding of the personal, then, is not, as Macmurray suggests, that personal action is non-causal and science presupposes causality. Rather it is that science of any sort provides systematic understanding or knowledge of the general, whereas personal action is particular and unique and therefore not generalisable or appropriate for systematic investigation. I wish now to turn to my third aim and to consider whether Macmurray's idea of a personal relationship can be extended, and if so how this would affect his idea of a community.

In order to develop this point I shall turn to an earlier thinker who is unlike Macmurray in that his methods are not those of philosophy, but whose thinking is in some ways similar to Macmurray's—Martin Buber. Let us begin by drawing Martin Buber's distinction between an "I-Thou" and "I-It" relationship. It will be helpful for my purposes to use his extended example of the range of attitudes one may adopt to a tree.

> I consider a tree.
>
> I can look on it as a picture: stiff column in a shock of light, or splash of green shot with the delicate blue and silver of the background.
>
> I can perceive it as movement: flowing veins on clinging, pressing pith, suck of the roots, breathing of the leaves, ceaseless commerce with earth and air—and the obscure growth itself.
>
> I can classify it in a species and study it as a type in its structure and mode of life.
>
> I can subdue its actual presence and form so sternly that I recognise it only as an expression of law—of the laws in accordance with which a constant

opposition of forces is continually adjusted, or of those in accordance with which the component substances mingle and separate.

I can dissipate it and perpetuate it in number, in pure numerical relation.

In all this the tree remains my object, occupies space and time, and has its nature and constitution.

It can, however, also come about, if I have both grace and will, that in considering the tree I become bound up in relation to it. The tree is now no longer It. I have been seized by the power of exclusiveness.

To effect this it is not necessary for me to give up any of the ways in which I consider the tree. There is nothing from which I would need to turn my eyes away in order to see, and no knowledge that I would have to forget. Rather is everything, picture and movement, species and type, law and number, indivisibly united in this event.

Everything belonging to the tree is in this: its form and structure, its colours and chemical composition, its intercourse with the elements and the stars, are all present in a single whole.

The tree is no impression, no play of my imagination, no value depending on my mood: but it is bodied over against me and has to do with me, as I with it—only in a different way.

Let no attempt be made to sap the strength from the meaning of the relation; relation is mutual.

The tree will have a consciousness, then, similar to our own? Of that I have no experience. But do you wish, through seeming to succeed in it with yourself, once again to disintegrate that which cannot be disintegrated? I encounter no soul or dryad of the tree, but the tree itself.

If I face a human being as my Thou, and say the primary word 'I-Thou' to him, he is not a thing among things, and does not consist of things.

The human being is not He or She, bounded from every other He and She, a specific point in space and time within the net of the world; nor is he a nature able to be experienced and described, a loose bundle of named qualities. But with no neighbour, and whole in himself, he is Thou and fills the heavens. This does not mean that nothing exists except himself. But all else lives in his light.[15]

Now this long passage contains many points with which Macmurray would be in agreement. For example, it is possible in the 'I-Thou' attitude, as described by Buber, to hold together a range of attitudes, scientific or aesthetic. This, for Macmurray, would translate as the point that a personal attitude can have an impersonal one as its "negative pole." But there are also important points of difference. For example, for Macmurray the personal attitude exists only between persons mutually perceived as equals,[16] but Buber seems to be saying not only that equality is not necessay for the "I-Thou" relationship, but that the "I-Thou" relationship can exist with a tree!

Now Buber himself does not make a lot of this; his main concern, like Macmurray's, is with persons, including God. Nevertheless, he clearly allows that we can enter into an "I-Thou" relationship with at least some aspects of the organic world. Macmurray, however, would emphatically reject that position. He is quite explicit that animal consciousness, far less trees, must be of a different moral order from that of human consciousness. Since Macmurray's position on this would be rejected by received opinion in socio-biology it might be instructive to consider his arguments.

Basically his claim (for in the end it is hardly an "argument") is that there is a radical difference, one of kind and not just of degree, between the conscious behaviour of animals and the informed intentional actions of persons. As he puts it, an action "is informed and directed by an awareness of the Other-than-self as other; and the ground of choice, that is, the determination of the action, lies therefore in the agent's knowledge of the Other."[17] Macmurray's claim is that the consciousness of animals cannot manage this. They cannot act intentionally, as he has characterised intentional action. He allows that they have "motives," but his use of the term "motive" is technical, not to say eccentric. He tells us[18] that "motive signifies, in general, that which determines movement. Its scientific equivalent is energy." It is motive in this non-cognitive sense which causes animal behaviour. Animals then cannot (logically) be said to act, but only to behave. Only persons can truly act, so it is only with persons that one can have a personal relationship.

Now supposing we agree, although the view seems questionable, that there is an unbridgeable gulf between persons and animals, what follows? It follows that only persons can have personal relationships. But there is a danger here of the thesis collapsing into triviality. We can have personal relationships only with persons—well and good—but that does not prevent us from having other sorts of relationships with animals and the environment. And they too can be meaningful in other ways. Some philosophers, such as Macmurray, maintain that we cannot be in a meaningful relationship with animals because there is an unbridgeable gulf between us and animals, but the very same philosophers also maintain that we can be in a meaningful personal relationship with God. Is the gulf there thought to be more easily bridgeable?

Like Macmurray I hold that the ideal of "community" is important, but unlike Macmurray I wish to avoid the tyranny of the personal. Macmurray says that our identity is constituted by our personal relationships. I wish to hold the more modest thesis that our identity is partly constituted by our personal relationships, but is also influenced by such factors as the environment, the arts, animals, and so on. Human beings are complicated and the relationships which constitute our identity and make us flourish are correspondingly diverse. Moreover, the human and natural environments which enable us to achieve our personal development place reciprocal obligations on us. This moral "ought" can be justified either humanistically, because we are trustees of our community and must hand it on, or mystically, because we live in a sacramental universe.

NOTES

[1] *Persons in Relation* (1961), 24.
[2] Ibid., 61.
[3] Ibid., 28.
[4] Ibid., 28.
[5] Ibid., 29.
[6] Ibid., 30.
[7] Ibid., 30.
[8] Ibid., 158.
[9] Ibid., 151.
[10] Ibid., 30.
[11] Ibid., 34.
[12] Ibid., 34.
[13] Ibid., 35.
[14] Ibid., 39.
[15] Martin Buber, *I and Thou*, translated by Ronald Gregor Smith, (Edinburgh: T&T Clark, 1937), 7–8.
[16] *Persons in Relation*, 158.
[17] *The Self as Agent*, 168.
[18] Ibid., 195.

CHAPTER SEVEN

Educating the Emotions

Esther McIntosh

"The heart has its reasons, which reason does not know."[1]
(Blaise Pascal, *Pensées*)

Macmurray's emphasis on the need to integrate reason and emotion is rooted in his concept of agency, which, in turn, stems from his concern with the nature of the person. By replacing Descartes' *cogito ergo sum* with the proposition "I do therefore I am," Macmurray makes action primary, rendering thought secondary and derivative. In so doing, he avoids instituting a reverse dualism, by presenting the logical form of the personal as a positive, which contains, and is constituted by, its negative.[2]

Further, according to Macmurray, it is the emotions that provide the impulse for conduct, since thought is not always prior to action. However, the emotions have traditionally been regarded as confused and irrational. Rejecting this formulation as needlessly divisive, Macmurray claims that the faculty of reason and, therefore, rationality, is the ability to act consciously in terms of the nature of the other. This endowment, then, is the capacity to behave objectively, or with self-transcendence, and it represents the second component of Macmurray's refutation of Cartesian dualism. That is, in conjunction with his axiom of agency, he asserts that the development of the personal is through the interrelation of persons. Consequently, he does not equate reason with the intellect; instead, he alleges that it is possible for both emotions and thoughts to possess rationality, inasmuch as they refer appropriately to actual items in the world. It follows from this, that these distinguishable elements of experience, are not, as Stoicism imagines, radically opposed. In addition, whilst accepting that the emotions are frequently irrational, Macmurray points out that this is also a commonplace for thoughts. Accordingly, in contrast to objective reason, an unreasonable emotion, or thought, is subjective and unreal. In the absence of adequate external grounds, then, irrationality, whether this be rooted in the intellect or the emotions, has an inward rather than an outward focus of reference; thus producing self-centred as opposed to other-centred behaviour.[3]

Although Macmurray began to formulate this thesis in the 1930s, his insistence on the potential rationality of emotion is now shared by other scholars. De Sousa, for example, claims that emotions supply information about the external world in the form of "axiological rationality."[4] From this standpoint it can be assumed that an object is loved because it is loveable, and is not merely regarded as loveable because it is loved.

Despite arguing for the rationality of emotion, Macmurray does not deny that the emotions could be unruly in the manner that tradition has alleged. However, this does not lead him to conclude that the emotions need to be repressed. In fact, he contends that is only primitive and uncultivated emotions that are disorderly. The concerted effort to educate the intellect, he explains, has a long history, but there is an absence of any corresponding exertion to educate the emotions. Consequently, whilst the intellect has had the opportunity to reach a stage of maturity that is compatible with rationality, the same has not been true of the emotions. Yet, if it is possible to teach children to think for themselves in this way, it seems plausible to suggest that they could also be trained to feel for themselves.[5]

An education in the emotions, Macmurray holds, would initially entail advanced training in sensuality. With enhanced sensory experience and awareness, he avers, the object which gives rise to an emotion would be valued for itself. Furthermore, a heightened sensitivity to the world would have inventive practical consequences, especially since the actions induced would involve the whole self, not just the intellect. At the same time, though, this spontaneous action, if rationally grounded, has to be appropriate to the object concerned, regardless of the category of the emotions stirred. The obstacle in refining sensibility, then, is the realisation that as the capacity for bliss is expanded, the capacity for pain is simultaneously enlarged.[6]

On this basis, it seems that inherent in the growth to emotional maturity, is the comparative development of emotional sincerity. In essence, this means that there is expression, rather than suppression of the felt emotions, and no pretence, or exhibition of unfelt emotions. Due to this preference for emotional liberty, together with his accent on the practical implications of any weighty theory, Macmurray finds himself committed to sexual freedom, even in conjugal relations. He qualifies this position by rejecting external controls as the correct criteria of virtuous conduct. Setting aside his Calvinist upbringing, he is certain that institutions, such as marriage, are designed for people, and not the other way around. Hence, whilst marriage itself is not deplored, he maintains that the proper internal control for moral sexual activity is love.[7]

It might seem, therefore, that promiscuity is admissible, and even advisable, if it is guided by emotional honesty, but the practice of emotional education, as we shall see, has more effectively increased fidelity than commands of abstinence, without explicitly pronouncing this as an intention.

The role of the school in the development of emotional rationality and sincerity, though, depends upon a particular understanding of the educational institution. In Macmurray's opinion, the sole justification for sending children to school is that this system equips pupils to live a full life. However, contrary to convention, he contends that the custom of emotionally void preparation is doomed to failure. He bases this allegation on the supposition that a competent intellect provides only the means for practical living, whereas the ends of action are differentiated emotionally. Emotional objectivity is learned, he suggests, through a relationship with an emotionally mature person. It is experiential, and is not governed by rules, nor is it a subject to be taught in the way that science, for example, is taught.

Moreover, whereas science supports intellectual development, it is in art and religion that the emotions are cultivated. Aesthetic attention, for Macmurray, is characterised by its apprehension of the intrinsic, as opposed to the utility value of an object. Artistic activity, therefore, expresses the artist's appreciation and enjoyment of the object, as an end in itself. In a similar manner, the religious attitude discerns the worth of persons, and is especially concerned with the conditions that influence the freedom and equality of persons in relation. On these grounds, according to Macmurray, emotionally immature individuals are overly pragmatic or contemplative in their actions, since they have an underdeveloped personhood, marked by fear. The benefit of an emotionally mature society, then, would primarily be the full realisation of personhood, with the by-product of an overall motivation towards heterocentric, rather than egocentric action.[8]

Although Macmurray does not offer any detailed explication of the methodology employed in teaching emotional appropriateness, the establishment of the Wennington School adds credence to his theory. As a co-founder of this educational institution, Macmurray harmonised the ethos of the school with his philosophical propositions. His elevation of the emotions, and their significance, is reflected in his perception of the working life as a means to the personal life;[9] hence, the school leaned more towards the provision of friendships, than to the improvement of efficiency or intellectual prowess.

Whilst this could appear to be an idealistic and impractical concept in a world revolving around examination grades and structured expression, the school was praised for the quality and standard of the work its pupils produced.[10] What Macmurray envisaged, and perhaps achieved, in terms of emotional rationality and education, is paralleled in Aristotle's analysis of virtue, where he states that: "The man who is angry at the right things and with the right people, and, further, as he ought, when he ought, and as long as he ought, is praised."[11]

There is not a great deal of secondary material available on any theme of Macmurray's writings, but education and emotion seem to be two of the most neglected areas, perhaps due to the fact that Macmurray's book on education remains unpublished.[12] Nonetheless, the claim that emotional responses are learnt in infancy and adolescence is one of the tenets behind the modern practice of psychotherapy, and its success relies on the capacity human beings have for relearning emotional behaviour.[13] Furthermore, the fact that emotions have biochemical determinants, insofar as this does not imply that an individual is merely the subject of his/her uncontrollable emotions, confirms Macmurray's claim that persons are embodied agents.

Likewise, Macmurray's labour can be supplemented by the recent work of Goleman, who examines the neurological and physiological changes that accompany an emotion, and also asserts that the emotional education of children is a feasible, and worthwhile pursuit.[14] His study seeks to ease the increasing instances of violence in schools, and the wider social problems of depression, drug addiction and broken relationships. Statistical data charting the IQ scores of children cannot reveal which of them, as adults, will experience one or more of these problems, so Goleman sets out to discover whether emotional intelligence is guiding their exuberance and social integration. He does not mention Macmurray, but, for the most part, he is describing what Macmurray refers to as emotional rationality. Emotional intelligence, he states, includes: "abilities such as being able to motivate oneself and persist in the face of frustrations; to control impulse and delay gratification; to regulate one's moods and keep distress from swamping the ability to think; to empathize and to hope."[15]

As depicted by Goleman, emotional intelligence is the master aptitude, affecting the employment of the other capacities, including the intellect. Education in the emotions, therefore, encourages the self-management of emotional reactions with the purpose of aiding the individual in retaining a realistic, but optimistic outlook. In addition, it includes training in the supervision of the impetus ensuing from emotion in order to assist the individual in choosing the types of conduct that society deems acceptable. As with Aristotle and Macmurray, then, this portrayal of intelligent emotion, which is intended to promote social adjustment and happiness, functions by balancing the emotions and the intellect, rather than subordinating one to the other.

By way of an example, Goleman cites "The Marshmallow Test."[16] This was an experiment begun in the 1960s with a group of four year olds. They were given a single marshmallow, and told that they could eat it straight away, or, if they waited about ten minutes they would have two marshmallows. Over the next fifteen years the progress of these children was intermittently reassessed. When collated, the data showed that those who had paused, and received the second marshmallow, were consistently more "successful," in terms of social assimilation and personal fulfilment, than those who had eaten the single marshmallow. Perhaps these findings are inconclusive; yet, the possibility remains that a persevering adult is the fruition of a child who can manipulate momentum and defer reward.

Moreover, according to Goleman, it is now considered to be medical fact that the so-called "negative" emotions, such as anxiety, hostility and despair, adversely affect the immune system, whereas the so-called "positive" emotions, such as confidence, enthusiasm and hope, have a beneficial effect on convalescence and general health.[17] Further, since, as we have already seen, the practice of psychotherapy confirms that emotional attitudes are acquired in childhood, the proposition that emotional intelligence is of distinct importance to an individual's well-being holds conviction.

Admittedly, a child's temperament is to some extent genetic, but parental figures and the wider society modify this, through their responses to the child's behaviour. Besides which, intellectual ability is similarly genetic, and it also begins its education in the home. Since a child is comprised of both intellect and emotion, then, it seems peculiar that the growth of both of these aspects is not addressed during a child's formal instruction. Within the school setting, as Goleman explains, children could be taught, by properly trained teachers, the habits that could actually prevent the onset of mental illness in later life.[18]

Some schools have discovered that emotional intelligence is most effective when it does not appear as a new subject on the curriculum, and it is not examined and graded, instead it is integrated into all lessons, addressing issues as and when they arise during the course of the day. In addition, the emotional attitudes cultivated are sustained by imaginative methods of discipline when official school rules are transgressed. To avoid the impression that this type of emotional literacy is a matter for small, private schools alone, Goleman cites its accomplishments in large, inner-city schools. In particular, violent children have been taught to monitor their animosity, reinterpret situations, consider alternative courses of actions and consequences, with the result that discipline problems have decreased. Likewise, melancholy children have been taught to label and re-evaluate their feelings, avoiding pessimism, with the effect that instances of childhood depression have halved. In a comparable way, the rise in numbers of children suffering from eating disorders and drug addictions has not only been halted, the numbers have decreased, whilst training in the empathic activity, of reading and responding to others" feelings, has reduced bullying and stabilised relationships.[19]

Goleman concedes that emotional tutelage is by no means a panacea for the vast range of personal and social factors that affect a child's well-being both in the present and the future. For this reason, even where emotional strategies are adopted, this cannot be used as an excuse to avoid addressing the other crucial issues. Still, if organised emotional direction is one way, however small, to reduce the risk of the problems cited, it is surely worthwhile. The recent efforts to provide children with factual information on drug abuse, suicide and teenage pregnancy are commendable, but their efficacy could be lowered in the case of emotional incompetence.

In the schools where emotional training is incorporated into the day's activities, the overall findings show that the community spirit is improved, since children are more compassionate and democratic, and also, IQ scores have increased, since children are more attentive, relaxed and buoyant. As a long-term anticipation these pupils are expected to grow into contented adults, who thrive on enduring relationships, and are less likely to require psychotherapy, or resort to crime. What is, at times, little more than a concept in Macmurray's writings, therefore, becomes both a scientific theory and an educational practice when defended by Goleman's contemporary study.

In closing, I will anticipate three conceivable objections to educating the emotions, and counter these by demonstrating that they are the outcome of misinterpretation.

First, it would be plausible to reject emotional education if this meant stultifying the emotions, and curtailing their immediacy; however, it is the unsuitable conduct accompanying an emotion that is to be re-directed, not the emotion itself. What constitutes acceptable action is determined initially by an individual's biology, partly by his or her character, and finally by the society of which he or she is a member; consequently, it is relative to one's culture, and any emotional education has to remember this.

Secondly, the reticent persons amongst us might be uneasy with the prospect of being forced to be effusive, but with the provision of emotional sincerity this is an unnecessary concern. Not only is emotional education carried out in a relaxed atmosphere, free from pressure, Goleman further asserts that it places children at a greater risk, in the event of sexual abuse, if they have previously been forced to express, or accept affection with which they are uncomfortable.[20]

Thirdly, it might be objected that the introduction of emotional education into our schools would instigate conformity; yet, an undeniable aspect of emotional competence is the extension of the diversity of feelings, and the encouragement of the rich and creative environment that the subsequent behaviour occasions.

NOTES

[1] "Le coeur a ses raisons, que la raison connait pas."

[2] John Macmurray, *The Self as Agent* (London: Faber, 1995), also known as *The Form of the Personal: Volume 1*, 84 ff.

[3] An irrational thought is a belief which is not true; likewise, Macmurray refers to sentimentality as an example of unreal emotion. Cf. John Macmurray, *Reason and Emotion* (1935), 3 ff.

[4] Ronald de Sousa, *The Rationality of Emotion* (Cambridge, Massachusetts: MIT Press, 1987), 169. Axiological rationality is concerned with value, in contrast to the duty dictated by deontological reason.

[5] John Macmurray, *Freedom in the Modern World* (1932), 141 ff.

[6] Macmurray, *Reason and Emotion*, 16 ff.

[7] Ibid., p. 68 ff.; John Macmurray, 'The Conditions of Marriage To-Day', typescript, (John Macmurray Microfilm, Aberdeen University Queen Mother Library: Items 1.31 and 2.40). This is a longer version of the published article 'Conditions of Marriage Today,' *Marriage Guidance*, 9 (1965), 379–385.

[8] John Macmurray, "Developing Emotions," *Saturday Review*, 41 (1958), 22 & 52; Macmurray, *Reason and Emotion*, 26 ff.

[9] John Macmurray, *Persons in Relation* (1961), 186.

[10] John Macmurray, 'They Made a School,' MS, 1968 (The John Macmurray Special Collection, Regis College Library, Toronto: Item 68.2).

[11] David Ross, tr., *Aristotle—The Nicomachean Ethics* (Oxford: Oxford University Press, 1980), 4.5, 1125b15-35. Although Macmurray does not explicitly state that he is borrowing this idea from Aristotle, he studied Aristotle's ethics extensively. Cf. John Macmurray, 'The Agent,' MS, undated (John Macmurray Microfilm, Aberdeen University Queen Mother Library: Item 3.8).

[12] John Macmurray, 'Lectures and Papers on Education,' typescript, undated (John Macmurray Microfilm, Aberdeen University Queen Mother Library: Item 1.46).

[13] Cf. Magda B. Arnold, ed., *Feeling and Emotions* (London: Academic Press, 1970); Klaus R. Scherer and Paul Ekman, eds., *Approaches to Emotion* (Hillsdale, N. J.: Lawrence Erlbaum Associates, 1984).

[14] Daniel Goleman, *Emotional Intelligence* (London: Bloomsbury, 1996).

[15] Ibid., 34.

[16] Ibid., 80 ff.

[17] Ibid., 164 ff.

[18] Ibid., 187 ff.

[19] Ibid., 229 ff.

[20] Ibid., 256.

CHAPTER EIGHT

The Relevance of Macmurray
for a Feminist Theology of Action

Susan Parsons

It is difficult for a feminist not to be wholly appreciative of the work of
the philosopher John Macmurray. In so many ways, he anticipated and
indeed gave expression to some of the outstanding themes of
contemporary feminism. In general terms, his work developed an
important challenge to the construction of the self in modernism, in its
philosophical, theological and political dimensions, a challenge which he
was not alone in making, but which takes a most sustained and careful
form in his writings, as one gathers it did in his teaching too. His concern
that the self of the modern age not only distorts the lived nature of being
self in the world, but ultimately deprives the fully human self of its most
distinctive possibilities, is a concern which feminists of all kinds and
persuasions have themselves been seeking also to demonstrate. So, for
example, one finds an echo of Macmurray's claim that the crisis of the
personal begins its first phase in modern philosophy with Descartes'
attempt to determine the Self as a thinking substance with mathematical
form,[1] in Genevieve Lloyd's description of Descartes' "most
thoroughgoing and influential version of Reason as methodical thought,"
in which, Lloyd suggests, something was to happen of crucial
significance for the development of stereotypes of maleness and
femaleness, and in particular for the formation of what she is to call the
"Man of Reason."[2] The correlation between Macmurray's primary effort
to reshape the form of the personal from the ground up as it were, and
feminist concerns to wrest the form of the personal from male
normativity is noteworthy, and suggestive I think of closer investigation.

In more specific terms, Macmurray's work also offers
encouragement to the feminist who is seeking to discover the positive

outcomes of this deconstruction of the modern self in particular recommendations for social ordering in the political and in the personal spheres. It will be important in this respect that Macmurray intended to overcome the sharp division of these spheres from one another, a division which in fact masks the dependence of the one upon the other, and this, a dependence which has been particularly troublesome and finally unbearable in the privately-constricted lives of women throughout the development of modern capitalism. Finding a way through this division by means of the common notion of "persons in relation," Macmurray not only preceded the explicit feminist claim that "the personal is the political," but also thereby opened out a shared terrain in which women and men may understand, may question, and may change the ordering of their lives in ways that are finally more fulfilling and whole-some in practice. Thus the general concern to reshape our modern understanding of the self issues in specific considerations of ethics and of politics in Macmurray's thought, considerations which link in so many ways with feminist moral and political agendas.

Our attention to these potentially fruitful connections between Macmurray and feminism has been drawn by Frank Kirkpatrick in his introduction to the new edition of *Persons in Relation* published in 1991. In the subsection entitled "Feminist Thought and Community," Kirkpatrick suggests an overlap between the emphasis on "mutuality and interdependence" in feminist thinking with Macmurray's work in the volume which is to follow.[3] Especially noteworthy for Kirkpatrick is the very suggestive research of Carol Gilligan into gender difference in human moral development, the results of which so significantly reflect some of the kinds of things that Macmurray also was seeking to illuminate. Thus specifically, it is important that Gilligan, like Macmurray before her, draws attention to the early parent-child relationship in which mutuality is born and nourished, and that she then further goes on to develop an ethic of interdependence, in which "the capacity for engagement" becomes more crucial to the emergence of authentic personhood than the detached reasoning of the "rationally autonomous and self-sufficient" ego. It is of course much disputed in the continuing Gilligan debate since the date of this introduction, whether in fact she was seeking to "replace" this concept of the autonomous self with another one altogether, as Kirkpatrick suggests, or whether she was setting two approaches to the self and its morality alongside each other so that they might hear and at least begin to recognize the different voices in which they speak the world.[4] However uncertain is the outcome of that debate, at least Kirkpatrick's point is clear, that he believes Macmurray to offer precisely the kind of philosophical framework which can support and sustain the heterocentric ethics of relationship that Gilligan and other feminists are pressing for.

For my purposes in this essay, it is helpful too that Kirkpatrick goes on to suggest that one finds in Macmurray's work "the metaphysical grounding for a religious view of reality," that while indeed his work "shares a great deal in common with the work of political, moral, feminist, metaphysical, and sociological scholars, at its most profound it is squarely rooted in a religious vision of reality as constituted by a universal community of 'persons in relation'."[5] At this point then, the work of Macmurray connects with that of feminist theologians who have recognized in the task of reshaping a more inclusive form of the personal, something which is of significance for the human understanding of and approach to the divine. Macmurray's commitment to discovering the form of the personal in the midst of human experience, as a way both of challenging the philosophical tradition and of constructing an understanding of God as personal Other, is to be admired for its systematic consistency as well as for its serious intention to address and to improve the conditions and institutions of modern social life. Feminist experiential theologians too have discovered the location of a relational God deeply implicated in the midst of the web of human relationships, as a sustaining presence that supports the forming of right relationship with oneself and others, as well as an atoning presence that brings wholeness out of broken and disabling relationship. In both then is the concern to discover the theological within the anthropological, and their resonance with one another is heard in their shared confidence that to speak of the divine is to speak of the human.

So it is that I too as a Christian feminist find much to recognize in Macmurray and derive encouragement in discovering a kindred spirit, whose line of argument in dismantling the modern self I am positively inclined towards, whose development of a morality and a politics of relationship I warm to, and whose very thoughtful effort at a contemporary humanism I also admire. In this essay, however, I want to examine more closely precisely those claims regarding the helpfulness of the relationship between Macmurray and feminist thinking, and I do this for two reasons. First, I do believe that there is much to be learned from Macmurray's attempt to discover a new starting point for humanism in the twentieth century. Since it is unpopular in some circles to declare oneself humanist, I want to draw as much insight as I can from one who so consistently thought in these terms, and I want to put pressure on his account to discover both its underpinnings and the framework that supports it. These things I believe may be helpful to my own interests, and this is my second reason, for I believe there are new developments needed within feminist theology, as it moves away from domination by the paradigms of the human sciences and the Enlightenment assumptions within which those are established. I understand feminist theology to be uniquely placed to help in this shift towards an appropriate theological humanism, but in order for it to do so, there will need to be a measure of self-criticism at least as deep as that with which I approach the work of Macmurray. I hope this will prove to be evidence of even-handedness in my treatment of him. So I propose to consider the relevance of Macmurray for a feminist theology of action, and to give critical attention to the questions that arise there. To begin this examination, it may be helpful for me to outline the three terms that shape my approach to his work, and thereby to the general contemporary context in which I understand this discussion to be taking place.

And so first to the term "feminist." There are still some of us who call ourselves feminists, but having said that, there is perhaps still more to be explained. Various versions of the end of feminism are around the place, so that some would call themselves post-feminist, giving attention to the kind of post-humanist thinking that one must do in post-modernity, while others would call themselves gender theorists, giving attention to the problematic nature of the category of gender for men as for women, and there is much to be said for these approaches. However, I do not think the critical and constructive work of feminism is by any means accomplished, and this leaves me with a primary question to ask of any work, namely - what is the place of woman within this scheme? The fact that there are still troubled places in which women are represented and unrepresented and misrepresented, and the continued search for the appropriate means of gaining some critical purchase on these places, constitutes for me the unfinished work of feminism, and shapes the project I do. This comes into the foreground in encountering a work like Macmurray's, which surely, one would think, has spoken about persons in a most inclusive way, and in a way which admittedly strikes deep chords within feminism itself. I however am not convinced that we can leave the matter there, and in directing to his work also the question, "what is the place of woman in your scheme?" I hope to bring to light some of his more troubling representations.

Secondly, the term theology. Since Macmurray's Gifford Lectures were themselves, as he says, "to direct attention to that aspect of our common experience from which religion springs," it is not surprising that this will resonate with so much of the theology which feminists have been writing from and to women's experience. The similarities and common interests are striking in that both are doing experiential theology which is to be of political consequence. This means for both an emphasis upon experience as starting-point and end-point of theological reflection. Theology so understood is a method which thinks about God from out of and in the midst of human experience, which shapes belief about God within the frame of that experience, and which uses experience as an evaluative, pragmatic test for those beliefs. Clearly for Macmurray the use of this method was so significant in his own turn from a Calvinist upbringing, so that as Jack Costello says, "Macmurray took God out of the sky and put God into history in a way that bewildered many people raised on dualisms between God and the world."[6] So Macmurray's real dismay at the silence with which his anti-war sermon was received following the First World War, such that from that time he was not a member of any Christian church, until becoming a Quaker upon his retirement.[7] There is a similar kind of defining moment in the collective story of contemporary feminist theology, born out of Mary Daly's dramatic walk-out of chapel of the Harvard Divinity School, in moral protest at the loss of dignity for women within its walls and in theological protest at the Father God whose word and will sustained this order. How much of this story we find also now in the challenging and serious work of Daphne Hampson. As with the word feminist, so too with the word theology, I want to raise a fundamental question, namely "what kind of theology is it that one is doing here?" and I raise this question because I am not wholly at ease either with this way of framing the task of theology, or with the legacy of post-Reformation Enlightenment thinking, that thinking which some call modern, which it bears. In questioning Macmurray on this account, I also therefore recognize the self-criticism of feminist theology which is thereby entailed.

Lastly to the word action. Living within the inheritance of Aristotelian biology, which for all its more recent scientific challenges still lives on in the social imagination, women have struggled within the dualism of action and passion. Identifying women within this dualism as passive sexually, driven by emotions, bound within the realm of the sensible, and defined essentially by their natural functions as wives, mothers, and carers of men, Aristotle was not able to account for the anomaly that women are also users of language, that women can speak, and therefore have at least some bare hold upon the exercise of the work of the soul. We know that Aristotle read this as evidence of woman's deficiency compared to man, a defect that renders her incapable of the use of the deliberative reason that shapes the distinctiveness of human being within the natural order and of human action within the social. Woman is thus an ineffectual human being. Feminists may discover in Macmurray someone who has thought consistently and helpfully about the phenomenon of human agency in a way that may transcend gender differences. For all the many pages of feminist text still being written to get around this dualism, Macmurray's work offers a way of thinking about the unity of action and passion, of reason and emotion, held together in the one human person whose effective agency is a defining feature of women and men, alike and equally. The question to be raised here is that nagging one of Luce Irigaray's "Equal to whom?"[8] and in the asking of it, we pose before Macmurray's work the sense in which his account of action still sits uncomfortably on boundaries that are problematic for an understanding of the action of woman. An investigation of these boundaries will conclude the paper and give us an opportunity for some overall assessment of Macmurray's relevance for a feminist theology of action.

In taking up our first question on the place of woman in Macmurray's scheme, our attention is drawn both to the symbolic function of woman and to the actual role of woman in Macmurray's discussion of growth in human mutuality, particularly in *Persons in Relation*. The title of the first chapter to take up this discussion is 'Mother and Child' and it is obvious to me throughout this chapter that the Mother as woman and the child as boy are the significant figures in the story, and thus that their specific gendered selfhood is essential to the narrative.

Now, it is fair to recognize that Macmurray does say "the term 'mother' in this connection is not a biological term. It means simply the adult who cares for the baby." And further that "She need not even be female. A man can do all the mothering that is necessary."[9] These are surely both bold and outspoken things to be saying in 1953, not so much because they had not been said before but because this was a particularly sensitive time in which to be saying them, and they suggest that Macmurray was ahead of much feminist insight into the nature of mothering as a kind of work involving a particular form of reasoning. Such ideas are later given systematic investigation in a book like Sara Ruddick's *Maternal Thinking*, which precisely suggests that the rational behaviour involved in the activity of mothering is not tied to a specific form of embodiment, and therefore that women like men have learned and are able to learn to do the necessary child-rearing in mutuality of relationship within the broader social context.[10] Despite what he says however, it strikes me that the narrative of growing up human which Macmurray presents is at critical points dependent upon the figure of woman, who both functions as an ideal female figure necessary for the ongoing plot of the story, and also must play a significant real part in what is to happen historically in individual boys' lives. Let me try to demonstrate this.

The symbolic presence of woman-Mother pervades the chapters on mother and child, the discrimination of the other, and the rhythm of withdrawal and return, throughout all of which we are aware of her presence, rather one should say more precisely we are aware of her presence-as-absence, in that she represents the primal unity out of which the young infant boy has been thrust by his birth. Dreams of such primal unity we find repeated of course in many forms throughout the history of western thought, but most recently in the background of Macmurray's work is the prevailing story of human maturity amongst certain developmental psychologists. Such a dream of unity functions in the human drama that Macmurray presents, and it also I suggest is a significant feature of the metaphysical drama that he unfolds. As one would expect, this dream explicitly invades the vocabulary he uses. Thus he says early on in his account, "The most obvious fact about the human infant is his total helplessness."[11] Compared to what, I wonder? And for whom is this the most obvious fact? Compared, I suggest, to the all-sustaining womb in which his life has been nurtured, the life of the boy is an experience of powerlessness, of urgent needs that require the actions of others to address, of loneliness in the moments of realisation of his mother's absence, and of struggle and of work to learn how to do things in a specifically human way. All of these things figure in Macmurray's description. That this is for him the most obvious fact of human infancy suggests to me that what we have here is a configuration of masculinity, a tale told by a man of his experience of human being, a tale in which woman is not herself present as herself, but in which she represents by her absence the limit of the space needed for the stage setting of this play.

But we have also the actual activity of woman in the process of shaping the boy's development in the real circumstances of his life. Here the most poignant chapter is the one on withdrawal and return, a chapter which describes in close detail the moral struggle that ensues between mother and child as she teaches him mutuality. It does not come naturally to him, for it is important to Macmurray to emphasize that uniquely human qualities are not simply given to us nor are they merely in our genes, but rather that they are forged in the give and take of human social and linguistic relationships. This production of the human begins in a critical moment when the boy's fantasies of complete satisfaction are shattered, and thereby "the basis of confidence and security is broken."[12] The role of woman here is precisely to cause, to bring about this disillusionment, for she is to "challenge," to "resist," to "govern," and finally deliberately to "refuse" his demands so that he may grow up to be fully human. These are all active verbs that Macmurray uses to describe the mother's actions. Thus he says that "at all of the crucial points" in the child's growing up, "the decision rests with the mother, and therefore it must take the form of a deliberate refusal on her part to continue to show the child those expressions of her care for him that he expects."[13]

The significance of this refusal grows in importance, as one notices that the word appears repeatedly in this one chapter of the book, and it appears precisely at the moments of the boy seeking a return to the unity which was and is no more. It is the mother's role to stand guard at these moments, so that he may grow in the proper sense of his own limitations in the real world in which he must live. Her refusal is to become balanced as the boy matures with a kind of loving acceptance so that his life may proceed without anxiety. I am wary however of the fact that Macmurray does not give attention to whatever is in the mother's own reasoning as she interacts with her son. The use of the phrase "deliberate refusal" disturbs me. Words have different meanings in Britain and

North America, so that I am conscious of the fact that we are divided by a common language, but when my mother said of me that I was being "deliberate," she did not mean it as a compliment to my rationality. What can Macmurray mean by calling this deliberate? My interpretation is that he understands her only in her role, so that there is nothing else she can have been thinking except about her son's needs and interests, and thus that her deliberation is significant only and in so far as it is shaped by the need for him to be taught mutuality and responsiveness to others. But is there something of an accusatory tone in this phrase as well, an accusation that, were it not for such refusal, how very different, nay better things might have been? The mother's presence in the actual life of her child is a thus a deeply ambiguous one, which again more precisely should be called her absence-as-presence, since she is here in role in the psychic life of man.

Since I believe there is a certain necessity about the symbolic function and the actual role of woman in Macmurray, I want to question the sense in which this early encounter of woman and man can or should be called "mutuality." It is true that the boy is learning to take others into account through and by means of interactions with his mother, and I don't want to diminish the significance of that learning for the general socialization of children. At some points in growing up, there need to be those who give some shape to our powerful desires, as well as guidance and direction to the different choices that we might make. What I think I am trying to get at is that mutuality needs at least two, and I am not convinced that there are two presences in the account that Macmurray gives. In his account there is one presence which is the important focus of attention, and there is another presence-as-absence and absence-as-presence in the form of the mother. Because she is not fully present as herself at all, there is no indication of the mutuality which is learned by or entered into by the mother, or indeed to give Macmurray the benefit of the doubt, by any parent of any child, and this points I suggest to the worrying consequence that because of the demands of the social, parents are forever to repeat their own upbringing, endlessly putting upon their children the same lessons they have themselves learned in their own time. Such repetition within the social sphere of roles and obligations does not give us the needed space to be able to consider the ways in which children teach their parents mutuality, or indeed sons their mothers, and so I doubt whether this order of repetition by itself can grow what I would want to call mutuality. For this we may need something that is altogether more disruptive of social patterns.

For this reason, I have to admit that I am disappointed in Martin Buber's uncritical response to Macmurray's work, for in Buber, there are at least two in the I-Thou relation. Perhaps there is even a note of irony in Buber calling Macmurray the metaphysician. As I think about this further, it so intrigues me that there is not an account of the adult relationship of woman and man, that from the time of establishing the rhythm of withdrawal and return within his discussion of persons in relation, Macmurray moves immediately into the realm of the moral. What the mother has provided by her actions and responses is the framework within which life in society can be accomplished and interactions between persons negotiated. She has played an essential part therefore in the establishment of law, and places new human beings very firmly within its constraints and expectations. Listen then to this from Macmurray:

> For since it was by his mother's action that the child's confidence was broken, it is only by her action that this confidence can be restored. If we may use the language of mature human reflection which, though its content is much richer, has an identical form, the child can only be rescued from his despair by the grace of the mother; by a revelation of her continued love and care which convinces him that his fears are groundless.[14]

Here the mother's actual role in teaching her son a proper mutuality merges with her symbolic role, for she is constructed within this text as an oppositional figure to man, a constant reminder of his finitude, a challenge to his efforts to escape being human, and a giver of momentary rewards of love so that his life within this space can be bearable. It is a finite end for which she is preparing him, and for which he must learn his lessons.

There are so many layers of meaning here that one might discuss. I am struck by comparisons with Augustine, and by the ways in which much of the psychology presupposed by and implicit within Macmurray's account is a secular version of Augustine's description of the growth of the human person in society and in language. There is too the sense in which Macmurray's is also a confession, like Augustine's, which is at least partly constituted as a confession of the situation of the human. For both, the danger of egocentrism looms large throughout, and indeed, and perhaps as a result of this, one also hears in both those significant and even ambivalent references to Mother. However, while there is a real sense of friendship as Augustine and Monica share the vision at the window in Ostia, Macmurray's confession, in a way that is not true of Augustine's, remains within this finite temporal world of the real, and it is woman's symbolic function and actual role to ensure this.[15]

To take the comparison one step further, both confessions are also and importantly constituted as confessions of the greatness of God. Here however, while Augustine turns to the trinitarian life of God as the context for the living of mutuality in relationship, Macmurray's moves in an altogether more Platonic milieu as a metaphysical story of separation and return. For in the finite life of man thrust out of primal unity, there is a remainder, a left-over of desire unsatisfied, and here again woman appears, this time as the mirror in which he sees reflected his own desire for immortality, his longing to escape the parameters of the real that the burden of being fully human has placed upon him. As he matures he will learn to abandon these impossible childish dreams, for they hold no relevance in the world as it is, and he will spend his time in the political sphere struggling to compensate for and make the best of the circumstances. Such a vision of life relies upon a metaphysical figuring of woman. How interesting it is to me therefore that we have in Macmurray a sense of the divine as woman, the woman as source in whom all life is originally conceived and sustained, the one whose refusal to give in to man's selfishness now stands guard barring the gates to paradise, forbidding thereby any complete return to full mutuality within the life of this world, nevertheless in spite of sin, the one whose continued gracious presence supports the fleeting and imperfect possibilities for love that characterise our life in this world, and finally the one who stands at the end waiting to receive in unity again all that has become separated from her.

We are already deeply into theological territory, and so I want to comment upon what kind of theology it is that is being done here. Macmurray's way of framing the task of theology sets the boundaries of theological discourse as well as the final end of its reflection very firmly within the realm of the human. Because the starting point of human agency is so compelling in his philosophical thinking, he moves out as far as his reasoning can legitimately take him to discover the matrix within which a community of personal agents in relation can flourish, and this he names the personal Other. The theological question that will not go away however is whether in fact he has missed altogether the divine, by positing the existence of a god made to serve the image of the human, a god essential for the sustaining of human living in its best finite expression. Already in response to the Gifford Lectures, Dom Illtyd Trethowan raised the suspicion that Macmurray's God "is, after all, only a function of the world, that he has no meaning in himself over and above the meaning which he gives to the world. He is not, that is, genuinely transcendent. He belongs, so to say, essentially to the world."[16] Whilst recognizing that attempts to speak of transcendence give rise to some of the most acrimonious debates amongst and invidious comparisons between theologians, nevertheless I too believe that the functional dimension of Macmurray's theology gives us reason to question in whose interests the scheme has been devised, and whether those of the human are rightly to take priority in the work of theology.

This is the point also in Lesslie Newbigin's very sharp attack on Macmurray's early work, *Freedom in the Modern World*. Recognizing the value of freedom in clearing away forms of mere mechanical conformity and blind obedience to authority, which Macmurray rightly challenges on behalf of an authentic rooting of morality in the development of persons, Newbigin questions whether the sustenance of persons in relation does not require precisely the kind of transcendent dimension Macmurray seeks so thoroughly to eliminate from his account. Newbigin calls this dimension the "element of unconditionality in our moral experience" which Macmurray misses by his refusal to acknowledge those moments in our experience when we confront an other who displaces us from the centre of the decision.[17] Without such an encounter with an "ultimate resistance" to our human will, without hearing some personal summons from God, the notion of God in Macmurray remains a purely formal one, a category which "stands in the same relation to particular personal relationships as "matter" does to particular lumps of matter."[18] What this criticism points to is the sense in which a theology which builds up from the human as presently configured does not in the end turn back in upon itself, having missed its object and thus having returned us to the order of the same. Theological models are thereby invoked as functional supports for practices that seem reasonable to us now within our present understanding of things. They may not serve to reconfigure that practice altogether.[19]

This brings into focus my concern regarding the signs of Enlightenment inheritance which Macmurray's account still bears. In seeking to overcome a range of dualisms that have appeared throughout the modern period, he contributed to the removal of the Cartesian man of reason and the Kantian man of duty as the central figures in the modern understanding of the self, replacing them with an acting social being whose nature is expressed in the quality of its relationships and whose purpose is to contribute to their most complete flourishing in the social and political order. The question which arises is whether this reshaped human self is not now the victim of its own success, and that this is so precisely because it reconfigures the self out of the framework of oppositions it has inherited. This limitation has very real and tangible results in the lives of women who are increasingly required in our present society to care for others, and who are worried now about the abuse of this human capacity. Because it can always be argued that more care is needed since its possible expressions are unlimited, it can always be the case that women's lives are stretched to meet these needs, and that they become used as providers of care within a regime that orders this activity from a distant place. There is a danger here that the loss of critical distance which such a reconfiguration of their moral lives as relational beings might entail becomes a new form of women's oppression, justified as more natural to them and more useful to the social whole.[20]

From this consideration of the legacy of dualism, I am drawn to those disturbing questions that emerge from Gillian Rose who asks in her critical re-reading of Hegel and Kierkegaard, whether we have not moved too hurriedly into the breach, seeking to heal the diremptions presented to us in the philosophical discourses of the past, out of the resources available to us in an equally ambiguous and difficult present. Philosophical attempts to describe higher forms of unity in which dualisms are believed to be successfully overcome place themselves in a position of new authority and delimit our questions and our challenges accordingly in the name of a so-persuasive pragmatic purposiveness. The logic of overcoming dualisms is powerful and seems to be such common good sense that it sounds a bit sour to refuse the kind offers of higher unity made by thinkers of all persuasions and political loyalties. Nevertheless, I pause in the project of a feminist theology of action to enquire what is at stake in these offers, to ask whether difference is affirmed therein or merely subsumed, to wonder in whose name these higher unities appear, and whether finally the search for unities in the human realm is really what the task of theology is about. I have deep reservations about a theology which believes that it can itself reconcile the divine with the human, and would abrogate to itself the work of mediation in the broken middle of modernism.

These doubts can be examined more closely in Macmurray's account of agency as the central feature of his humanism. There is much to be admired in this emphasis upon agency as a fundamental truth of the human person and as the site of inter-action between persons. That agency already requires the reality of the social and already therefore places us in a personal and relational context seems to me to be the right way to think about the human person and about the interaction of divine and human persons. What proves more problematic is that Macmurray's work, being dedicated to the construction of a new common platform on which humanity may meet within the terms provided by his account of agency, is required to draw the boundaries rather carefully around what it is that constitutes the human as such, in order both to affirm and to protect its distinctiveness. It is precisely in the drawing of these lines however that his account nonetheless reveals the influence of the normative man in ways that prove difficult for the fullest appreciation of the action of women. Thus, I am left with Irigaray's question regarding sexual difference, a difference which she emphasises by asking to whom woman is to be deemed equal. A brief demonstration of two of these difficult points at which his description of agency is less than fully inclusive of women will bring us to a final assessment and appreciation of the relevance of Macmurray for a feminist theology of action.

The first point of difficulty is in Macmurray's quite sharp division between the organic natural realm on the one hand and the personal human realm on the other, a division which leaves the figure of woman in a most awkward position. Like many developmental thinkers of his day, Macmurray's account of human personal development begins not with giving birth nor with conception, but rather with infancy, with the already-born child. He says, "We start then where all human life starts, with infancy."[21] Now, while it is true that his attention to the mother-child relationship is certainly an improvement upon Hobbes' request that we "consider men as if but even now sprung out of the earth, and suddenly, like mushrooms, come to full maturity, without all kind of engagement to each other," I wonder what kind of advance has really been made.[22] Beginning with infancy has importantly left out of account that unity of action and passion in conceiving, in child-bearing and in giving birth, precisely those experiences of human agency in which women uniquely act. So I am struck by Macmurray's statement that it is the impulse to communication by the infant that "is sufficient to constitute the mother-child relation as the basic form of human existence, as a personal mutuality, as a 'You and I' with a common life."[23] By leaving out yet again the woman's active role in shaping or constituting the personal, Macmurray has also found it impossible to move, or as he says, "to ascend from the organic to the personal," since for him the beginning of the personal is already after the birth has happened.[24] How interesting then that he says an infant "is born into a love-relationship," rather than saying he is born out of one.[25]

This further means that Macmurray cannot accept the analogous way in which Aristotle speaks of embodiment, finding the belief that "the human infant is an animal organism which becomes rational" to be "radically false." "The root of the error," he says, "is the attempt to understand the field of the personal on a biological analogy," and it is in order to break this continuum that he begins the form of the personal in a place and at the moment of separation from nature, where there can be no cause for confusion between the animal and the human, between instinctual behaviour and intentional action.[26] He says "To affirm the organic conception in the personal field is implicitly to deny the possibility of action."[27] The line which is drawn precisely here however traces its way on across the distinctive nature of woman and results in her being torn apart by the division Macmurray seeks to impose. This leads me to believe that the border here between the natural organic and the personal human is a troubled one for Macmurray. He opts to emphasise the distinctiveness of the latter, but he does so at the expense of some of the embodied wisdom of women for whom this border is less troubling, and at some cost to the inclusiveness of the account of action that he is hoping to give. His thoughts at this point highlight what I have called elsewhere the dilemma of difference for feminist thinking, since women are to be understood as fully and equally personal here, provided they put away the things of the flesh.

The second boundary which is problematic in Macmurray is that between persons. It is important to acknowledge that Macmurray sought to shift the emphasis within philosophical arguments regarding other selves from attention to the sense of sight, by which we see other persons who are distant from ourselves in space, to the sense of touch in which we encounter persons in greater physical and bodily immediacy. Once again, his account assumes however that the first experience of such immediacy is as an independent self inhabiting a space in which one is already a separated being. He thus presumes the boundary that his account now seeks to cross. His vocabulary is therefore interesting. He claims that our perception of another person begins in an experience of resistance. This resistance is both because the sense of touch as a tactual sense is comprised of pressure that one can feel on one's nerve endings, and because we have practical experiences in which our will is resisted by the presence of another agent who at that moment is an obstacle to our acting. This is not the language in which a woman speaks of her perception of an other, either when growing and coming to life within her womb, or later in her fundamental assumption of the connectedness of persons one with another. It is to Macmurray's credit that he opened up this field of enquiry which so many empirical studies have now explored, but in the process we may find that we need to challenge his vocabulary as normative.[28]

Macmurray's rendering of our awareness of the other may be the result of his description of agency as causal efficacy in an external objective world of things. As a feminist, I would need to say that this seems inappropriately to emphasise a technical or manipulative view of agency, that reintroduces the dualism it has sought to avoid in a new guise. The man who makes tools for the reshaping of the natural world and whose reason is directed to the accomplishment of purposes in this external sphere is no more inclusive a figure than those Enlightenment selves that Macmurray has already summarily dispatched from the scene. Once again, I do recognise that Macmurray's is an attempt most seriously to engage with some of the worst errors both of individualism and intellectualism which he inherited in the modern philosophical tradition. That one still however finds the traces of what Grace Jantzen has termed "the adversarial model of human relationships" suggests that the pervasive legacy of remoteness, of isolation and of disconnectedness may require more than the efforts of one man's philosophical endeavours to overcome.[29] The urgency of this difficulty is to be felt very keenly I think in the debate about abortion in which women are claiming both their right to decisions about their own bodies, thus affirming that they are more than a mere organic function, and at the same time their significant agency in bearing and birthing children. Macmurray's vocabulary, and indeed the more widespread use of this model of agency, may not be helpful to us in the resolution of this debate.

This investigation of Macmurray has led me more fully to appreciate the precarious and creative place in which a feminist theology of action is poised in our contemporary context. Challenges to the problematic inclusiveness of the philosophical tradition, such as I have tried to demonstrate in Macmurray's account of the development of the personal and of the nature of agency, have resulted in the search for a greater inclusiveness in our understanding of the human, so that women's embodied experiences are brought more completely into the account. To take this path is to require of a humanism that it rise to a higher unity of understanding in which all the diverse possibilities of experience can be gathered up and valued. It is in this context that the proposals for a more Aristotelian reading of humanism offered by Martha Nussbaum are so richly suggestive.

At the same time, these challenges have opened up a deep seam of suspicion regarding this kind of philosophical task, accompanied by a troubled and troubling awareness that within this approach, it becomes less clear to whom is to be entrusted the task of sketching out this inclusive account, and who will be there to appreciate all of it when it is complete. To question the presumption that it is possible to present the unity of the human in thought is to sound a Heideggerian note regarding the Western obsession with being—it may sound anti-humanist, even atheist, but it may also point to the newly relevant place of theology in our present context. It may open up a place in which to consider an account of divine action more directly encountered and expressed than in Macmurray. That a feminist theology of action finds itself drawn increasingly towards an account of divine action incarnated in the normative humanity of Christ, suggests that the renewal of a theological anthropology, which has learned from but also outgrown its forebears, may be a most significant and timely task.

NOTES

[1]   John Macmurray, *The Self as Agent* (1959), 33.

[2] Genevieve Lloyd, *The Man of Reason: Male and Female in Western Philosophy* (London: Methuen, 1984), 39.

[3] Frank Kirkpatrick, Introduction to *John Macmurray, Persons in Relation* (London: Faber & Faber, 1991), xix-xx.

[4] Seyla Benhabib, *Situating the Self: Gender, Community and Postmodernism in Contemporary Ethics* (Cambridge: Polity Press, 1992), Chapters 5 & 6.

[5] Kirkpatrick, op. cit, xxiii.

[6] John E. Costello, S.J., Introduction to John Macmurray, *Reason and Emotion* (London: Faber & Faber, 1995), viii.

[7] See the discussion of this incident in Jeanne Warren, *Becoming Real: An Introduction to the Thought of John Macmurray* (York: Ebor Press, 1989).

[8] Luce Irigaray, 'Equal to Whom?', *Differences*, 1.2 (1988), 59–76.

[9] *Persons in Relation*, 50.

[10] Sara Ruddick, *Maternal Thinking: Towards a Politics of Peace* (London: The Women's Press, 1990), 40–45.

[11] *Persons in Relation*, 47.

[12] Ibid., 88.

[13] Ibid., 89.

[14] Ibid., 90.

[15] Augustine, *The Confessions*, Book IX.

[16] Dom Illtyd Trethowan, *Absolute Value: A Study in Christian Theism* (London: Allen & Unwin, 1970), 236.

[17] L. Newbigin, *Christian Freedom in the Modern World* (London: SCM, 1937), 40.

[18] Ibid., 69.

[19] Cf. The very critical piece on Sallie McFague in John Milbank, *The Word Made Strange: Theology, Language, Culture* (Oxford: Blackwell, 1997), 263–267.

[20] This issue has been addressed by a number of contemporary feminists. See Jean Grimshaw, *Feminist Philosophers: Women's Perspectives on Philosophical Traditions* (Brighton: Harvester Press, 1986) chapter 7; and Joan Tronto, *Moral Boundaries: A Political Argument for an Ethic of Care* (London: Routledge, 1993).

[21] *Persons in Relation*, 47.

[22] *Thomas Hobbes, Man and Citizen*, ed. B. Gert (Gloucester, Massachusetts: Peter Smith, 1978) 205. See Christine DiStefano, *Configurations of Masculinity: A Feminist Perspective on Modern Political Theory* (Ithaca: Cornell University Press, 1991) Chapter 2.

[23] *Persons in Relation*, 60–61.

[24] Ibid., 47.

[25] Ibid., 48.

[26] Ibid., 44–45.

[27] Ibid., 46.

[28] Cf. David Fergusson, *John Macmurray* (Edinburgh: Handsel Press, 1992), 18.

[29] Grace Jantzen, 'Connection or Competition: Identity and Personhood in Christian Ethics', *Studies in Christian Ethics*, 5 (1992), 1–20.

CHAPTER NINE

Macmurray and the Role of Ethics in Political Life

Brenda Almond

Although rightly claimed as a Scottish philosopher, Macmurray was more familiar to the present writer as A.J. Ayer's predecessor as Grote Professor of Mind and Logic in the Philosophy Department at University College, London. In style and philosophy, however, there could hardly have been a greater contrast between the two. As far as his personal life was concerned, a teenage enthusiasm for evangelism, open-air testimony and tent crusades could be set against Ayer's life-long religious scepticism. And although Macmurray later came to an honest though reluctant recognition of the impossibility, notwithstanding that early religious commitment, of accepting the literal truth of the doctrines of the Christian Church, this was not a sceptic's rejection, and he later found an acceptable home in the Quakers, the Society of Friends, with their lack of formal preoccupation with doctrine.

In his professional life, too, Macmurray trod a distinctive path, which has only recently been seen as a legitimate path for philosophers to follow. For Macmurray was as a philosopher distinguished by his commitment to popular philosophy, to philosophy with practical relevance, and especially to recognition of the need for ethics to link directly with politics and social policy. As he himself put it in introducing the second volume of his Gifford lectures, these lectures were "concerned to exhibit the primacy of the practical in human experience, and the need to transfer the centre of gravity in philosophy from thought to action."[1]

Macmurray was, then, what is today called an "applied philosopher." He was not, however, a resident of today's world. The world he confronted posed different challenges and no doubt suggested different solutions. The nineteen-thirties, when he was at his prime philosophically, was a period of stark contrasts, and it is hardly surprising that, faced with the contrast between fascism and communism, his political sympathies should have led him in the direction of socialism rather than fascism. It is understandable, too, that he was a sympathetic reader and exponent of the early Marx, although a critic of Marxism as it was taking shape in the Soviet Union.

Macmurray, however, could not accept the secular, indeed atheistic, basis of Marxism and remained a *Christian* socialist. By no means, though, could he be called a doctrinaire Christian, as his perceptive remarks about faith in *Freedom in the Modern World* make clear. Pointing out that references to faith in the Gospels cannot be interpreted as referring to "belief" in the sense of holding *that* some proposition or set of propositions is true, he describes faith as a quality of personality, a person's "supreme principle of valuation."[2] Believing that "Christianity had to be rediscovered and reinvented,"[3] he wrote: "Instead of believing in the idea of God, we should seek and find God in this world."[4]

As this implies, he was not in any sense a social determinist. On the contrary, for him, the political was firmly embedded in the personal, and the fact that he saw persons, not as abstract entities—units out of context—but as located in a network of relationships with other people, gives his philosophy a surprisingly contemporary flavour. There are several important respects in which this is so. First, it is easy to see it as articulating themes developed very recently in feminist ethics for, as Kirkpatrick notes in his introduction to the 1991 edition of *Persons in Relation*, there is indeed some similarity between Macmurray's notion of "mutuality" and the conception of caring and being cared for that is regarded as central by writers such as Nell Noddings and Carole Gilligan.[5] Indeed, for many contemporary feminist writers, it is this notion of personal responsibility for close "others" that marks out a distinctively female moral perspective, that can be contrasted with traditional abstract notions of justice, moral distance, and impartiality.

Secondly, in rejecting the traditional dualism of body and mind, the material and the immaterial, Macmurray could be said to have anticipated in a low-key but nevertheless recognisable way the new environmentalism: explicitly, he reminds us that "Man is... part of

Nature; and we individual men and women are not merely members of the human community but elements of the natural world."[6]

Thirdly, there is a resonance with some versions of virtue ethics in Macmurray's emphases on context and particularity, for virtue theory, too, attaches importance to the notion of what is appropriate to a particular role in a specific situation. And finally, it is possible to see Macmurray's philosophy as developing, as far as political philosophy is concerned, an emphasis on community as opposed to what is sometimes described as "radically unencumbered" liberal individualism.

This point, however, needs qualification. Liberal individualism is much misunderstood and indeed vilified today, because people forget—except when it suits them to attack patriarchy—that liberal individualism was in fact conceived of within the assumed context of the institution of the family. It was never the idea of *unencumbered* men, but of men whose own identity encompassed also wife, children, and no doubt other household members, whether related by blood or by service. Its point was to claim a right to live that family-life unimpeded by excessive external interference whether by hereditary ruler or by government. So liberalism should not be understood as self-centred in an egotistical sense but as already focussed on the small but biologically natural community of the household.

If one accepts this understanding of liberalism, one might even go on to position within it an alternative version of Adam Smith's "hidden hand" thesis: applied to family relations rather than economics, it would amount to the claim "Leave families free to pursue their own good and the 'community' will take care of itself."

This may be, of course, to move too far from Macmurray. Undeniably, however, close relationships and the emotions they engender are very much a part of his agenda. In *Persons in Relation*, he presents love and fear as polar motives, love representing the positive, fear the negative, and says that in both domestic and international politics, negative motivation is destructive of the possibility of community. He sees communication—and this is not simply "speech"—as a primary feature of human beings, and says that it is in relation to others in their family that children gain their sense of personal identity and come to recognise their own individuality. Children are not, however, mere passive receivers of experience, and Macmurray says that to be a person is to be someone who is *active* in the world. "Persons are agents; and the relation of persons is a relation of agents."[7] It is this relationship that provides the ground of morality or, as he puts it, "The moral rightness of an action... has its ground in the relation of persons."[8]

Macmurray's Notion of Community

Persons in relation may be described as a community, and this term can be given a specifically moral interpretation. So while Macmurray is prepared to recognise the practical possibility of moral pluralism—of different subcultures within a society—and also the conflict this may produce, he insists that: "The interrelation of agents, which makes the freedom of all members of a society depend upon the intentions of each, is the ground of morality... *My* freedom depends upon how *you* behave."[9] It is this harmonious interrelation of agents that he calls their "community" and he asserts unambiguously that "a morally right action is an action which intends community."[10]

Macmurray distinguishes this notion of "communal" morality from two other modes of morality: the contemplative and the pragmatic. The contemplative mode is exemplified by Rousseau. In this mode, individuals identify with the state and its edicts through the "general will." Macmurray describes this as the idealist view in which individuality is absorbed in a "mystical identification" with the state.

The pragmatic mode, in contrast, is illustrated by Hobbes' "aggressively egocentric individuals" and it yields a mechanical view of a society composed of "atomic units inherently isolated or unrelated, and ideally equal."[11] Dismissing as "emotional prejudice" the usual liberal democratic approach to Hobbes which finds it "a revolting theory, immoral and cynical,"[12] Macmurray says that, according to Hobbes, the function and effect of state power is to make society possible by bringing together self-interest and rational obligation.

He holds, nevertheless, that neither of these accounts of political society gives adequate recognition to the idea of individuals as *persons*, a term which Macmurray interprets in a rich and full-blooded way, saying that, while morality is indeed a matter of relationships, this, "misses an essential element in the truth if it considers the agents as isolated individuals."[13] But both the contemplative (idealist) and the pragmatic (empiricist) types of society depend on negative motivation and provide essentially impersonal bonds between individuals. While the organic view leads ultimately to totalitarianism, he says, the pragmatic view is mechanistic and ultimately anarchic in its consequences. So neither of these types of society can generate "communities." This term must be reserved, according to Macmurray, for "such personal unities of persons as are based on a positive personal motivation. The members of a community are in communion with one another, and their association is a fellowship. ...Every community is then a society; but not every society is a community."[14]

Both the two rejected modes of morality centre on the self—the contemplative seeing the self as seeking spirituality and harmony, the pragmatic seeing it as set in pursuit of purely material goals. The "communal" mode, in contrast, is expressed by the Golden Rule "Love your neighbour as yourself." Community in this sense, Macmurray says, is comparable to Kant's "kingdom of ends," and can be supplemented, too, by the Christian admonition, "Love your enemies." In this way, Macmurray's philosophy goes beyond a standard secular conception of both community obligations and socialist fraternity.

It is worth noticing, however, that while Macmurray does indeed emphasise the social nature of morality, he also wants to retain the idea that society is made up of individual persons. This, after all, is his reason for rejecting the idealist view of society as an organic unity. It was this point, no doubt, that Margaret Thatcher intended to convey when she— famously or infamously—said "There is no such thing as society," and Macmurray, too, rejects the idea of society as an entity over and above the individual persons it contains, and with it the idea of social teleology or evolutionary goals. Such a view appears to make any theory of society (any social science) impossible, and Macmurray, far from backing away from this conclusion, argues that since anyone who tries to frame a theory of society is necessarily also a participant in it, they are, as participants, in a position to act to falsify the theory they have already propounded.

But if Macmurray is concerned to preserve, within his social community, the notion of irreducible individuals, he does at the same time insist that these individuals – these *persons* – are not amoral and not separate: they are already deeply social and caught in the "seamless web" of moral relationships. So in reply to the Sophists' question "Should man live by nature or by custom?" Macmurray echoes Plato's response: "For men, to live by nature *is* to live by custom. Human nature is social and custom is the bond of society."[15]

Politics Today

Contemporary politics and contemporary political philosophy have recently become much more sympathetic to such views. It is possible to see them as reflected in British New Labour and American Democratic talk of a "third way" between capitalism and communism—and there are those who would describe this as a communitarian alternative. This is, however, a term to be applied with some caution. Nor is it particularly welcome to politicians in the mainstream political parties, who already have an independently-defined agenda. But I do not, in any case, propose to say very much about this aspect of Macmurray's influence, interesting though it is. Instead, I want to focus on what Macmurray's philosophy might imply about the relation between the political and the ethical—and to develop the thought that part at least of its "message" is the desirability of bringing together the world of practical politics and the world of ethics or serious moral concern. As Macmurray puts it:

> We cannot just distinguish morals and politics, and leave it at that; we must know their relation to one another, if only to enable us to devise laws which will not come into conflict with the requirements of morality... political obligation is a derivative and indirect moral obligation.[16]

It is something of this sort that I take to be implied by Prime Minister Tony Blair's endorsement of Macmurray's philosophy and one reason at least for his willingness to provide an Introduction to the selection of Macmurray's writings collected in *The Personal World.*[17] But this is not, of course, to suggest that adopting an ethical approach to public policy is a matter of *party* politics. For there are a number of areas today in which many people who are neither doctrinaire nor partisan are concerned to emphasise the ethical dimension of public policy issues. This desire often finds its expression through single issue groups or campaigns, from feminism and animal rights to Friends of the Earth. It is also implicit in the setting up of expert committees on a number of controversial issues which raise genuine ethical dilemmas for policy-makers, especially in the areas of science and technology.

The desire to set moral and legal bounds in public policy is not, however, a new aspiration. In particular, it has long been recognised as a reasonable and desirable goal in relation to war and armed conflict, from the sixteenth and seventeenth centuries when the early 'just war' theorists—Grotius, Suarez, Pufendorf—sought to apply notions of justice or morality to the waging of war, both in its initiation and in its conduct, to the present century, when similar goals led to the Geneva Convention which provided, amongst other things, for the humane treatment of prisoners of war, and to the Nuremberg trials, which confirmed the principle that even within the context of all-out war, there are moral boundaries which individual soldiers are expected to recognise.

But while international conflict continues to be the subject of ethical debate, from Vietnam, Suez and the Falklands to the recent confrontation with Saddam Hussein in Iraq, war is no longer the only, or even the most important, subject of ethical and political controversy. Other issues in public life are increasingly being shifted from the amoral vacuum in which they germinated to increasing recognition as moral as well as practical problems. These more recent issues include environmental concerns, principles involved in the conduct of business, not only at the micro-level, but also in the international dealings of multinational companies, and a host of developments in science, technology and biomedicine.

Any of these would repay detailed discussion, but here I want simply to raise some very general questions about the place of ethics in public affairs. First, what is it to have an ethical *foreign* policy? And second, what does it mean to be guided in *domestic* policy by ethical considerations? In particular, what, if anything, does *ethics* dictate in areas such as welfare and taxation?

If one is concerned to seek an answer to these questions that owes something to the inspiration and influence of Macmurray, it is, of course, important to remember that, as far as the first is concerned, Macmurray was writing, at least until the later stages of his career, when Britain was a world power—and one which took empire for granted—while as far as the second was concerned, his reflections *preceded* the creation of the welfare state.

The International Context

The desire to moderate the unfettered pursuit of national self-interest with a more ethical approach is most often articulated in the international context when political support is made conditional on reform in key humanitarian areas. The kind of reform the advocates of ethical policies look for has most typically been a matter of upholding human rights, and condemning their violation. Increasingly, however, wider issues are being brought into the picture. There is, for example, a new emphasis on seeking to encourage policies to safeguard the environment, reduce pollution and avoid the careless depletion of resources, whether forests, oil reserves, or species. While these, too, are in the end, also issues that involve human rights, they do so in a much broader and more indirect way.

None of these goals is unproblematic, however, and difficulties tend to arise when richer or more developed nations seek to influence the traditions and cultural practices of other countries, particularly if change is made a condition of aid and trade. An interest in population control, for example, may be seen, not as a helpful intervention, but as a form of neo-imperialism or worse still, genocidal racism. The population issue carries with it, too, views about the position of women which may violate the religious beliefs of some countries, thus coming into conflict with another ethical "human rights" objective: freedom of religion. Nor is it difficult to see that people regarded as brave campaigners or activists from outside may seem like ill-motivated and pernicious influences from within—a destabilising threat to the body politic.

Even if pressure is confined to the more modest objective of correcting explicit human rights violations—the detention or execution of political prisoners, and other abuses of power such as torture and summary punishment—the foreign statesman's ethical agenda may well be viewed with suspicion, generating impatience and resentment rather than gratitude.

As far as environmental issues are concerned, this suspicion is deepened by the fact that developing countries often aspire to a chance to catch up with the envied standard of living of the wealthier nations: to buy fridges, drive cars, receive advanced medical treatment or higher education. Again the charge of neo-imperialism may surface when these aspirations are criticised, this time accompanied by the claim that the rich countries have a vested interest in keeping others poor—that it is only natural that they should want to continue with policies of economic exploitation that allow each individual inhabitant of a city like New York to consume a disproportionate share of the world's limited resources. It may be hard to persuade them of what is undoubtedly true: that the threat to future generations posed by uncontrolled pollution, significant climate change and the loss of important species of animals, should matter equally to all, and that there is a case for a reasonable consensus on sustainable development at least in the sense of not doing irreversible damage to the earth's capacities or causing irreplaceable loss of its resources.

These problems point to a much more general difficulty, and one familiar within liberal theory: this is the way in which liberalism's commitment to toleration impales it on its own liberal hook. Cultural tolerance, particularly when differences of colour, race and religion are involved, can conflict with other principles which are equally important to liberal theory, not least respect for individual human life. Two questions seem to be involved here. First, a factual question: if no attempt is made to conduct a foreign policy with ethical objectives in mind, is this neutral strategy neutral in its practical consequences? And second, a moral question: do the leaders of liberal democracies have a moral obligation to adopt/observe such a policy? As far as the first of these questions is concerned, liberal politicians—and also individuals doing business, travelling, or offering other services—are likely to find that the mere fact of *not* speaking out in criticism, and carrying on doing business regardless, may well be interpreted as endorsement of any rights violations that are current. Speaking out, then, may be morally incumbent. But this conclusion can easily be confused in practice with an attitude capable of bringing the notion of an ethical foreign policy into disrepute, i.e., the sort of arrogant interference in the affairs of another sovereign nation in which insensitive pronouncements are made about matters which are genuinely the concern of other countries and perhaps vital to their survival. This applies particularly to boundary disputes and deep-rooted internal schisms. In certain important respects, then, moral and practical judgement have still to be kept apart. But in maintaining this distance, it is important to recognise the difference between practical toleration of a practice and moral endorsement, and to recognise, too, that while the first is sometimes unavoidable, at least in the short term, there is never any reason to regard the second as an option.

The Domestic Forum

But the problem of combining moral condemnation with practical toleration is a well-known dilemma for liberals, and one which is encountered, too, in the narrower arena of domestic politics. In this area, the issues raised may be different—they may be issues of distributive rather than formal justice—but the problem is not dissimilar. Macmurray says the question one must always ask is: "How far does the State succeed in achieving and maintaining justice in the indirect or economic relations of men?"[18] The tests he offers are the "absence of complaint," that "the peace is kept" and that there is "cooperation without compulsion." Macmurray, no doubt, shared the general feeling which came to a head at the end of the Second World War that cradle-to-grave security was a good thing. But before enrolling him in "old Labour" rather than "new Labour," we should review some of the considerations that led very recently to the renaissance of the free-market ideal, not only in business, but also in welfare policy.

Domestically, it is easy to see "being ethical" as helping the poor by bolstering benefits and by governments enhancing the security of individuals through the tax system. The Robin Hood principle of equalisation, taking from the rich and giving to the poor, has immediate ethical appeal, and the provision of health-care and education, old-age support and disability cover, has evolved as a minimal ethical requirement in developed societies today. But half a century of research and argument has forced the questioning, not only of the practical value and affordability of such strategies when over-zealously or carelessly applied, but also of their ethical basis.

Macmurray, in particular, could hardly have anticipated the disenchantment half a century on with abuse of the welfare state ideal: the funding of broken promises between couples that has cast a generation of children into the strained family life of step-relations, or, worse, onto the streets where they become exploited objects of either pity or fear; the housing estates of single parent "families"; the breakdown of community; and the evolution of lawless groups of young males dispossessed of either work or family responsibilities. The ethical point may well need to be reiterated: that some things are, after all, better done by individuals than by the state. Small committees, for example, administering personal donations may well be more careful than state employees in allocating help where it is needed, and better able to hold off where it is not. And while there are many worthy causes, there is a case for saying that it is better to help these on a voluntary basis through charitable donations than through the compulsory levy of the tax system. For apart from the question of liberty, or choice, there is also the consideration that charity is *good* for the giver, in a way in which tax-paying is morally indifferent. Finally, there is an important point to be made about the nature of responsibility both on the part of the giver and the part of the recipient, for in both cases the fact is that you can't be truly "responsible" if you know someone else will pick up the tab if you fail to do so. Being ethical, then, cannot in itself supply an unambiguous direction for all political and economic policy. Even given an agreed goal of helping people who are not currently helping themselves, there is room for dispute as to how to achieve that goal.

Public Life, Private Persons?

Finally, there is one other area of public life in which the question of a link between ethics and politics may arise; this is the area of personal ethics. I do not mean by this the "dirty hands" issue already familiar in political philosophy in which it is asked whether a statesman may order in that capacity things which would be morally repugnant if ordered by a private citizen, but rather the question currently exercising the media about politicians' conduct of their own private life.

There may seem to be a *prima facie* case for regarding that private life as private, despite the well-known fact that example is in itself important, since it can be either inspiring and uplifting, or corrupting and demeaning. Much will depend, however, on what the failings are that are at issue. Sexual misdemeanours may seem trivial to some—bribery and corruption hardly so, while instances of murder, or the ordering of murder or torture, are indisputably unacceptable, and likely to call to mind Acton's warning of the corrupting effect of power. But when what is at issue is the private rather than the public person, and especially the area of sexual behaviour, debate swerves confusingly between two distinct questions: is the conduct itself right or wrong? Or is the wrongdoing of public figures none of our business?

These questions are not necessarily intrusive or irrelevant. Watchful democrats are entitled to look for signs of corruption in their leaders, and there is a popular view that proneness to wrong-doing cannot be contained in one area of a person's life. Devlin's view that morality is a "seamless web" is often shared by ordinary people, and I have already suggested that it is implicit in Macmurray's approach. Yet a new virtue, described as "compartmentalism" has been cited in respect of some current difficulties in both the USA and Britain. In the British case, this may well be prompted by a desire where these issues are concerned to distinguish New Labour from the policies of both Thatcher and Major, who were seen to have fallen down by talking, in the first case, of Victorian values and, in the second, of a return to "basics," just at a time when major figures in their circle were caught in a number of flagrant sexual scandals. As is well known, this generated charges of hypocrisy and inconsistency. However, there is a certain aura of inconsistency about "compartmentalism" itself. For consistency requires that one should accept the possibility of tolerating *without* condoning. Again, as in the two areas discussed earlier, there is no need to pursue a *moral* hands-off policy just because an area is recognised as inappropriate for *practical* interference. In other words, there is no need to defend the indefensible just because it must be socially, legally or politically permitted.

But defending the indefensible is not a policy likely to appeal to a Christian socialist and Macmurray would not, I feel, have had much sympathy for today's politicians caught in the spotlight of public exposure of behaviour which, nevertheless, from the ordinary person's point of view, could be said to be "their own business." For he would no doubt have taken the view that public life demands higher, not lower, standards. And with his emphasis on the personal, and his tendency to locate that in the family, he would not, I believe, have leaned to the "compartmentalising" view. For Macmurray, personal relations were fundamental, and the good society and the good community were only likely to flow from their cultivation at all stages—in bringing up children, in the mother-child relationship, in the relation between husbands and wives, in family life, in community relations. It seems, then, that he would have had difficulty discounting personal behaviour and personal relations at any level of community life.

Conclusions

Macmurray's ideas seem to have a new currency in today's politics, but events in the real world seem already to have caused a distancing from the fundamental conception of "ethical" politics on each of the fronts I have mentioned: foreign policy, welfare reform, politicians' private lives. Nevertheless, if a "people's philosopher" is needed for today's world, then Macmurray may indeed have at least some of the right qualifications. He was a philosopher who believed in objective reason, believed that the emotions, too, can be rational, and that education is a tool for achieving this. He was also a philosopher who took from Christianity a perspective which is both individualistic and internationalist, setting as a goal a world community of persons endowed with human rights, and one who defined as the problem of our own day "...the achievement of an effective world unity."[19] But he had a suitably modest view of all this, and of the people who must carry it out. I cannot do better than end with his own surprisingly sympathetic comments on the State and the politicians and civil servants who service it.

> Leviathan is not merely a monster, but a fabulous monster; the creature of a terrified imagination. If we track the State to its lair, what shall we find? merely a collection of overworked and worried gentlemen, not at all unlike ourselves, doing their best to keep the machinery of government working as well as may be, and hard put to keep up appearances.
>
> If we insist that it is their business to make peace on earth and hand us the millennium on a platter, what will happen? Those of them who are wise enough to know their limitations, and to be immune to the gross adulation of their fellows, will resign; and government will be carried on only by megalomaniacs, who are capable of believing themselves possessed of superhuman attributes and whose lust for power is the measure of their weakness.[20]

NOTES

[1] *Persons in Relation* (1961), 11.

[2] J. Macmurray, *Freedom in the Modern World*, 25.

[3] Philip Conford, (ed.), *The Personal World: John Macmurray on Self and Society* (Edinburgh: Floris Books, 1996), 38.

[4] Ibid., 190.

[5] See N. Noddings, *Caring: A Feminine Approach to Ethics* (Berkeley: University of California Press, 1984), and C. Gilligan, *In a Different Voice* (Cambridge: Harvard University Press, 1982.) Second revised edition, 1993.

[6] *Persons in Relation*, 212.

[7] Ibid., 91.

[8] Ibid., 116.

[9] Ibid.,119.

[10] Ibid., 119.

[11] Ibid.,137.

[12] Ibid., 136.

[13] Ibid., 16.

[14] Ibid., 146.

[15] Ibid., 128.

[16] Ibid., 196.

[17] Philip Conford (ed.), *The Personal World*, op. cit.

[18] Ibid., 203.

[19] *Conditions of Freedom* (1950), 65.

[20] *Persons in Relation*, 200–1.

CHAPTER TEN

Responsibility as First Ethics: Macmurray and Levinas [1]

Hwa Yol Jung

Goethe's idea[2] that "in the beginning was the Deed" marks the genesis of a paradigm shift in contemporary philosophical thought for the celebration of which I wish to invoke the names of two epochal and inimitable philosophers of the twentieth century: John Macmurray and Emmanuel Levinas.

Both Macmurray and Levinas challenge the logocentric tradition of Western philosophy since its inception in ancient Greece, that is, in Plato whose central importance is encapsulated in Alfred North Whitehead's view that the history of Western philosophy is a series of footnotes to Plato. The logocentrism of ancient Greece reaches its summit in modern philosophy in Descartes'' "epistemocracy" and Hegel's dialectical theoretism. On the other hand, the philosophical root of Macmurray and Levinas stems from the Judaeo-Christian tradition, that is, the "other" root of Western civilization, which prompted Levinas to declare that heterocentric—or, as he calls it, heteronomic—ethics is the Judaic contribution to Western philosophy. The Hebraic *nephesh* (living being) is embodied in dynamic movement, whereas the Greek *psyche* (soul) is ensouled in timeless Being.[3] The Hebraic *dabhar* became associated with the Deed or practical, while the Greek *logos* completes itself in Reason. Goethe dramatized this problematic by frowning upon the theoretic "I think" as "grey" and was determined not to dull the primary colors of the practical "I do." He was deeply suspicious of the truth of the Delphic oracle—"Know thyself"—which is the principium of Socratic wisdom and synonymous with the beginning of philosophizing in the West as "a device of priests secretly leagued to confuse man by impossible demands and to divert him from activity in the world about him to a false introspection." For Goethe, "[m]an knows himself only in so far as he knows the world, becoming aware of it only in himself, and of himself only in it." Furthermore, he contends that "[o]thers know me much better than I do myself. It is only [through] my relations to the world about me that I can learn to know and appraise correctly."[4]

The seminal importance of Macmurray and Levinas lies in their mutual confirmation of the sacrament of coexistence or the sanctity of "interbeing," handicrafted in Auguste Rodin's sculptural masterpiece (with the feminine title) *La Cathédrale* (1908). For Macmurray and Levinas, the Other (*l'autrui*) or the dialogical "You" after the fashion of Martin Buber's "Thou" (*Du*) is the topic of first magnitude, and the primacy of the other over the self is indispensable to and prerequisite for ethics. Indeed, the primacy of the other is the most basic grammar of ethics and responsibility as first ethics. It certifies ethics as heterocentric or, indeed, ethics itself. The contemporary relevance of heterocentric ethics to social and political thought may be translated into the notion of "taking responsibility seriously" which would reverse and replace the mainstream (even "malestream") Anglo-American political and jurisprudential notion of "taking rights seriously."

Western modernity has been hypnotized by the Cartesian *Cogito* with which is theoretism par excellence and the exemplar of Macmurray's self as (epistemological) subject, that is, of the "I think" in contradistinction to the "I do." The theoretic or epistemological subject is by necessity egocentric. As Macmurray claimed, the self is to be conceived not theoretically as a subject, but practically as an agent. Since human behaviour carries a social reference, the isolated subject is a fiction. The *Cogito* as theoretism typifies a thinker's desire to seal himself or herself off from the world and to keep his thinking pure or uncontaminated by the presence of the other.[5] The true philosopher is for Descartes, the inventor of the *Cogito*, one who, as he himself characterizes it, is "alone but secure in a heated room on a cold winter's day"[6] and takes infinite delight in the permanent state of solitude, social isolation and hibernation. The Cartesian mind as *res cogitans*, in the final analysis, is in the perpetual state of social paralysis and is incapable of socializing.

By identifying my being or existence with that I think of it, the *Cogito* valorizes that mind which is disembodied, monologic, and even ocularcentric. As it is the activity of the mind as "thinking substance," the *Cogito* is inherently monologic because it is always and necessarily ego *cogito* (the "I think")—the epitome of an "invisible man" in total isolation from others, both other minds and other bodies. To use the language of Macmurray: *Cogito ergo non-sum*. As a thinking substance, the mind needs nothing more than itself to think. Once the self and the other are viewed as disembodied substances, two self-contained substances, monologism, or even solipsism *in extremis*, is inevitable. For Descartes, moreover, the mind as *Cogito* erects the privatized, insulated, and echoless palace of "clear and distinct ideas," three visual terms, in which nobody else can live. Thus the *Cogito* is identified with ocularcentrism, with a kind of epistemological prison-house not unlike the Panopticon which Jeremy Bentham designed as a perfect prison system. As a matter of fact, Cartesian panoptic metaphysics goes hand in hand with the monologism of the *Cogito* because vision tends to deny the sociability of the other senses. To put it simply, there is an identity between the "I" and the "eye." The *Cogito* is really *video ergo sum*, or the mind's *I* is the mind's *eye*. The "eye-viewpoint" of the Cartesian *Cogito* highlights the subjectivism or egocentrism of modern philosophy, of the modern (TV) age itself.

Contrary to Descartes for whom the certitude of existence is guaranteed by the solitary *Cogito*, Macmurray certifies the certitude of existence by the social "I do." The form of the personal, according to Macmurray, is not only relational through and through but also ruled by the dialogical primacy of the other as "You," by "altarity"[7] in which the other as "You" is placed on the altar or *above* the self. In Macmurray's formulation of the "I do" the self does not and cannot exist in isolation. To be a person means "to be in communication with the Other."[8] The unit of the personal is not the "I" alone but the "You and I" together. We humans are inextricably "enmeshed in [a] network of relation[s] that binds us together to make up human society."[9] In the very concluding sentence of *The Self as Agent* Macmurray unequivocally rejects the "atheistic" formulation of Sartre's existentialism that "hell is other people" (*l'enfer, c'est les autres*).[10] Morality is not only essentially social but also inherent in human action or the "I do." Macmurray understands well, moreover, that the personal is relational only by way of the agents as bodies. It is first and primordially an embodied relation, that is, it is intercorporeal.

However, we cannot speak of the dialogical primacy of the other without relationality which is based on the distinction or difference rather than the identity between the self (ipseity) and the other (alterity) both as singulars. Difference in the relationality between the "I" and the "You" is the force that pulls "us" together rather than pulls us apart. For Macmurray not only is human *difference* constituted in the "I do," but he also speaks of the "discrimination of the other." Without the discrimination of the self from the other, of the "I" from the "You" and vice versa, the field of the personal would be a flatland of the same. The discrimination of the self makes the self open to the other—the process of which is neither homogenizing nor being homogenized. Without discrimination, therefore, communication among humans is unnecessary.[11]

By way of relationality, difference, and the primacy of the other, Macmurray continues the Copernican revolution of human thought which Ludwig Feuerbach enunciated in modern philosophy. It may be called Copernican because what Copernicus's heliocentrism is to Ptolemy's geocentrism, heterocentrism is to egocentrism. Feuerbach's Copernican discovery of "Thou" (or "You") is promulgated in principle 59 of his *Principles of the Philosophy of the Future* (*Grundsätze der Philosophie der Zukunft*) which was originally published in 1843. He writes:

> The single man for himself possesses the essence of man neither in himself as a moral being nor in himself as a thinking being. The essence of man is contained only in the community and unity of man with man; it is a unity, however, which rests only on the reality of the distinction between I and thou.[12]

With this enunciation of Feuerbach is the birth of heterocentric thinking and doing. Indeed, the term *heterocentric ethics* is redundant because any ethics worth its name is by definition heterocentric, that is, founded on the primacy of the other.

Levinas, too, continues to trek the path of the Feuerbachian revolution. He attends directly to the question of *ethics as first philosophy* which is his paramount contribution to phenomenology as a philosophical movement in the twentieth century. Based on the asymmetrical relation of the self and the other in which each is different because he or she is unique or singular, not the other way around, *the other as other (alterity) is ethically prior to the self (ipseity)*. Alterity, in other words, is the site of the ethical. It is of utmost importance to emphasize the point that Hannah Arendt's controversial discourse on Adolf Eichmann's "banality of evil" is grounded in his "thoughtlessness." By thoughtlessness Arendt means one's inability to think from the standpoint of another. It led Eichmann to commit the ir/responsible acts of "crimes against humanity" (*hostis generis humani*) for which he deserved to be hanged.[13]

Levinas's ethics as first philosophy is tantamount to the ethics of responsibility, a heteronomic ethics for others or, as he himself puts it, an ethics without concern for (absolute) reciprocity. It is noteworthy that in Hebrew, responsibility (*ahariout*) and "other" (*aher*) share the same etymological root.[14] Because each person is singular and thus different from another, moreover, his or her responsibility for the other is also unique and thus non-transferable.[15] Cruelty or brutality, in all forms of its manifestation, is condemned because it results from disrespect for the other's difference, for alterity. Violence, whether it be war, revolution, or capital punishment, involves cruelty or brutality. It aims at the defacement or complete effacement of the other from the surface of the earth. Thus it may be said that violence is the price we pay for the abolition of differences, of alterity which signifies each person's integrity and dignity as a human being. Violence results from the intolerant and uncompromising affirmation of the self's epistemological infallibility and moral inculpability against the other that violates the fundamental principle of human coexistence based on respect for difference. It is ignorant of and oblivious to what Hans-Georg Gadamer[16] calls the soul of hermeneutics as the possibility of the other being right. Michael Walzer puts the matter concisely, "tolerance makes difference possible; difference makes tolerance necessary."[17] What is, then, the ultimate *telos* of coexistence based on alterity? For Levinas who witnessed the Holocaust as for Macmurray who was a Quaker pacifist, it is peace without qualification. With the idea of peace, the question of the ethical merges with that of the political. In merging with the ethical, however, the political does not refer to "a fabulous monster" that Hobbes created as Leviathan with "a terrified imagination" or the purpose of overcoming the state of nature in which we are condemned to the fear of violent death because it is the warlike condition of each against every other. We are reminded here of Picasso's extraordinary and magnificent depiction in

Guernica (1937) of the horror and terror of war painted in the faces of humans and animals, a depiction that nullifies Rodin's sacrament of coexistence. Contrary to Karl von Clausewitz, peace, not war or carnage, is the continuation of politics by other means. Arendt declares,

> Power is actualized only where word and deed have not parted company, where words are not empty and deeds not brutal, where words are not used to veil intentions but to disclose realities, and deeds are not used to violate and destroy but to establish relations and create new realities.[18]

Levinas is particularly concerned with the ethical gridlock in Heidegger's "fundamental ontology" as phenomenology in *Being and Time*.[19] In his opposition to Heidegger's ontology, Levinas chooses the term *meontology* which affirms "a meaning beyond Being, a primary mode of non-Being (*me-on*)."[20] Thus "meontology" is proposed both to negate and to transcend Heideggerian ontology. In a nutshell, the ethical is "otherwise than Being" (autrement qu'être).[21] "I am trying to show," Levinas says, "that man's ethical relation to the other is ultimately prior to his ontological relation to himself (egology) or to the totality of things which we call the world (cosmology)."[22]

There is indeed an ineradicable gulf between Heidegger's fundamental ontology and Levinas's ethics as first philosophy. In *Being and Time*, Heidegger defines *Dasein* as "Being-in-the-world" (*in-der-Welt-sein*) which includes the province of *Dasein's* relation with others (*Mitsein* or *Mitwelt*). Since "in" in "Being-in-the-world" is ecstatic in the existentialist tradition of Kierkegaard, humans are radically distinct from non-human beings and things in nature. For Heidegger, the "authenticity" (*Eigentlichkeit*) of *Dasein* as *Mitsein* is distinguished from the "anonymous they" (*das Man*) which implicates *Dasein*s fallenness to "inauthenticity" (*Uneigentlichkeit*) from the grace of authenticity. While Levinas's ethics as first philosophy is predicated upon the primacy of the other, Heidegger's *Daseinsanalyse* is self-centered (*eigentlich*) and concerned with "interiority" which is inside the self. Heidegger's *Dasein* is never "ec/centric" and as such is not concerned with "exteriority" which is outside the self. Therefore, Heidegger's egological "fundamental ontology" is incapable of birthing or fashioning an ethics[23]—an ethics of responsibility which is held together not by the "resoluteness" (*Entschlossenheit*) of "authentic" selves but only by the responsivity of dialogical others. Therefore, Heidegger's egological "fundamental ontology" is incapable of fashioning an ethics, an ethics of responsibility which is held together by the resoluteness of "authentic" selves, not of the dialogical others.

The face (*visage*) is for Levinas capable of facing or interfacing the singular other as "You." It is the ethical surface of humanity: "the epiphany of the face is ethical."[24] Levinas defends vigorously "the defenseless nakedness of the face" as an ethical hermeneutic.[25] "The approach to the face," he emphasizes, "is the most basic mode of responsibility. As such, the face of the other is verticality and uprightness; it spells a relation of *rectitude.* The face is not in front of me (*en face de moi*) but above me."[26] The phenomenologist Erwin W. Straus, too, is forthright when he speaks of the "upright posture" of humans which signifies humanity's ethical posture of rectitude as much as its physiological characteristic.[27] By the same token, the *look* of the face as an ethical gesture in crying, laughing, pain, or joy is not and cannot be determined by the objective color of an eye.

As an ethical gesture of first magnitude, the face does not just look but also "speaks" albeit in silence. The language it speaks (i.e., "saying") is the language of rectitude as "ethical sincerity."[28] Saying, in other words, has an ethical force and fortitude. Here Levinas, consciously or unconsciously, speaks of the language of Confucian ethics, the Confucian ethics of saying as ethical performance which is plainly called *sincerity* (*ch'eng*).

In the primacy of the ethical, subjectivity is affirmed never for itself (i.e., never monologic or egocentric) but only for the Other (*pour l'autrui*). Subjectivity comes into being or existence as "heteronomic." "It is," Levinas affirms, "my inescapable and incontrovertible answerability to the other that makes me an individual 'I'."[29] Thus the notion of responsibility (answerability) is, first and foremost, the confirmation of the I which is what Levinas calls the "meontological version of subjectivity," based on the face as its most basic and expressive manifestation. He writes that responsibility is "the essential, primary and fundamental structure of subjectivity. For I describe subjectivity in ethical terms. Ethics, here, does not supplement a preceding existential base; the very node of the subjectivity is knotted in ethics understood as responsibility."[30]

It would be wrong, however, to think that responsibility contradicts or opposes freedom. Macmurray's distinction between the "I do" and the

"I think" finds its parallel in Arendt's distinction between the *vita activa* and *vita contemplativa*. Unlike the "necessity" of labor (*animal laborans*) and the "utility" of work (*homo faber*), freedom is for Arendt the distinguishing characteristic of human action. For her, the irreversibility of human action can be redeemed only by the human faculty of "forgiving," whereas the unpredictability or uncertainty of action in the future is guaranteed by the human faculty of making and keeping promises. Defining the irreversibility and the unpredictability of human action, she asserts that "forgiving and promising enacted in solitude or isolation remain without reality and can signify no more than a role played before one's self (without interaction or the other in mind)."[31]

Levinas, too, would agree with Arendt when she says that action is the human answer to the existential condition of natality as *initium* (initiative).[32] As a matter of fact, the insertion of oneself into the human world is likened by Arendt to "a second birth." It is noteworthy here that there is an unbridgeable gulf that separates Arendt and Heidegger. While Heidegger contemplates *Dasein's* "authenticity" (*Eigentlichkeit*) or its "own innermost sphere," Arendt pursues the *vita activa* as the locus of human plurality. More radically, there is a stark contrast between Arendt and Heidegger in that the former invests natality as the beginning of the *vita activa*, whereas the latter deems or redeems *Dasein* as "Being-towards-death" (*Sein zum Tode*). It is the sheer difference between natality and mortality—the two extreme spectrums of human existence. Man is for Heidegger the mortal of all mortals whereas he or she is for Arendt the beginning of all beginnings within the boundaries of the all-embracing earth which constitutes the quintessence of the human condition. The radical implication of natality for the philosophy of action lies in the twofold fact that each and every human being is unmistakably an *initium*, a new beginning and that he or she has the native or inborn gift of transforming and shaping anew the world because he or she is an *initium*. In other words, the human faculty of action is ontologically rooted or anchored in the simple facticity of natality. Phenomenologically, power, the central category of politics, is ancillary to the advent of natality. As its cognate etymology shows, it connotes "potentiality" as in the Latin *potentia* or *potestas*, the Greek *dynamis*, and the German *Macht*. Arendt writes,

What makes man a political being is his faculty of action; it enables him to get together with his peers, to act in concert, and to reach out for goals and enterprises that would never enter his mind, let alone the desires of his heart, had he not been given this gift—to embark on something new. Philosophically speaking, to act is the human answer to the condition of natality. Since we all come into the world by virtue of birth, as newcomers and beginnings, we are able to start something new; without the fact of birth we would not even know what novelty is, all "action" would be either mere behavior or preservation.[33]

Faith and hope, Arendt adds, are two correlatives of natality. As they pertain to "Jesus of Nazareth," they are Biblical creations. Greek antiquity, which invented the *vita contemplativa*, knows nothing of them. "It is," Arendt intimates, "this faith in and hope for the world that found perhaps its most glorious and most succinct expression in the few words with which the Gospels announced their "glad tidings": "A child has been born onto us."[34] This does not mean, however, that for Arendt as for Macmurray they are divine or "other-worldly." Rather, they are primarily human or "this-worldly" and belongs to the public order of the *vita activa*.

By virtue of natality, Levinas would insist with Arendt that human existence is *invested as freedom* rather than condemned to it. The investment of human existence in freedom, however, can never be absolute: there is no unconditional freedom insofar as we, the individuals, inhabit and share the same spatiotemporal arena of action with others in the world and on this earth. The aim of political theory itself is to ensure, according to Levinas, "the most complete exercise of spontaneity by reconciling my freedom with the freedom of the other."[35] Nevertheless, Levinas opposes Heidegger's ontology for affirming "the primacy of freedom over ethics."

To be sure the freedom involved in the essence of truth is not for Heidegger a principle of free will. Freedom comes from an obedience to Being: it is not man who possesses freedom; it is freedom that possesses man. But the dialectic which thus reconciles freedom and obedience in the concept of truth presupposes the primacy of the same, which marks the direction of and defines the whole of Western philosophy.[36]

In the end, responsibility is not only compatible with, but also weightier than, freedom because one can be free without being responsible but one cannot be responsible without first being free.

According to Fergusson, Macmurray, under the sway of Kant, claims that "without freedom responsible action becomes impossible."[37] Freedom, then, is the necessary but not sufficient condition of responsible action. For Macmurray as for an existential phenomenologist, freedom and action are imbricated and imply each other. Freedom is inherent in the very structure of action. Freedom, according to Macmurray, is "the capacity to determine the future by action."[38]

We would be remiss if we do not take notice of Viktor Frankl who gives us a glimpse of responsibility as "self-transcendence" (or "altarity") which deserves, I think, more than a passing comment. He was a survivor of Nazi death camps and founded logotherapy or psychotherapy with a human face, as it were. Logotherapy calls for the affirmation of life at all cost as opposed to the abolition of life relying on Nietzsche's single dictum that "he who has a *why* to live can bear with almost any *how*." Like Levinas, more importantly, Frankl prompts and promotes an elegant way of formulating the concept of responsibility as "self-transcendence" which is "the cue to cure" the feeling of life as meaningless or worthless. By self-transcendence, Frankl means the discovery and recovery of life's meaning by engaging actively in the world, in the other rather than one's own inner psyche. Self-transcendence is embodied in the idea of responsibility.

> Freedom… is not the last word. Freedom is only part of the story and half of the truth. Freedom is but the negative aspect of the whole phenomenon whose positive aspect is responsibleness. In fact, freedom is in danger of degenerating into mere arbitrariness unless it is lived in terms of responsibleness.[39]

Responsibility as heterocentric ethics based on the hermeneutics of the face in Levinas and the interpersonal "I-You" relation in Macmurray is embellished by the contemporary ethics of care as a feminine *gift* of life. For I consider the ethics of care as having the primordial structure of responsibility with a feminine face and a feminine distinction. In *In a Different Voice*, Carol Gilligan voices the feminine ethics of care in the following terms:

> The moral problem arises from conflicting responsibilities rather than from competing rights and requires for its solution a mode of thinking that is contextual and narrative rather than formal and abstract. This conception of

morality as concerned with the activity of care centers moral development around the understanding of responsibility and relationships, just as the conception of morality as fairness ties moral development to the understanding of rights and rules.[40]

The ethical basis of "taking rights seriously" is at best one-sided and at worst illegitimate because it thinks the unthinkable, that is, the ontological fabric of the self as completely autonomous and self-reliant being rather than an interdependent ensemble of social relationships. In this sense, responsibility as first ethics deconstructs the mainstream ("malestream" as feminists would call it) philosophy of rights.

It is fashionable today to invoke the "care of the self," the "care of the soul," the "care of the body, "healthcare," "medicare," and even "earthcare." Heidegger defines care (*Sorge*) as the ontological soul of *Dasein* as "Being-in-the-world." However, as we have above argued, Heidegger's fundamental ontology is incapable of generating an ethics or an ethics of responsibility because individual *Dasein* is conceived stubbornly as egocentric (*eigentlich*). Foucault, too, speaks of "the care of the self."[41] His analytics of the sex/power nexus has been rightly attractive to feminism in an attempt to empower women. For Foucault,[42] power is both ubiquitous and relational and as such it penetrates deeply the module of sexuality as nothing but a nexus of human relationships turned into carnal contact which is abbreviated often as powerplay. Thus sexuality is really a relational function of power or a strategic form of powerplay. However, I think Foucault is as misguided as Heidegger because he is totally oblivious to care as heterocentric. Care means for Foucault taking care of oneself rather than others. In the form of a corpus of knowledge and rules, Foucault declares that the healthcare of medicine, for example, defines "a way of living, a reflective mode of relation to oneself, to one's body, to food, to wakefulness and sleep, to the various activities, and to the environment."[43] His reference to the other in care is confined to pay "the attention one devotes to the care that others should take of themselves the injunction of which is regarded as "an intensification of social relations."[44] Thus care as relationality and responsibility are marginalised and secondary to the "care of the self."[45]

In conclusion, let me reiterate what I stated at the outset: it would be an intellectual travesty to fail to recognize that Macmurray and Levinas are paradigm shifters in twentieth-century philosophy in inaugurating the dialogical primacy of the "I do" over the "I think," ethics as first philosophy, and responsibility as first ethics. In relating Macmurray and Levinas, who are truly philosophical soulmates, it must be emphasized that the primacy of the "I do" is the (ontological) precondition for ethics as first philosophy. They implicate and complement each other. For the "I do" and ethics are two reversible sides of the same process. They together herald and propel a paradigm shift of Copernican proportion and magnitude. Yet in reversing or deconstructing, if you will, the theoretic or theory-centered tradition of modern Western philosophy since Descartes, their work has not, unfortunately, reached the shores of ethical and political thinking even if for Macmurray the personal is concerned eminently with politics as ethics.

Mary Ann Glendon is outspoken in criticizing the long-held tradition of "rights talk," as she calls it, in Anglo-American political, social, legal and moral philosophy from Thomas Hobbes and John Locke to William Blackstone and Ronald Dworkin. The true American Way, she contends, is unmistakably the Way of Rights that places the self as the center of the world and universe. The American Way shows a genuine genuflection for the *I's have it*. "The American rights dialect," she writes, "is distinguished not only by what we say and how we say it, but also by what we leave unsaid."[46] She argues further that as the *lingua franca* of American social and political thought, the language of rights knows no bound and "no compromise." It is indeed the confessional *reductio ad insanitatem* of American culture itself. In this light, Locke's old observation that in the beginning all the world was *America* becomes ageless and acquires a new twist of meaning in the context of Francis Fukuyama's recent provocation of "the end of history." It turned out to be even prophetic, that is, in the end (as well as in the beginning) all the world *is*, again, America.

The real question, I think, is why altruists have increasingly become victimized in the land of "rights talk" which is tied to choices, contracts, and entitlements. Kristen Renwick Monroe's recent work *The Heart of Altruism* has a decisive bearing on the ethics of (caring as) responsibility which, as a paradigmatic moral theory, is an alternative to "rights talk."[47] It is heartening when the kind face of compassion transfigures and prevails upon the nasty and ugly face of contempt and cruelty. Altruism is a matter of the heart or what Macmurray calls "emotional rationality." Monroe attempts to answer James Q. Wilson's cogent question, "[i]f rights are all that is important, what will become of responsibilities?"

Altruism, Wilson contends, may not be "a strong beacon light" but is "a small candle flame" that is capable of dispelling the darkness and warming our soul once it is brought close to our heart and cupped in our hands.[48]

Altruism lands a mortal blow to the cherished tradition of "rational choice theory" whose center is "economic rationality." Wilson echoes Monroe when he claims that "the teachings of the heart deserve to be taken as seriously as the lessons of the mind."[49] Economic rationality in rational choice theory as an indispensable and integral part of "rights talk" is based on the premise that "rational man" is one who chooses to maximize his or her own self-interest, "enlightened" or otherwise. He or she is a self-centered person, while the altruist is heterocentric. The altruist has the natural disposition and propensity to linking himself or herself to (distant) others through the moral sense of "a shared humanity." In essence, the "heart of altruism" refutes the twofold character of rational choice theory: (1) rationality and (2) choice. Neither rationality nor choice explains the good deeds of altruists. As Monroe emphasizes, altruists are left with "no choice in their behavior towards others. They are John Donne's people. All life concerns them. Any death diminishes them. Because they are part of mankind."[50]

It is high time that "rights talk" should give way to the language and ethics of responsibility which has been instantiated in Macmurray and Levinas. Only by "downsizing," "rights talk," do we hope to make responsibility the center of ethics and the moral universe. For Levinas as for Macmurray, transcendence signifies an ethical gesture and turn of the first order. Ethics as first philosophy, indeed, involves the philosopher's responsibility to commit himself or herself to the welfare of humanity and the betterment of the world. It is deeply rooted and inheres in the *vita activa* of the Hebraic *dabhar* in contrast to the *vita contemplativa* of the Greek *logos* which Friedrich Hölderlin, in the footsteps of Goethe, would disdain as full of thought but poor in deed. What "rights talk" is to the usual art of the possible, responsibility is to the unusual art of the impossible—to appropriate the recent expression of the Czech President Vaclav Havel who read Levinas closely in his prison years and intends to promote the idea of "living in truth" and the new vision of "politics as morality in practice."[51] Then and only then does responsibility as first ethics become an ethics of the future, and ethics as first philosophy—a philosophy of the world which is hurrying into a global village.

NOTES

[1] While finishing this paper, I heard the sad news of the death of George Tyler who had been a friend, gentleman and scholar. It is fitting for me to dedicate it to his memory.

[2] Johann Wolfgang von Goethe, *Goethe's Faust*, trans. Carlyle F. MacIntyre (Norfolk, CT: New Directions, 1941), 82–83.

[3] See Thorlief Boman, *Hebrew Thought Compared with Greek*, trans. Jule L. Moreau (Philadelphia: Westminster Press, 1960).

[4] See Johann Wolfgang von Goethe, *Wisdom and Experience,* trans. & ed. Hermann J. Weigand (New York: Pantheon Books, 1949), 206–7.

[5] See Gerald L. Bruns, 'What Is Tradition?', *New Literary History*, 22 (1991), 1–21.

[6] See Wolf Lepenies, 'Interesting Questions' in the History of Philosophy and Elsewhere," in *Philosophy and History*, Richard Rorty, J. B. Schneewind and Quentin Skinner (eds.) (New York: Cambridge University Press, 1984), 141–71.

[7] Here I am appropriating the neologism of Mark C. Taylor, *Altarity* (Chicago: University of Chicago Press, 1987).

[8] Macmurray, *Persons in Relation*, 77.

[9] Macmurray, *Reason and Emotion*, 14.

[10] See *The Self as Agent*, 222.

[11] Cf. Hannah Arendt, *The Human Condition*, 2nd ed. (Chicago: University of Chicago Press, 1998), 175–76.

[12] Ludwig Feuerbach, *Principles of the Philosophy of the Future,* trans. Manfred H. Vogel (Indianapolis, IN: Bobbs-Merrill, 1966), 71.

[13] See Hannah Arendt, *Eichmann in Jerusalem*, revised ed., (New York: Penguin Books, 1977).

[14] See Catherine Chalier, 'The Philosophy of Emmanuel Levinas and the Hebraic Tradition,' in *Ethics as First Philosophy*, Adriaan T. Peperzak (ed.) (New York: Routledge, 1995), 8.

[15] At the moment of its inception in the latter part of the nineteenth century, responsibility was identified with the "accountability" of the self for himself or herself. See Richard McKeon, 'The Development and the Significance of the Concept of Responsibility,' *Revue Internationale de Philosophie*, 11 (1957), 3–32. Responsibility as heterocentric ethics in Macmurray and Levinas is thus a new paradigmatic idea.

[16] See Jean Grondin, *Introduction to Philosophical Hermeneutics,* trans. Joel Weinsheimer (New Haven, CT: Yale University Press, 1994), 124.

[17] *On Toleration* (New Haven, CT: Yale University Press, 1987), xii.

[18] *The Human Condition*, op. cit., 200.

[19] See Martin Heidegger, *Being and Time*, trans. Joan Stambaugh (Albany, NY: State University of New York Press, 1996).

[20] See Richard Kearney, *Dialogues with Contemporary Continental Thinkers: The Phenomenological Heritage* (Manchester: Manchester University Press, 1984), 61.

[21] See Emmanuel Levinas, *Otherwise Than Being or Beyond Essence,* trans. Alphonso Lingis (The Hague: Martinus Nijhoff, 1981).

22 See Kearney, *Dialogues*, op. cit., 57.

23 See Emmanuel Levinas, *Basic Philosophical Writings*, Adriaan T. Peperzak (ed.), Simon Critchley & Robert Bernasconi (Bloomington, IN: Indiana University Press, 1996), 1–10.

24 *Totality and Infinity,* 199.

25 Emmanuel Levinas, *Outside the Subject,* trans. Michael B. Smith (Stanford, CA: Stanford University Press, 1994), 158.

26 See Kearney, *Dialogues,* 59.

27 Erwin W. Straus, *Phenomenological Psychology* (New York: Basic Books, 1966), 137–65.

28 See Kearney, *Dialogues,* 64.

29 Emmanuel Levinas and Richard Kearney, 'Dialogue with Emmanuel Levinas,' in *Face to Face with Levinas,* Richard A. Cohen, (ed.), (Albany, NY: State University of New York Press, 1986), 20.

30 Emmanuel Levinas, *Ethics and Infinity,* trans. Richard A. Cohen (Pittsburgh: Duquesne University Press, 1982), 95.

31 Arendt, *The Human Condition*, 237.

32 Ibid., 177.

33 Hannah Arendt, *Crises of the Republic* (San Diego, CA: Harcourt Brace Jovanovich, 1972), 179.

34 *The Human Condition,* 247.

35 *Totality and Infinity*, 83.

36 Ibid., 45.

37 David Fergusson, *John Macmurray*, 15–16.

38 *The Self as Agent*, 212.

39 See Viktor E. Frankl, *Man's Search for Meaning*, revised ed. (New York: Washington Square Press, 1985), 133. Cf. Erich Fromm, *The Art of Loving* (New York: Harper and Row, 1956), 1, who writes poignantly that "[m]ost people see the problem of love primarily as that of *being loved* [i.e., self-centered or *taking*], rather than that of *loving*, of one's capacity to love [others] [i.e., *giving*]."

40 Carol Gilligan, *In a Different Voice* (Cambridge, MA: Harvard University Press, 1982), 19.

41 See Michel Foucault, *The History of Sexuality*, vol. 3: *The Care of the Self,* trans. Robert Hurley (New York: Pantheon Books, 1986).

42 See Michel Foucault, *The History of Sexuality*, vol. 1: *An Introduction*, trans. Robert Hurley (New York: Pantheon Books, 1978).

43 *The Care of the Self,* 100.

44 Ibid., 53.

45 It is extremely important to note that we often forget to recognize the notion of self-identity as a misnomer because the self is always in the process of *becoming* and thus in the state of *incompletion* until death. The self as a process is, in other words, heterogeneous. See Madan Sarup, *Identity, Culture and the Postmodern World* (Athens, GA: University of Georgia Press, 1996), xvi.

46 See Mary Ann Glendon, *Rights Talk* (New York: Free Press, 1991), 76.

47 *The Heart of Altruism* (Princeton, NJ: Princeton University Press, 1996).

[48]   James Q. Wilson, *The Moral Sense* (New York: Free Press, 1993), 245 & 215.

[49]   Ibid., 238.

[50]   *The Heart of Altruism*, 216.

[51]   The best known political idea of Havel is "living in truth."   The most recent collection of his essays under the title of *The Art of the Impossible*, trans. Paul Wilson et al. (New York: Alfred A. Knopf, 1997) is concerned with the related question of "politics as morality in practice."

CHAPTER ELEVEN

Public and Private: The Search for a Political Philosophy That Does Justice to Both without Excluding Love

Frank G. Kirkpatrick

One of the persistent dilemmas of contemporary social life has to do with the relation between the public and the private dimensions of human life. In the United States, in particular, the private dimension, usually associated with the family, has been elevated to such a high moral status that the public, especially the political dimension, has been treated as corrupt, overly intrusive, even the enemy of what some have come to call family values. One result of this split between private and public has been the increasing removal of the economic dimension from regulation and oversight by political[1] values. The ironic consequence is that as market economic practices run free of political control the principal victim is the very family so cherished by those who insist upon splitting private and public.

John Macmurray's philosophy, with its stress on direct personal relationships (the mutuality of the personal), can easily become a pawn in this contest between the private the public. His emphasis on direct personal heterocentric mutual love as necessary to the fulfillment of the self could be rhetorically exploited to devalue concern with more impersonal, indirect relations associated with public, political, and economic issues, including issues of social justice that transcend the intimacies of mutual love. But using Macmurray to pit private against public is absolutely contrary to both the spirit and the substance of his philosophy. In this essay, I shall establish a framework, drawn from Macmurray's philosophy of the personal, for understanding the nature of the private as well as its proper relationship to the public spheres of life.

Standing at the heart of this relation is the family as a locus of personal relationships. (It is not the only form of mutual direct and positive relationships, but for Macmurray it is the (or one of the) most basic. It is also private in the sense that the intimacies of its relationships are not duplicated in the impersonal relations of public, societal associations). Macmurray is no apologist for the hierarchical, patriarchal patterns of family life that have historically overridden women's rightful demand for justice and equal opportunity for flourishing, including those opportunities to help shape the public policies which impact family life. David Fergusson has nicely captured Macmurray's philosophy of the family, especially ways in which he provides justification for its reform.[2] I take my point of departure from Fergusson's work and want to draw out some of its more societal implications. What I want to suggest is that there is a well-stitched unity (which preserves and does not annul vital distinctions) between the development of deeply personal relationships and the work of statecraft at the political and economic level. What makes the relationship a unity, rather than an opposition, are the conditions necessary for the full development of mutual relationships and of the selves that participate in them. We are ultimately selves fulfilled only in and through the kinds of relationship that Macmurray calls "mutual" and which develop most fully in what he calls "community." But he warns us against setting in opposition what he refers to as the "minor mutualities" of limited loves and the public structures and principles of social justice. One way in which Macmurray holds private and public together without subsuming one to the other is through his all-important distinction between "society" and "community," a distinction often ignored by contemporary philosophers of both liberal and communitarian stripes. The distinction between direct and intimate relationships and those that are indirect and impersonal must not be used to sever them from each other, though they play different and mutually supporting roles in the full lives of individuals in relation.

One Macmurrian principle that holds them together is his appeal to the universal intention of community: his belief that fruitful human relationships can only be fully rational when they intend a universal community that in principle is open to all persons and not just those with whom we are in the most direct intimate contact. Since not all actual relationships can be direct, personal, and mutually loving, there must be a place for relationships that are indirect and impersonal, but *potentially* (and intentionally) able, in any given instance, to become personal.

One axis along which the public/private debate is often played out in political philosophy is that which stretches between communitarian and liberal political philosophies.[3] Macmurray, I suspect, would be loath to be pulled fully into either the communitarian or the liberal camp. And the lynchpin to his position is, I believe, the dialectical relation between what he calls the positive and negative poles of human relationship. One part of the negative pole is the "resistance" and "withdrawal" of the lover for the sake of the beloved's full development as an individuated self who will be able to stand in the deepest, most fully personal relationships while realistically involved in the impersonal relationships necessary for sustaining personal relationships and the larger society in which they are embedded. Resistance is both necessary to the full development of the self and is most fruitfully and initially expressed in the context of the family. This means that the self is not absorbed into a "minor mutuality" that would eliminate its ability to stand back critically from the entanglements of that community. Nor is the self able to become the critical, reflective, and fully developed self that it can be apart from the nurturing relations that throughout its life, but most especially at its beginning, instill in it both the experience of love and the experience of resistance to and discrimination of the "Other" as other.

Some people are apt to read Macmurray as if he wants to merge persons into each other or at least to have them relate to each other as if individual differences are either to be overcome or subsumed in what he calls "heterocentric" love for the other. This can lead to a romantic reading of Macmurray, drawing upon images of love in which the beloved becomes one with the lover. Macmurray himself may have given rise to this misinterpretation of his own work: when he talks about the goal of personal community being one in which each cares for all the others and no one for himself, he seems to be saying that one should literally sacrifice his "self," his very "person," to the Other. But this is, I think, a misreading and can be corrected only by a fuller exploration of how Macmurray understands our relationships not just at the deeply mutual level, but at the political, impersonal, or societal level as well, a level he never disparages even while attempting to relate it instrumentally to the deeper mutual level. Justice is not identical with nor a substitute for love, but love cannot override or swamp the imperatives of justice as long as persons stand in a relationship with each other that respects each partner's uniqueness and integrity. One important implication of this point is that the family cannot be exempt from the imperatives of justice, just as society cannot escape entirely from the imperatives, and the vision, first developed in the family, of care and compassion as moral guideposts for the fullest possible human life. If the family is removed from public scrutiny it can become an enclave of unjust domination and oppression, especially for women. If the family is made little more than the servant of the state, it loses those capacities that make it a model (but not the only model) of a community in which persons can relate to each other directly, personally, intimately, and mutually, in a way that is not possible among all the members of a society. Relationships within communities are never to be summed-up or reduced solely to ones of justice. But love without justice is subject to the temptation of tyranny in which the self loses itself either out of fear of the other or out of an inappropriate desire to destroy itself for, or to allow itself to be swallowed up by, the other in the name of love. The trick is finding the proper, just, and personally enriching way to establish the relationship between communities and societies, between private and public.

It has become a commonplace in the literature today to observe that women in particular must be wary of jumping from the frying pan of the falsehoods of an alienating liberal individualism into the fires of a cloying communitarianism. Liberal theory valorizes the individual who is able, through ascent to the heights of formal moral calculation, to make rational choices of life plans, goods, and modes of satisfaction unconstrained by the fetters of dogma, tradition, and the bonds of relatedness to others whom one has not chosen to be with. The more one can stand apart from or above all inherited constraints, the more one can exercise an unbounded freedom to do as one chooses, propelled only by one's rationality and personal dispositions. This liberal self, ideally, has only its own self-interest to consider, until it comes into contact with others. Then it adjusts the modes for realizing its self-interest in order to accommodate the interests of others, so that each and all can best, under the conditions of reciprocal restraint, continue to pursue their self-interest.

For many reasons, not least of which are the bonds of motherhood and the experience of love which is not always a rational choice, many women have been highly skeptical of the presuppositions of a liberal theory of the self and its corollary, rational choice theory. As a result, many have been attracted to communitarianism which stresses the embeddedness of human life in given traditions. Communitarians often extoll the relational self that is as much defined by its entanglements, commitments, and boundness to others as it is by unconstrained rational choice and individual freedom.

But as some feminist theorists are now pointing out, communitarianism poses its own dangers to relational thinkers, especially to women. Communitarian thinkers such as Alasdair MacIntyre have rightly been criticized for being insufficiently attentive to the ways in which "communities"[4] have perpetuated forms of tyranny and domination of women in the name of tradition and embeddedness. Communitarianism runs the risk of giving individual members of a particular tribe or community no critical distance on their situatedness. If I "am" nothing but "a bearer of a particular social identity" given to me even before I rise to consciousness, then it is hard to see how I could reject or criticize those identities that define me as a slave, subordinate, inferior, without equal rights, powerless, etc. As Marilyn Friedman has pointed out, communitarianism's emphasis on the social nature of the self gives us no purchase on a criticism of those "situations" which are not morally justifiable, such as ones that reify hierarchies of gender domination and subordination. She also points out that most of the historical communities, especially the family, appealed to by communitarians have not been particularly friendly to women.[5]

Now it is at this point that Macmurray can enter the conversation. While it is true that he leans far more to the communitarian side of the axis (or to be chronologically correct, they move closer to him), his philosophy contains some important qualifications on excessive communitarianism and a strong and necessary link between the family and the public social order which permits a critique of false "traditions" and unjust tribal identities.

For Macmurray, the family is "the original human community and the basis as well as the origin of all subsequent communities. It is therefore the norm of all community..."[6] This is an extremely strong statement and could easily be deployed by the advocates of "family values" in support of their position. But it is crucial that we sort out *how* Macmurray intends his claim to be taken. It is not, I would argue, to be taken as a descriptive statement. He is not saying that the family as presently constituted (e.g., in Britain in the 1950s or perhaps at any particular historical period) is *in fact* a perfect model of community. We have to remember that the Gifford Lectures, from which this quote has been taken, were intended to develop what he called the philosophical "*form* of the personal." Macmurray was attempting to lay out a philosophical model, a metaphysical account, that would delineate the elements in human nature that constitute the "fullness" of human life. His conception of the family falls within this account with respect to its ideal philosophical form. The actual family falls far short of the ideal. That is why, I believe, Macmurray talks of the family as the "norm," not the actuality, of all community.[7]

It is also important to note that Macmurray talks of the family as if it is a chosen form of relationship. The family, he says, "is established and maintained by natural affection; by a positive motive in its members."[8] But empirically this can't be entirely right. Families are not always chosen forms of relationship. Children are born into families and their "positive motive" towards their parents becomes fully conscious only over time. There are biological, anthropological, and sociological conditions and constraints to existing families that Macmurray's ideal form of the personal simply doesn't deal with. We have to conclude, therefore, that when he discusses the family, Macmurray is to be taken as writing about an ideal form of relationship. Thus, what he says about the ideal family can stand as a critique on existing families, giving him the critical distance from the traditional family in western societies that Fergusson and feminist thinkers are rightly calling for.

Why does Macmurray single out the family as the ideal form of community? To get at this question we have to remind ourselves of what constitutes community (as distinct from other forms of association, especially society and the state). A community is "a group of individuals united in a common life, the motivation of which is positive... its members are in communion with one another; they constitute a fellowship. . . It is constituted and maintained by a mutual affection... Each member of the group is in positive personal relation to each of the others taken severally." The relation between the members is "positively motiv[at]ed in each. Each, then, is heterocentric; the centre of interest and attention is in the other, not in himself... The other is the centre of value... He cares for himself only for the sake of the other. But this is mutual; the other cares for him disinterestedly in return."[9]

Before we unpack other parts of this section of Macmurray's development of the idea of community, we need to note the centrality of the concept of a "positive motivation" and its negative corollary. This concept first emerges in Macmurray's discussion of the relation between personal and impersonal relations (a distinction, as we shall see, vital to the difference between the private and the public). A motive accounts satisfactorily for behavior in the absence of an intention. When we treat other persons as mere objects (with no freedom of their own) we assume that their behavior is solely the result of motives, whereas a free agent is guided by intentions as well. But, employing an unfortunate Hegelian way of putting it, Macmurray claims that a positive motive always contains and is constituted by its own negative. What this means concretely is that even when I intend a personal relationship with another person, I carry with me, as it were, a negative motivation insofar as I regard that other person as an object, a not-self. Our relations with these others can be either personal or impersonal. If I intend a personal relationship I know the one with whom I am in relationship as a free agent. If I intend an impersonal relationship, I can, for practical purposes, treat the other as an object determined by causal law. I can "negate" (provisionally and situationally) the personal character of the other (i.e., ignore his freedom as an agent) and treat him as "completely conditioned in his behaviour."[10] And this view of the Other can never be entirely absent even from the most intimate of relationships given Macmurray's notion of the negative as *always* contained within the positive. "Even in the most personal relationships the other person is in fact an object for us. . . The impersonal (or negative) aspect of the personal relation is always present and necessarily so."[11] We do not relate fully to beings that have no objective dimension to them. The other person's "otherness" always stands as an object to me, even when I am in the deepest possible personal relationship with her. This means that I cannot subsume or absorb her into my own self: she retains an obstinate, recalcitrant objectivity that I cannot (and ought not to try to) nullify by making our personal relationship so falsely intimate and mutual that her own unique particularity, and stubborn otherness disappear in me or in the relationship. My relationship with her, while intending the fullest possible personal mutuality, "includes the impersonal as a matter of fact."[12]

Now Macmurray insists that a personal relationship that is positively motivated is one that intends mutuality, to know the Other personally, not impersonally. And this kind of relationship requires no justification because it is the norm for all personal relations.[13] This means that all impersonal relations have to be justified by showing how they are "for the sake of the personal," or why the negative is subordinated to and *for* the sake of the positive.

> The other person may be treated rightly as a means to the realization of our intentions, and so conceived rightly as an object, only so far as this objective conception is recognized as a negative and subordinate aspect of his existence as a person, and so far as our treatment of him is regulated by this recognition.[14]

This is the foundation on which Macmurray builds his treatment of the relation between community, society, and the state, in which the family plays a critical role. But note that even in the family, the model of the closest kind of positive personal relations, there is an objective, negative, impersonal dimension always present. And to the extent that principles of justice apply to our impersonal relationships, they should also apply to those dimensions of our most mutual relationships that contain the impersonal as a negative subordinated to a positive.[15] Thus, the family itself (and any other form of constituted social arrangement, such as those the communitarians appeal to) ought to be subject to the principles of justice even when there are essential elements in family life such as mutual love that go beyond the impersonal, objective dimensions of justice.

One of the most direct relations possible is between mother and child.[16] Macmurray insists that this relation is not to be understood solely in biological terms since the survival of the human infant requires the free, intentional action of its parent. The infant has motives which are responded to by the parent's intentions. If it relied on its motives alone it would die since it is helpless without the aid of supportive agents.

> Nature leaves the provision for his physiological needs and his well-being to the mother for many years, until indeed he has learned to form his own intentions and acquired the skill to execute them and the knowledge and

foresight which will enable him to act responsibly as a member of a personal community.[17]

The acquisition of these skills takes place in the framework of the mother-child relation which Macmurray claims is that "basic form of human existence," a 'personal mutuality,' a 'You and I' with a common life."[18] The personal, therefore, is a relationship, not an individual. This relation is constituted by the infant's impulse to communicate with the world which, originally, *is* wholly the mother before he can begin to discriminate the various forms and modes of "otherness." Now out of this mother-child relationship are developed positive and negative poles of the infant's motivations. They are respectively love and fear. Fear is of isolation from the Mother: love is the delight in being cared for and in intimate communion with her. Consistent with his earlier treatment of positive and negative, Macmurray argues that the negative pole (fear) falls within and is subordinated to the positive (love). When the positive is fully functioning the child and mother enjoy their relationship as an end in itself, for its own sake. There is a mutual delight in the relation "which unites them in a common life" expressed through various symbolic gestures.[19]

Nevertheless, the infant is not yet able to fully intend the relationship with the parent. He must be brought through the developmental process to the point where he can exercise his agency so as to freely and consciously intend a positive relation with others. And one crucial part of this process is the *resistance* that the parent provides to his motives. The resistance of an object to my action is, for Macmurray, the essential basis of my knowledge of the Other *as Other*. The resistance the Other offers to me "is a frustration of the [or my] will." In practical experience "self and Other are correlatives discriminated together by their opposition; and this opposition constitutes the unity of the experience."[20] The first "other" the infant experiences is the mother. Before the process of gradual differentiation completes itself, the mother is to the infant "the whole community of persons of which [it is] an individual member."[21] Some different others that resist the infant do so actively and are eventually differentiated and characterized as agents: other beings do so passively and are characterized as non-agents (either as material and/or organic). In short, the practical process of differentiation begins with a characterization of the whole as personal and gradually distinguishes on a purely practical basis between those parts of the whole that respond personally (and hence are taken as persons) and those that do not (and are taken as non-persons). This process is essential to the full development of the individual self. "Personal individuality is not an original given fact. It is achieved through the progressive differentiation of the original unity of the 'You and I'."

What is particularly significant about this is that "the child discovers himself as an individual by *contrasting himself, and indeed by wilfully opposing himself to the family* (italics mine) *to which he belongs*; and this *discovery* of his individuality is at the same time the *realization* of his individuality."[22] This means that individuality requires resistance from the Other (or least some "critical distance" or ontic space) and therefore the actualization, within a particular context, of the negative pole of relationality. The personal Other, originally the mother, must *withdraw* from a fully positive relation with the child in order to help the child differentiate positive from negative. If the Other simply melted away at our touch, or absorbed us into itself with no resistance, there would be no possibility of distinguishing ourselves as individual persons. We need the resistance of the Other to become ourselves since central to our self-identity as persons is our agency. "Without the support of a resistance there can be no action; and the resistance must... be the resistance of a personal Other."[23] Within the family, he says, "the normal positive motivation is usually sufficient to dominate [not eliminate] the negative motives of self-interest and individualism."[24] Eventually, of course, the infant must learn that there are non-personal Others in the world which will also offer resistance. Without this knowledge, the developed self will be a helpless and ineffective agent in the world.

Of course, within the context of a relationship that is intended to be mutual, direct, and personal, the resistance of the Other is a strategic means to an end: first to the development of a fully functioning healthy individual self and second to that self's mutual relationship with others in community. One part of this process is the necessity of the child's learning to distinguish between negative and positive. Macmurray believes that his distinction undergirds the later distinctions the adult will have to make between real and unreal, good and evil, beautiful and ugly, true and false.

Now the trick is to develop a true understanding of what is truly negative (i.e., not personal) without remaining stuck in negativity (i.e., becoming so fearful of the non-personal withdrawn and resisting Other that one adopts an egocentrism out of fear of that Other). The ideal is to use the knowledge of the reality of the non-personal in the service of developing healthier personal relationships. The child will develop a healthy will of his own: but he will have to choose whether he will exercise that will to wall himself off from potential Others who, he believes, intend him harm, or to guide him toward personal others who, he hopes, will welcome him into community and mutuality. The resistance and opposition that the mother, and more expansively, the family, provide the infant must be delicately and carefully handled.[25]

This leads directly to what Macmurray takes to be the basic problem of life itself: the problem of reconciliation. If the child responds to the mother's strategic and lovingly intended withdrawal and resistance out of fear, the negative motive will dominate his later egocentric actions. He will become either submissive to or aggressive toward the other as a way of dealing with his fear that the Other intends him harm. But egocentric behavior toward the Other is self-defeating because the only thing that will truly fulfill the self is "the full mutuality of fellowship in a common life, in which alone the individual can realize himself as a person."[26] Only if one intends this state of mutuality can one be understood as positively motivated. But this requires the opposite of fear, which is love: love for the other as other. That is why Macmurray calls it "hetero-centric" since its object is the other, not the self. "The centre of reference... is always the personal Other."[27] But this heterocentricity is possible only in community, in which the unity of persons is based on positive personal motivation.[28]

But every positive contains its own negative, and the negative in relation to community is society. A society is a unity of persons and it must be maintained by intention. But the social unions that constitute societies are also primarily negatively motivated by fear for oneself and therefore fear of the Other. These fears do not annul our social relationship but they determine them egocentrically. Our relationships become ones of forced cooperation "for such ends as each of us has an interest in achieving."[29] In this sense, Macmurray has articulated the basis of the liberal society: it exists to foster bonds of association that permit the individual the greatest possible latitude to pursue her own interests without violating the interests of others.

Society is necessary, of course, because not all relationships in fact can be mutual, direct, and personal. There are simply too many persons with whom we are in social but not mutual relationship.[30] Because societies are configured at a less than fully mutual level, they will serve different purposes than direct fellowship, but the purposes they serve ought to support, complement, and enhance community. Societies can be instrumental to community without becoming themselves communities. And if the model community is the family, then it follows that societies are to serve the family. (And by implication any other form of community). To this extent the conservative critique of liberalism is correct. But if society is the negative that is contained within the positive, it is also the case that the family (or any form of fellowship or mutuality) ought to adequately prepare its members to participate in and serve the society so that it, in turn, can serve the community. We have here, in effect, a dialectical dynamic, a form of what Macmurray calls the rhythm of withdrawal and return, or of resistance and response. In our terms, the private needs to prepare its members to play public roles so that society can best serve community without becoming confused with or reduced to it.

Just as the mother must withdraw temporarily from complete engrossment in the infant in order to allow it to grow and develop as an individual self, so the family must recognize the need of the individual to enter into relations that are not fully personal, mutual, and direct. All personal bonds need nurturing and support from persons who themselves often are not parties to those bonds. You literally cannot live on love alone: lovers need among other things such social goods as food, clothing, shelter, education, health care, etc. When they live in social union with multiple others, they also need justice, law, order, and the complex political, economic, institutional and systemic structures that make living with others in non-direct, impersonal ways humanly and humanely possible. This means that we all depend on others whom we don't know personally to function effectively in various social roles: as trainmen, doctors, nurses, engineers, teachers, etc. A society will be characterized to a large extent by the way in which it determines which social roles are necessary, what training must be provided to help people perform those roles effectively, and how those roles are efficiently integrated. At the same time it must not succumb to the false view that serving a societal role is an end in itself or that the full exercise of meaningful action is exhausted by successfully performing our societal functions.

But if society is to serve community then individuals need to be given training in distinguishing the negative and impersonal dimensions of life from the positive and personal ones and subordinating the former to the latter. This is where the family can be crucial.

The family might best be seen as the most effective forum for cultivating the essential traits and capacities of full personhood (love, trust, mutuality) without neglecting training in the negative elements necessary for societal relationship: i.e., resistance, impersonal relations, withdrawal, justice, cooperation, and healthy self-interest. If the negative is never entirely absent from even our most personal relationships, the best families will be those that prepare their members to integrate or balance the personal and impersonal relations that constitute the relation between society and community. This means, among other things, preparing their members to take active and responsible roles in helping to shape the political and economic life of society. Unless justice, law, order, and the structures of society that provide for the most efficient distribution of necessary goods work well, the private life of individuals will suffer. The self will either drown in the cloying and absorbing quicksand of too much intimacy and too little critical distance from it. Or it will become the victim of impersonal forces the control of which it has ceded to other hands and structures. The family must not allow false barriers to be established around it, cutting it off from political and public policy-making.

What are the capacities for both personal and social life that the family ought to nurture?

(1) The capacity for informed free action: action without knowledge or self-reflection is blind. This means cultivating the habits of learning, rational thought, investigation, imagination, and critical analysis that maximizes the self's freedom of action. This would be one part of Macmurray's antidote to the myopic limitations of inherited traditions that pass themselves off as genuine communities in some communitarian philosophies. As Will Kymlicka has argued, even the situated self needs liberty to critically examine what is most valuable for it. Precisely because our projects are so important "we should be free to revise and reject them, should we come to believe that they are not fulfilling or worthwhile."[31] This includes the capacity for objectivity in both thinking

and feeling with respect to the objects with which we are in relation. We need "ontic" space in which we can distinguish ourselves from others so that their individuality and uniqueness is respected while they respect ours. Clear thinking is one way to do this.[32]

(2) The capacity to distinguish between those objects that have the capacity in themselves to bring flourishing and joy to the self, and those that instrumentally support and sustain the relationship without being intrinsically joy-bringing. Moments of mutual joy with the mother requires the availability of a variety of basic, but not strictly personal goods, among which are food, shelter, clothing, education, health care, meaningful employment, opportunities for relaxation, art, culture, etc. Learning the appropriate relationship between the primary material/social goods and the persons whose relationships they enrich is a capacity that is essential for understanding the transition from the family into the political/economic order; this suggests another capacity;

(3) The capacity for understanding the importance and function of impersonal relations. The primary supportive goods must be delivered in some way, usually with the aid of other persons. Not all these deliveries will establish personal relationships between the providers and the receivers. I may need the services of health care personnel, but my relationships with them (in their societal roles as doctors, nurses, hospital administrators) will be for the most part impersonal. And I need to know the difference between these relationships and ones "outside" the societal context with the same persons.[33] Learning the utility of impersonal relations is an essential part of the full development of any person. Since impersonal social relations are structured by principles of justice, it is crucial for these principles of justice to apply within the family itself under the appropriate conditions. Justice abstracts from personal idiosyncracies in order to structure relationships by universal principles or, impersonally.[34] Children need to know that there are many uniquely distinguishing traits they cannot appeal to for special treatment by their parents in matters of discipline (e.g., being more beautiful or athletically gifted than their siblings).

(4) The capacity to both express and receive love: true love develops, of course, over time and presupposes a certain level of intentionality, emotionality, and free choice. Within the family the encouragement to express one's love toward others and the opportunities for doing so ought to be maximal. Not only should one be nurtured in

giving love, but also in learning how to receive love from others. Only by learning how to be loved, can one keep the negative motivation of fearing the other in check. And if fear is the basis of individualism, learning how to receive love is integral to balancing the excesses of self-reliance. Part of what it means to love, of course, also includes learning how to love as many others as possible. Genuine love cannot arbitrarily foreclose the boundaries of the community that love is willing to embrace. (This is where Macmurray's notion of a "universal community" can play a role). Such love is so central to Macmurray's philosophy that its full articulation is unnecessary here.

(5) A capacity for trust. Trust is an essential component of love. It is one crucial way of subordinating the negative motivation of fear of the other. Laurence Thomas has argued that the parental love which gives the child "basic psychological security" makes it possible for fear not to be a motivating factor in the life of the child.[35] And this requires what Thomas calls the establishment of "basic trust," trust that "others will treat one in accordance with the precepts of morality."[36] If this trust is established through good parenting, the child who becomes an adult will be much more able to will the flourishing of others without denying an interest in his own flourishing. In fact, it is primarily because others have loved us that we can love ourselves (contrary to the popular wisdom that we have to love ourselves before we can love others.) Out of trust and love, therefore come the capacity to love oneself in a healthy way. And the venue for learning what it is like to be loved and to love others is the family.

One crucial implication of learning basic trust, Macmurray argues, is that we can then establish the basis of some kind of political order.

> The possibility of the State depends upon an existing habit of co-operation which needs no enforcement; upon the existence of a society in which people do trust one another for the most part, though not under every condition or in all cases [but] provided we do in practice trust the majority of people to do in most circumstances what is expected of them, it is possible to devise mechanisms for dealing with the exceptions.[37]

It is this last point that suggests the transition from family to society. Not all families are the Swiss Family Robinson. Most families exist in complex webs of interrelationship with other families and with a whole host of other forms of association and support structures, personal and impersonal. Among these the two most important are the political and economic institutions of society. The latter provides the material goods which make human life possible: the former determines the moral principles and structures through which these goods can be most fairly provided for all the members of the society. Politics is the "maintaining, improving and adjusting [of] the indirect or economic relations of persons."[38] It expresses itself best in principles and institutions of justice which, in this sense, is the minimum of reciprocity and interest in the other; it is a kind of "zero or lower limit of moral behaviour." And it can be summarized, I think, pretty much as John Rawls does, as "fairness." Justice is the negative aspect of morality necessary to the constitution of the positive. It does not require direct, personal, mutual relations, but it does require a set of mutually agreed upon principles of fairness that keep our impersonal relations from degenerating into "minor mutualities" that mask injustice and unfair treatment under the rhetoric of love.

One crucial implication of this view is that the freedom of the individual within a personal community should not be confused with the freedom of the market place within an impersonal society. It is precisely this confusion that has marked much of the debate about the relation between public and private in the United States. A market place is where economic goods (without which personal life is severely impoverished both materially and spiritually) are produced and exchanged. It necessarily presupposes disproportional degrees of freedom. Those without adequate resources to produce or purchase those goods necessary for a good life become less well-off. But if the economic order is a means (the negative) to a fully personal life (the positive), then the freedom necessary to maintain the market must *always* be qualified and conditioned by the end it serves. The rhetoric that extols unlimited freedom in the market place (i.e., no governmental regulation) overlooks both the degree to which unequal freedom prevails in practice and the more fully personal ends such impersonal economic freedom is supposed to serve. Macmurray was highly critical of the liberal view of society which denied to the government the "power to use the economic resources of the community for the benefit of the community."[39] Thus Macmurray had no problem endorsing what he called positive government which, ideally, sees its duty to be using the resources of the people for the welfare of the people. And this means determining the economic life of the society.[40] In contemporary terms it means the regulation of the economic order by society in the service of community and justice. And society's vehicle for determining control and regulation of the market is politics.

As I mentioned at the outset, there are many proponents of family values who steadfastly decry government regulation of the market place, confusing the freedom necessary for the full development of personal life with the freedom of the free market. What they fail to see is that in an unregulated market negative forces of greed and self interest are unleashed that are inimical to family life.[41] A family, to take only one example, that cannot afford health care because it is offered only as a market product (and therefore the providers systematically deny access to the sick, the poor and un- or underinsured because it is not profitable to do otherwise), is effectively denied the very resources necessary for a healthy life and strong personal relationships. But the provision of health care is a public issue: the politics that will determine its availability, cost, and quality will be determined in the public sphere of political power according to some public agreement on social principles of justice. It cannot remain an entirely private matter even though one of the ultimate effects of such public action will be upon persons in their most private intimate relationships.

Public life is necessary to the full constitution of the self, just as the impersonal and negative is necessary to the full constitution of personal relationships. Without a strong public life, private life would close in upon itself. It would have no access to primary goods necessary for the completion of the personal life: goods which neither the individual nor the family alone can provide efficiently and effectively. Private life would be shunted from the necessity of maintaining an intention for inclusive community. Such a community, while not capable of being fully instantiated in practice, must nevertheless always be a norm against which the tendencies of the private self to close itself off from others must be checked. The more we nurture our public, albeit impersonal and societal relations, the more we open ourselves to extending the boundaries of our communities, without ever succumbing to the totalitarian impulse to impose universality upon unwilling and unprepared persons and distinct national or ethnic societies.

Private and public, therefore, are mutually complementary dimensions of human life which stand in the same relation of positive to negative as do personal to impersonal forms of human relationship. Understanding the complex dynamics of that relation will inform both our understanding of the family and of the public life with which it is integrally involved. To divide them is to conquer them: to sustain their dynamic relationship is to nourish and complement them.

NOTES

[1]   It should be obvious throughout that I intend to use the notion of the political to refer to those spheres and values of life that have to do with our social relations. Every society has political values: and "politics" is the means by which these are determined. As I will argue the political is a direct outgrowth of personal relations even though it does not contain some of the most important elements in those relations which are direct, mutual, loving, and intimate.

[2]   David Fergusson, 'Macmurray's Philosophy of the Family,' *Appraisal,* 1.2 (1996), 68–74.

[3]   I mean to refer here to political philosophies, not to particular political programs.

[4]   Communitarians' use of the term "community" is misleading if it is taken to incorporate or be equivalent to what Macmurray calls "community." In fact, most communitarian thinking uses "community" synonymously with "society." In failing to distinguish the two, communitarianism leaves itself vulnerable to most of the charges of its critics, a vulnerability Macmurray's philosophy is not subject to.

[5]   See especially Marilyn Friedman, *What Are Friends For?* (Ithaca: Cornell University Press, 1993), 'Feminism and Modern Friendship,' 237.

[6]   John Macmurray, *Persons in Relation* 155.

[7]   He may well be influenced here, as elsewhere in his philosophy, by Hegel, who called the family the "ethical root" of the state G.W.F. Hegel, *Hegel's Philosophy of Right*, trans. with notes by T.M. Knox (London: Oxford University Press, 1967), 154.

[8]   John Macmurray, *Persons in Relation*, 156.

[9]   *Persons in Relation*, 157–8.

[10] *Persons in Relation*, 34.

[11] *Persons in Relation*, 33–34.

[12] *Persons in Relation*, 34.

[13] *Persons in Relation*, 35.

[14] *Persons in Relation*, 37.

[15] We should note, as Macmurray does, that the distinction between personal and impersonal relations is not identical to that between direct and indirect relations with others. Direct relations involve a personal acquaintance with the other. Indirect relations are between persons who do not know each other personally. Thus all indirect relations are impersonal but not all direct relations are personal. I may know you (have a direct relationship with you) but not choose to have a positively motivated personal relationship with you. See *Persons in Relation*, 43.

[16] In light of the feminist critique of traditional views of the family, Macmurray explicitly argues that his use of the term "mother" is not a biological one. It simply means the adult who care for the infant. "The mother may be an aunt, or an elder sister or a hired nurse. She need not even be a female. A man can do all the mothering that is necessary, if he is provided with a feeding-bottle, and learns how to do it in precisely the same fashion that a woman must learn." *Persons in Relation*, 50. This assertion both opens up the boundaries of what a family can be and might be argued to have overlooked the importance of breast-feeding that is now regarded by many as essential to the physical as well as emotional health of the developing child.

[17] *Persons in Relation*, 53.

[18] *Persons in Relation*, 60.

[19] *Persons in Relation*, 62–3.

[20] *The Self as Agent*, 108.

[21] *Persons in Relation*, 80.

[22] *Persons in Relation*, 91.

[23] *Persons in Relation*, 92.

[24] *Persons in Pelation*, 156.

[25] This is why, perhaps, Freud and other psychologists have rightly focused on the importance of the early years in child-raising and why they are so fraught with danger and expectation. It also suggests some interesting connections between Macmurray's work and that of object-relations theorists who stress the importance of relationality, and in particular of the "good enough mother" in the development of a healthy self. It may be no accident that Macmurray's work and the development of object-relations theory both occur at the same time and in the same place: W.D. Fairbairn was a contemporary Scot and Harry Guntrip was Macmurray's student.

[26] *Persons in Pelation*, 105.

[27] *Persons in Pelation*, 122.

[28] Even within the family itself, over time, relations will wax and wane between personal and impersonal. There will be times when members of the family need to withdraw from each other both to deepen their own individuality and to challenge abusive and perverse forms of "love."

[29] *Persons in Pelation*, 150.

[30] Macmurray reminds us that no one person ought to be intentionally excluded from the mutual relationships of community because such exclusion would be based on fear. But while open to the possibility of entering into mutual relations with everyone, not everyone will be capable of entering into those relations nor will we in any given instance or contingent social arrangement.

[31] Will Kymlicka, 'Liberalism and Communitarianism,' *Canadian Journal of Philosophy*, 18 (1988), 185 & 187.

[32] Objectivity in thinking is intimately related to the capacity for emotional objectivity: Macmurray insists that we need to develop appropriate emotional responses to others congruent with their "objective" natures. Emotional obsession with a toy to the exclusion of persons is not objectively appropriate, nor is emotional withdrawal from those with the capacity and willingness to love the child

heterocentrically. But learning how and upon what appropriate objects to express one's emotions needs to be learned within the context of the family.

[33] This fact explains why many physicians and psychiatrists do not have "personal" relationships with their patients.

[34] This is one aspect of John Rawls' famous argument that we develop the principles of justice behind a veil of ignorance without knowing anything about ourselves or others that are directly personal.

[35] Lawrence Thomas, *Living Morally* (Philadelphia: Temple University Press, 1989), viii & 88.

[36] Thomas, *Living Morally*, 176–77.

[37] Macmurray, *Persons in Relation*, 191.

[38] Macmurray, *Persons in Relation*, 188.

[39] Macmurray, *Constructive Democracy* (London: Faber and Faber, 1943), 15.

[40] Macmurray, *Constructive Democracy*, passim. Macmurray at that time leaned heavily toward a socialist determination of the economic order. But in this respect he was, I think, a pragmatist and would permit varying kinds and degrees of government control under different circumstances, provided only that the end of such control was the just and fair provision of economic resources for people who need them in order sustain and nourish more direct personal relationships.

[41] For a thorough and persuasive discussion of how de-regulation in America has affected private as well as public life, see Robert Kuttner, *Everything for Sale* (New York: Alfred A. Knopf, 1997).

CHAPTER TWELVE

The Point of Politics: Friendship and Community in Macmurray[1]

Michael Fielding

There is no doubt that an awful lot of pious and pernicious nonsense is talked about community. This is not, of course, a new phenomenon. Its capacity for inwardness, for exclusion, and for the comfortable curtailment of human aspiration is too often matched by the bright celebration of a partial past and an orderly, if predictable, future. Even as we approach the twenty-first century, the combination of benign atavism and nostalgic aspiration continues to have a visceral appeal, at least for those whose historical presumptions are protected and whose proposed futures seem less fragmented and forlorn than the persistent uncertainties of an increasingly fractious present.

Ray Pahl has long been amongst those who have both reminded us of questions we need to ask and posed possibilities and alternatives to which we can respond. 'The Politics of Friendship,' jointly authored with Liz Spencer,[2] is the latest in a series of timely interventions[3] that engage with dilemmas of social cohesion and individual flourishing, issues which remain as centrally important to personal and political experience as they do to sociological and philosophical attempts to understand their nature and guide our action.

Pahl and Spencer on the Politics of Friendship

At the heart of their negative thesis is the charge that communitarianism is likely to worsen our current crises of social cohesion for three main reasons. First, it is historically myopic. It retrieves from communities of the past what it finds congenial and ignores what it does not. Thus, insufficient recognition is given to aspects of community which trade the emergence of significance, meaning and identity of its members against the diminution, marginalisation or exclusion of those who, both internally and externally, offer alternative views of what the community might become. Secondly, its valorisation of a supposedly golden age not only skews its historical perception, it distorts its capacity to see the present. Communitarianism is likely to further moral panic rather than reduce it because "the moral weapons of a fuzzy communitarianism"[4] obscure the true nature of changing reality; an ill-informed, essentially superficial perception of social decay rests upon a propensity, not merely to glamorise a chimerical past, but to demonise a complex, contested present. Thirdly, this double misreading of the past and the present is exacerbated by an obsession with what *ought* to be to such an extent that it blinds communitarians to the necessity of "building on what *is*."

Against what amounts to an ill-considered, often frightened, response to dilemmas and difficulties of postmodernity Pahl and Spencer argue for a reconsideration of current social trends which recognises what is positive, creative and liberating in the uncertain, risky reality of contemporary life. Central to Pahl and Spencer's positive thesis is the argument that friendship is "a positive, new and important theme in contemporary society."[5] There are broadly four aspects to their advocacy. First, we need to re-engage with deeper understandings of friendship, such as those offered by Aristotle in *The Nicomachean Ethics*, which suggest a threefold bond based on enjoyment of each other's company, functional utility, and common commitment to the good. Secondly, we need to deepen our understanding of the nature of micro-social realities and go beneath the surface of taken-for-granted notions like "social networks" which tell us very little about the meaning and content of specific relationships. Thirdly, we need to develop new terms which, in reflecting new realities rather than old aspirations, are more helpful to us in the challenge of creative social policy. In this regard, the concept of a "social convoy" is suggested as a useful term "for the real, as opposed to the imagined sets of relationships that people carry with them through their lives."[6] Lastly, the key issues and concerns underlying the anachronistic vagaries of communitarianism can be more appropriately met by encouraging the third component of the Aristotelean notion of friendship—namely, friendship "as a common commitment to the good." It is here that we see "one of the clearest hints towards the politics of friendship"[7] which provides their substantive and preferred alternative to the "confused rhetoric of community."[8]

Critique of Pahl and Spencer

There is much to applaud in Pahl and Spencer's advocacy of the politics of friendship; its challenge is at once authentically and engagingly contemporary, properly impatient with dissembling rhetoric, challenging of past and present status quo, and imaginatively and responsibly probing, both in its analysis and its alternatives. It is, however, deeply flawed in two important respects.

First, it is superficial, not in the sense of being trite or uninteresting, but in the sense that, despite its claims to the contrary, it fails to probe far enough beneath the surface of human interaction to provide us with sufficiently robust alternatives. It lacks a convincing philosophical account of human being and becoming on which any adequate articulation of friendship or community must rest. Whilst Aristotle may provide a good starting point, there is also much to be said, if not for an alternative ending, at least for an alternative route. The account of friendship implied and intermittently articulated in their account too often misses the point or hits it unwittingly, and, therefore, less convincingly than it might. Thus, it is not clear what the relation is, if any, between friendship and community. Are they now one and the same thing, and if they are not, are we to write off community as irretrievably unhelpful, doubtfully and questionably attainable, or both? And what of the insistence that we concentrate on what *is* or what works, rather than what *ought* to be? Even if we were to be clearer about what "it" is, would it not also be helpful to know *why* it works and whether there is some relation between its efficacy and the moral quality of what it is intended? Is the connection between means and ends not important here?

Secondly, it lacks clarity at the very point at which it is most needed. This is most evident in its failure to tackle the relation between the personal, the social and the political. Certainly, there are references to social policy and taking politicians to task for not only ignoring the promise and possibility of friendship as a social adhesive, but also failing to devise social policy which promotes it. However, other than recommending the development of a more sensitive form of interpersonal mapping in the context of care for the elderly, it does not give us any hints as to what a friendship-friendly social policy might mean, let alone what it might look like. And what about the very notion of the politics of friendship? In the contested context of post-modernity rather than relative homogeneity of Athenian civic republicanism, is there no sense in which this unlikely combination might be seen as problematic? No sense that the very spontaneity and freedom entailed in friendship might sit uncomfortably within the framework of politics?

Having suggested major reservations about the adequacy of Pahl and Spencer's position, I believe nonetheless that, in identifying friendship as a matter whose importance is matched only by its neglect, they are on to something which is of immense significance in our current efforts to understand the nature of human association and its relation to individual and communal flourishing. What we need is, first, an account of friendship and community which not only helps us to understand the nature of the two more clearly, but also answers the quite proper concerns of those who see in community the perpetuation of much that is regressive and perniciously anachronistic. What we need is, in effect, an emancipatory account of community at the heart of which lies an individuality conditional upon the kind of vibrant mutuality that friendship typically offers. Secondly, we need an account of community which helps us to understand, not just its nature, but also its relation to the political, the social, and the personal dimensions of human experience. We need to understand the distinctions between them, which is prior to what and why. Above all else, we need to understand how we might create community of the sort that is both the means and end of an inclusive human fulfilment.

Towards an Emancipatory Account of Friendship and Community

Such an account does exist and is to be found in the work of Macmurray, a life-long socialist and Scottish philosopher whose work had such a profound impact on many thousands of people between the two world wars and, more recently, on Tony Blair. Writing from a standpoint which engaged energetically, not only with the work of Marx, but, remarkably for the period, with the early Marx, Macmurray argues for the significance of friendship and community as the centrally important

condition of human freedom. For Macmurray we become ourselves, we
develop as human beings through trying to understand and take into
account the nature and value of what surrounds us. Particularly important
in our development as persons is our encounter with other persons and
central to that encounter is the persistent and insistent fact of mutuality.
The notion of an isolated, unencumbered self turns out to be a nonsense.
"We need one another to be ourselves. This complete and unlimited
dependence of each of us upon the others is the central and crucial fact of
personal existence. Here, Macmurray says, "is the basic fact of our
human condition."[9]

There are, however, some kinds of relationship between human
beings that enable us to be more fully ourselves and pre-eminent
amongst them is friendship, a relationship which Macmurray regards as
absolutely basic and absolutely universal and one which does not differ
in any fundamental respect from community. The importance of
friendship lies in the nature of its ground motive and in the principles
which govern its emergence. Its motive is essentially other-regarding; it
is about concern for, care of, and delight in the other person as a person.
It is a relationship that has no point or purpose other than the mutual
expression of fellowship. If you ask what the purpose of a friendship is,
the asking of the question implies that it is not a friendship at all, but
rather a relationship which, despite having the veneer of friendship, in
fact has ulterior or instrumental reasons for its existence.

The guiding principles of friendship provide one of the most
interesting aspects of Macmurray's account and it is in them that the
emancipatory potential of friendship and community emerge most
strongly. Here, at last, we have a philosophical account of community
which enables us to cut through the undergrowth of paternalism,
hierarchy and repression that have disfigured so much of its history and
its misuse for so long. For Macmurray, at the heart of friendship and
community lie the two mutually conditioning, constitutive principles of
equality and freedom.

> Equality is a condition of freedom in human relations. For if we do not treat
> one another as equals, we exclude freedom from the relationship. Freedom,
> too, conditions equality. For if there is constraint between us there is fear; and
> to counter the fear we must seek control over its object, and attempt to
> subordinate the other person to our own power. Any attempt to achieve

freedom without equality, or to achieve equality without freedom, must, therefore, be self-defeating.[10]

Two further points are pertinent here. First, because Macmurray offers us a clear philosophical account of friendship and community, he also enables us to distinguish between, on the one hand, the changing forms of these relationships, and, on the other hand the underlying energy and integrity which provide their emancipatory edge. For example, debates about the family too often ignore the fundamental issues at stake, issues which have to do with motives and principles, not with the specifics of their historical articulation. It is only thus that we can gain access to the fundamental rather than the peripheral issues. It is only thus that we can appreciate the nature of Macmurray's prescient suggestion in the mid-1930s that "the family as we have known it, *must* cease to function as the social unit. For it rests upon the refusal of individual personality and individuated life to women."[11] It is not the family *per se* that is important, but what the family has, at least on some accounts, traditionally expressed and enabled. Should it cease to do so, it must be replaced or supplemented in much that same way as Pahl and Spencer advocate. What Macmurray offers us that they do not is some way of understanding *why* this might be appropriate; whilst they interestingly, but merely, describe the facts of change, Macmurray helps us to *understand* that change in relation to what is centrally important in human flourishing.

Secondly, because it is so intimately bound up with the conditions under which we can be most fully ourselves, friendship is for Macmurray "the supreme value in life, and the source of all other values."[12] It is the one true measure of success. Despite the quite other values which our society proclaims, he urges us to understand that our success "will have only one measure; it will be measured by the extent and depth of your friendships with men and women. That alone will benefit the world; within that, and within that alone, all other value for yourself or the world will grow."[13]

The Nature of the Political and the Communal

Another key feature of Macmurray's account of community which is particularly pertinent today is its capacity to help us understand the difficult, but crucially important, interrelationship between community, society and the realm of politics. There are two stages in Macmurray's argument here. First, we need to understand the differences between these forms of human association. Secondly, we need to understand the relationships between them and the relative importance of each. Only then can we develop a proper understanding of what we might wish to achieve and how we might set about its accomplishment.

One way of coming at this first stage of clarifying the broad differences between the social, the political and the communal is to grasp Macmurray's central distinction between two fundamentally different ways in which human beings relate to each other. On the one hand we have what he calls "functional" forms of unity and on the other hand we have forms of human association that he terms "personal."

Functional relations, which are expressive of the twin realms of the social and the political, are those in which human beings relate to each other for a particular purpose and it is those purposes that define the relationship. At the micro level an example might be a customer buying an item from a shop assistant; at the macro level the reference point is society in which human beings co-operate in a range of ways to achieve common purposes.

Whilst functional relationships are important in getting our daily work done they do not allow us to enter into them with anything other than a part of ourselves. They seem to require of us "a willingness to overlook and suppress the peculiarly personal elements in our relationships with one another," or, as he puts it later in the same paper, "the institutional life of society can never be free... we must always be less than ourselves in it."[14]

In contrast to a functional relation, a *personal* relation, in Macmurray's special use of the term, is one in which two persons enter into relation with one another as whole persons. Their relationship exists for its own sake, and not for the sake of some function or particular purpose. At the micro level, friendship is his preferred exemplar; at the macro level it is expressed in community which consists, not in the conjunction of common purposes, but in the sharing of a common life.

This is not, of course, to say that relations of friendship or community do not involve the practicalities of purposes and action. A personal or communal relationship produces purposes, but, and this is the key point, it is not defined by them. Those purposes may change and those very changes contribute to the richness of the relationship; they are expressive of it. However, the reverse is true in a functional relationship. Because functional relations are defined by their purposes, a change of purposes automatically dissolves the relation.

Achieving Community: On the Importance and Impotence of Politics

If the social and the political are essentially functional ways in which human beings relate to each other, and the communal is essentially a non-instrumental expressive relation of mutuality, what is the proper relation between them? Which is prior? What is the relation between community and politics? Which is most important and why?

With regard to priority, for Macmurray, the answer is quite clear. Community is prior to politics in at least two important senses. First, it is prior in the sense that the whole point of politics is the provision of conditions under which human beings can be and become most fully themselves. All functional, that is to say social, political and economic activity must be brought within the compass of human well-being and not the other way round. Their sole justification resides in their capacity to further rather than diminish human flourishing. Thus, in a memorable observation, as pertinent to day as it was when it was uttered over twenty-five years ago, Macmurray reminds us that "an economic efficiency which is achieved at the expense of the personal life is self-condemned, and in the end self-frustrating... the economic is for the sake of the personal."[15]

Secondly, community is prior to politics in the very practical sense that without community there can be no politics of a democratic kind. In one of his most remarkable short books on the nature of community, *Conditions of Freedom*, Macmurray argues that "a democratic polity is possible only for a human community which has established a common way of life upon a basis of mutual trust; and the extent and quality of the freedom it provides depends upon the extent to which those it governs and organises are in communion with one another."[16]

If politics is for the sake of community and community alone can provide the conditions of a developing democratic polity, how are we to understand the relation between the two in a practical, not just a theoretical sense? What are we to do now? If community is both the end and means of human fulfilment, how are we to achieve it?

Three further points may be helpful here. First, we need to be absolutely clear that community cannot be organised; it cannot be ordered into existence any more than friendship can be imposed on us. The capacity of politicians, and indeed, whole societies, to ignore or misunderstand this point has led to disasters exemplified by the horrors of fascism and the totalitarian betrayal of the Soviet Union. Macmurray's observation that we live in an age of "unparalleled effort and unparalleled frustration" and that whilst "man's power of achievement has grown vast beyond belief... his capacity to achieve any serious human purpose is diminishing at an alarming rate"[17] refers primarily to the catastrophic misunderstanding of the relation between the realm of politics and the realm of community, between the functional and the personal.

Secondly, whilst there is no technique for achieving community a centrally important understanding of its nature brings us back to the motives which sustain it and those which destroy it. Amongst the most insistent strands of Macmurray's arguments arises from his conviction that fear is the greatest single obstacle to community, whether it be community on a local or international scale, or whether it be community in its quintessential form of friendship between two persons. For Macmurray, "The problem of community is the problem of overcoming fear... All other problems are contained in the problem of maintaining the network of positive personal relationship which constitutes a human community."[18] Such a network of positive personal relationship is essentially about the development of a common way of life informed by the inclusive values of freedom and equality.

Thirdly, whilst politics cannot create community it is nonetheless necessary to it. Whilst the functional and the personal, the political and the communal, are fundamentally different from each other, they are inextricably linked. What then is their proper relation? This is perhaps best summed up in Macmurray's suggestion that "The functional life is *for* the personal life; the personal life is *through* the functional life."[19] It is neither possible nor desirable to keep the two separate because "the shape of one decides the outlines of the other."[20]

Politics, then, impacts on and contributes towards the reality of community. Community, for Macmurray, is not about "the mere sentimentality"[21] of endless, ungrounded talk; community must attend to the practical needs of our common humanity. Indeed, this co-operation for the satisfaction of one another's distinct individual needs is the only way in which a community can become real. "This," he says, "is the absolute law of personal nature."[22] The common stock of wealth that we produce through our economic and political co-operation is the stuff out of which we can care for each other's material needs and it is the distribution and use of this resource that provides an indispensable basis on which to judge the sincerity and the authenticity of our communal aspirations. "Our fellowship as a community only becomes real—only gets hands and feet—when in our daily work we provide for one another's needs, and rejoice that we are doing so."[23]

Politics is hugely important. It is, as Macmurray reminds us, "necessary to freedom; the more necessary the larger the society it embraces."[24] However, we must never forget that the meaning of the functional/political lies in the personal/communal, and not the other way around.

> The state is for community; the community is through the state.... The state must be the servant, not the master of the people.... A good political and economic system is one which provides as fully as possible for the personal life of its citizens, and for all of them equally... Where the state serves the community, its power is used by the community, for personal, human ends. But if the state becomes master of the community, it can only use human life as a means of power.[25]

For Macmurray, "persons, not purposes are absolute."[26]

The Wider Relevance of Macmurray

Macmurray is one of the great unsung figures of twentieth-century British philosophy. Seventy years ago he was arguing that understanding the nature of the self and community constituted the central problem of western philosophy. Despite holding prestigious posts at Balliol College, Oxford, University College, London (where, ironically, he preceded A.J. Ayer as the Grote Professor of Logic and Mind), and the University of Edinburgh he was sidelined for most of his life by what Jonathan Rée has delightfully and tellingly described as "the logic louts" of analytic philosophy.[27]

Yet here was someone who argued for a distinction between what he called "real philosophy" and the central problems of the academic tradition. Here was a person who rejected the individualism of so many of his academic contemporaries and argued that the task of philosophy was essentially communal in the sense that its impetus, its focus and its validity should be grounded in the cultural dilemmas facing society, rather than in the freewheeling preferences of individual philosophers.[28] Here is a philosopher who attracted enormous audiences through his radio broadcasts in the summer of 1930 and January 1932 to such an extent that, although he was strongly attacked by some of the right wing press as the "Red Professor of Gower Street," his (very reputable) publishers, Faber & Faber, claimed that *Freedom in the Modern World*, first published in 1932 with five large reprintings in three years "has probably had a deeper more lasting effect than any other book of a philosophical character published this century." Here is someone who had great faith in the ordinary person and their entitlement to engage in debate and what he called "real thought" and who believed that philosophy would benefit, since "where the effort to popularise philosophy is a sincere effort of self-expression the philosopher will find himself forced, not into superficiality, but into deeper realisation of his own meaning."[29] Here is a philosopher who was centrally involved in the Christian-Marxist dialogue in the 1930s and who argued for the necessity of establishing an adequate understanding of persons which acknowledged the insights of Marx, but went the next crucial and difficult step in developing what he then called a "superdialectical," and later, "personal" understanding of human unity.

Here is a philosopher who, unlike so many within the current liberal-communitarian debate, explores and articulates a notion of community which is actually and insistently attentive to its philosophical nature. Here is a philosopher whose account of community avoids the watchful self-absorption of atomistic individualism and the earnest self-abrogation of its organic counterpart. Here is a philosopher whose understanding of community is inclusive, emancipatory and utterly central to the point, the practice, and promise, not only of philosophy, but of what it is to be and become more fully human.

It may be that Macmurray's time has come. The renewed interest in community, in the nature of persons, in the relation of the political and the communal, in the true nature of religion, and in the importance of education, not just of schooling are all issues with which he wrestled throughout his long life. The fact that Ray Pahl and Liz Spencer invite us to look again at friendship as a pivotal issue in contemporary society adds further weight to such a judgement. Macmurray is certainly a writer whose elegance and insight are immediately engaging and persistently profound; without what Bernard Crick once tellingly described as "the ugly carapace of footnotes," he draws us in to reflection which is invariably authentic, always properly and quietly demanding, and always linked to a revitalised re-engagement with the world. As Macmurray himself insisted, "All meaningful knowledge is for the sake of action, and all meaningful action for the sake of friendship."[30]

NOTES

[1]   This essay originally appeared in *Renewal*, 6.1, 1998, 55–64, and is reproduced with minor revisions by kind permission of the editor.

[2]   Ray Pahl and Liz Spencer, 'The Politics of Friendship,' *Renewal*, 5 (1997), 100–107.

[3]   Ray Pahl, "Friendly Society", *New Statesman & Society* (10 March, 1995), 20–22.

[4]   Pahl and Spencer, ibid., 101.

[5]   Ibid., 102.

[6]   Ibid., 104.

[7]   Ibid., 103.

[8]   Ibid., 106.

[9]   Macmurray, *Persons in Relation*, 211.

[10] Macmurray, *Conditions of Freedom*, 74.

[11] Macmurray, 'The Social Unit,' *New Britain Weekly*, (12 July 1933), 235.

[12] Macmurray, *The Kingdom of Heaven,* sermon preached at Balliol College, Oxford, 19 May, 1929 (Oxford: Oxonian Press, 1929,) 9pp.

[13] Ibid., 8.

[14] *Reason and Emotion*, 96, 105.

[15] *Persons in Relation*, 187, 188.

[16] *Conditions of Freedom*, 105.

[17] 'Freedom in the Personal Nexus,' in Anshen, R. (ed.), *Freedom: Its Meaning* (London: Allen & Unwin, 1942), 191.

[18] *Persons in Relation*, 161.

[19] 'Two Lives in One,' *Listener*, 36, (December, 1941), 822.

[20] Ibid.

21 *Persons in Relation*, 176.
22 *Creative Society*, 117.
23 'The Community of Mankind,' *Listener*, 36 (December, 1941) 856.
24 *Conditions of Freedom*, 105.
25 'The Community of Mankind,' op. cit., 856.
26 'Freedom in the Personal Nexus,' op. cit., 190.
27 J. Rée, 'Selflessness", *London Review of Books*, 8 May, 1997, 18.
28 'Dialectical Materialism as a Philosophy' in Levy, H., Macmurray, J., Fox, R., Page Arnot, R. Bernal, J.D. & Carritt, E.F., *Aspects of Dialectical Materialism* (London: Watts, 1934), 31–5.
29 *Freedom in the Modern World*, 17.
30 *The Self as Agent*, 15.

CHAPTER THIRTEEN

Universal Community and Justice

Nigel Dower

In this brief essay, in part a response to issues raised by several other essays in this volume, I want to explore what Macmurray means by "intending universal community". This is a rich concept, in some ways similar to Kant's "legislating for a kingdom of ends," and worth exploring in its own right. My approach is that if we are to make sense of this, we may need to adjust what we say about love and justice.

I approach this issue via two other questions, one to do with the relationship between community and society, the other to do with the relationship between love and justice. How one handles these two issues will turn out in the last analysis to be closely connected. My theme is that, if we can relax Macmurray's penchant for over-precise contrasts (which are not necessary for us still to retain the kernel of important truth in his thinking), we can make better sense of the complexity of personal relations and in particular we can make sense of the idea of "intending universal community."

Macmurray talks a lot about the value of community—whether it is the framework of a close community of a family or emanating out of friendship, or world community. Community is contrasted with society which, as a set of relationships can be based on various motives and interests. Community on the other hand is a set of relationships based on love and mutual respect. When Macmurray talks of "intending universal community" he is clearly postulating the possibility of a world of persons in relation, altogether richer than mere co-operation for mutual benefit (though we are of course far from achieving the latter in the world anyway). But he is also, I suggest, saying something important about the *present* relations we now stand in vis à vis all human beings.

Before looking further at Macmurray's idea of community, let me introduce the other issue I mentioned. As Kirkpatrick's essay brings out, Macmurray sets out a set of contrasts between love and justice, personal and impersonal, subjective and objective, recognition of free agency and the interpretation of behaviour as causally determined. Although in all relations, as Kirkpatrick and Downie show, Macmurray understood the impersonal to be involved in the personal (just how is a matter of interpretation), there is a clear picture that the sphere of justice, the public or the political is part of the "negative" phase and is "for the sake of the personal"—that is it is a means to the personal. We need good government, robust citizenship, democracy, justice as a framework in which the personal life can flourish and be extended.

Now there are two comments to be made about all this. First, it is in a way surprising that Macmurray seems to downgrade the political/public/sphere of justice as "negative" and not as of intrinsic importance or value. Given his intense rejection of the liberal tradition in which there is accepted the "contract of mutual convenience" so criticised by Plato and Aristotle, that is that the state is a necessary evil to tackle our selfishness and "unsociable sociability" (as Kant called it), it is surprising that he does not see more common cause with Plato, Aristotle and others in affirming our "political" nature in the sense that *part* of human flourishing consists precisely in participating in the governance of our common affairs. It may be true that good/flourishing cannot *consist in* such activities, that something would be missing and that this is the level of personal relations in the "private" sphere which Macmurray is keen to stress. But conversely life wholly conducted in the personal sphere, without any participation in the life of society (not community in Macmurray's sense) may be seen to be lacking too.

Need Macmurray be involved in denying the intrinsic importance of a certain kind of participation in the public sphere? There are two reasons for thinking not. First, picking up the statement "the functional is for the sake of the personal," the personal is expressed through the functional (where functional refers to creative work, public life or other social roles we enact), it seems possible to see the value of personal relations as embedded in a whole range of practices ranging from the private to the public. This however does not get us far enough. For it may still be held that in the public sphere e.g. that of a judge, administrator, politician or even teacher, one is essentially treating another being fairly/ impartially/

justly but it would only be accidental if one *happened* to have a personal relation of love/acceptance of real equality though in one's being a teacher, administrator and so on.

Part of what makes the activity valuable (and expressive of personhood) is the treatment of others as having a certain status as free, equal rational beings. Macmurray seems to make the recognition of this problematic because of his alignment of love and the personal with freedom and his alignment of justice and the impersonal with determinism. But this seems unnecessary. Both love and justice (and moral relations generally) presuppose freedom, as contrasted to a socially scientific view of others as subjects of a deterministic science, or a view of them as objects of manipulation, as things to be caused to do what one wants. So long as in whatever I am doing, as teacher, administrator or political activist, I am identifying the other as a free agent, equal in status as myself, that I am acknowledging their (and my) personhood.

It is furthermore difficult to see how Macmurray could deny this extension of the personal/free to justice/respecting rights and acceptance of the latter's intrinsic importance if we are to make sense of his claims about universal community. It strikes me that "intending universal community" is very similar to Kant's "willing a kingdom of ends" which is an expression of the will in one formulation of the Categorical Imperative. Kant's formulation is not a statement that we do, in any real sense, already exist in such a community. In one sense we do not and as we see in his work *The idea of a universal history with a cosmopolitan intent* Kant saw a "cosmopolitan" order of a world state as lying in the distant future. Nevertheless Kant is also a cosmopolitan in the sense that the same categorical imperative commits me *now* to treating all human beings as rational agents and as persons. I suggest that this double sense should also be applied to Macmurray's analysis of intending universal community. It is intending (and thus working towards) something that will exist in the future, but it is also acting now in a certain way towards all humans in the present (but with less emphasis upon rationality than Kant, both as the essence of the human and as the source of motivation).

This strongly suggests that Macmurray was really a *cosmopolitan* who accepted as a starting point the idea that all human beings are equally persons (with whom we could enter into personal relationships, were the circumstances right) and this is parallel to, though not identical to, Kant's idea of all human beings as "rational ends." The development of actual lived community (in the sociological sense of actually existing) is something to be aspired to as an expression of (ideal) universal community.

In this sense Macmurray is not on the side of modern communitarianism at all, insofar as the latter, as in MacIntyre, which wants to question or deny universal community precisely because moral values, identities and loyalties arise from and are sustained by shared practices and traditions of actual communities.

But how do we take the idea of intending universal community? It is not, I have suggested, merely a potentiality—something we will to come into existence in the future—but the expression of a current *attitude* towards all fellow human beings—to treat them as persons, as equal, etc. and precisely to work against practices and policies which frustrate the expression of this attitude. But two things need to be said about this.

This attitude cannot be expressed in the kind of love of another that Macmurray sees as the ideal of friendship and close relationships. It is nothing if not the affirmation of a certain status of all others as the basis upon which respect is grounded. This is none other than the basic stance of justice/fairness—not as an acceptance of a set of cold rules but a recognition of a certain equal status. This recognition is not personal in the full sense of a personal relationship of love or friendship, but it is in the *actual* affirmation of a certain status here and now combined with the *counterfactual* affirmation that were one to be in appropriate circumstances it would be possible to develop fully personal relations. (That we will never be in this situation vis à vis more than a tiny minority of the billions of people making up universal community is neither here nor there.)

Resistance to this way of taking Macmurray might come from two related moves. First universal community exists only in a second order way as a community of communities. Human beings belong to various communities—often geographically extended (like communities of academics or NGOs) and so the world community develops as an actuality through the growing membership of people in smaller communities which together make up the evolving world community or universal community.

Now this as a matter of fact may be how wider identities are formed and may be the catalyst to persons accepting the reality of being members of a world community (world citizens as some would say). But it need not be. Some world-wide communities, for instance with a strong sense of inclusion and exclusion, might indeed be hostile to others and thus antithetical to intending universal community. The only way such communities will point their members in the direction of "intending universal community" is that in addition to the loyalty within the group, they also affirm the common vision of human beings as equal persons.

It may be said that those communities which do show Macmurray's ideal of friendship and mutuality, unlike many actual communities or associations, do implicitly affirm universal community, and the more such communities exist the nearer the social reality of universal community will come. Kant is famous for supposing that in any moral decisions one is implicitly legislating for all, so any real personal relationship will implicitly contain a way of affirming all other with like personhood.

There are however two corollaries of seeing affirming universal community implicit within the genuinely lived community Macmurray commended. First, there is the need to affirm in my own actions the rights and equal status of *all* human beings with whom I actually interact, whether or not they are inside a richer community, and for this the framework of justice is clearly presupposed. Second, to intend universal community is to engage in actions which are neither expressions of such close community relationships nor expressions of respect for any other person one interacts with, but are done to create the structures in which wider community can occur—through social and political action.

One way of capturing the idea universal community being implicit in particular community is to make a point made by Mayeroff in *On Caring* that if x loves or cares for the "other" (y), x wills y's "good". If y loves another (z) he wills z's good. Now if we assume that in loving another one identifies with another in that one's good in a sense is partly constituted by that good, a grand chain of love can be postulated whereby if x love y and y loves z, x implicitly affirms and wills the good of z (because y's good is by y's love identified with that of z) Thus a community of all human beings in which networks of human beings affirming each other's good would be a community in which each of us affirms the good of anyone. Thus although I could not stand in personal relationships to more than a few of the billions of people of the planet, I would still affirm their equal personhood through the recognition of this network.

Whether Macmurray's position is helped by the last suggestion of the chain of love, we remain with the challenge of tying together into a single account Macmurray's emphasis upon the centrality of personal relations based on love with his affirming of universal moral community. Some account of the latter is needed and my suggestion is that aligning the complex apparatus of justice as a principle of equal treatment (not as equivalent to laws) on the love/personal side of the personal/impersonal divide (with social sciences on the other) and thus seeing the attitude of love and justice as both different ways of affirming the personal, makes better sense of his idea of intending universal community and may be helpful in other ways too.

CHAPTER FOURTEEN

Privacy and the Form of the Personal

Iain Torrance

Although John Macmurray was not a systematic thinker, his work is immensely suggestive and provides hints for much constructive development across a range of areas. The aim here is to quarry from him, so as to clarify what we may mean by "privacy."

In what way is the notion of privacy unclear or an area of difficulty? The public/private boundary became contentious during the pursuit of the Princess of Wales by the media, and the counter claim was made that she had "invaded her own privacy." The situation has been made ridiculous by attempts to muzzle disclosure of the costs of the Lord Chancellor's Pugin-style lavatory and hand-painted wallpaper. The issue is that there is an area of our lives many of us claim is private, but it is difficult to know precisely where to draw the boundary, and even harder to know on what basis it is to be policed. What is it that we are defending? The appeal to privacy in Western society is so various that, to take the discussion further, we might consider several dimensions. There could be many others.

First, at a meeting of the Society for the Study of Christian Ethics in 1988, Trudy van Asperen attempted to explicate the concept of professional confidentiality.[1] This required a prior account of why some things are secret. She offered both a word study and pointed to certain anthropological contexts. Thus, "secret" comes from the Latin *secretum*, meaning "that which is set apart." Here secrecy has connotations of sacredness, prohibition and the numinous. There is also a link, illustrated by the German *heimlich*, between what is secret and what belongs to the home. Yet another dimension is marked by the Greek *arretos* which marks that which cannot or should not be spoken because it is 'shameful, dishonourable or abominable."[2] Anthropologically, van Asperen suggested that in many societies the ability to deceive is recognised as a sign of social competence, and that behind this there lay the development of a sense of an inner self which is hidden from view. The person who speaks of intimate matters to strangers is considered disordered, unable to distinguish between self and others. The adult, she suggests, has an inner core, and respect for a person is, in part, to do with respecting this. Our picture of a nightmare society is of one where human life is totally transparent. There are, she suggests, activities in which we may appraise our performance even as we act, but also another range where the actor is so immersed that self appraisal is impossible. Prayer,[3] sex and religious ecstasy might be examples of such immersed activity. If here the agent may not tolerate even self-observation, the observation of another is downright intolerable: "The eye of the observer is destructive of intimacy."[4] With this, van Asperen might have thought that she had made her case, but she was confronted by an extraordinarily perceptive observation from Nicholas Peter Harvey.[5] He questioned her underlying notion of what it is to be human, with its attendant suggestion that adult wisdom consists in balancing disclosure and concealment. Harvey suggests that this is to confuse social adjustment for moral advance.[6] Rather than cultivating balance, he suggests we pin our hope on "a transfigured humanity, where openness and privacy are not at odds, where 'what is said in the chambers will be shouted from the housetops' (Luke 12:3)."[7] What is interesting here is the linking of privacy and fundamental understandings of what it is to be human.[8] Harvey reminds us of Jesus, who had nothing to lose, nowhere else to go and nothing to conceal.[9]

Second, it may be suggested that there is an interesting, but often unexamined, assumption of privacy behind the constructive proposals of contemporary non biblicist writers on Christian ethics. The Scottish theologian Elizabeth Templeton has, on a number of occasions, reminded the Christian community that we do not worship a God "who has his binoculars trained on the bedrooms of the world."[10] I believe that her instinct here is right, but it is easily misheard. A sense of privacy is indeed defended, but this is not the negative sense of privacy enshrined in the phrase "what consenting adults do in private." Privacy there means a right to freedom from interference, provided that one's actions are not abusive, and do not interfere with others. Privacy is then a defensive notion, rooted perhaps in Mill's *Essay on Liberty*, and it is nothing to do with Christianity. Elizabeth Templeton, I believe, is saying something different and more profound. The curtains are not peeked at, because God is not prurient.[11] What goes on behind them is private because it is personal. The specifics are not fundamental and may be disattended from. Despite this, Christians yearn for openness, for the fuller integration of which present sexual activity is merely the sign. This is neither saying that God is not there, nor that what goes on is a matter of indifference, but that there is a limited space for human difference. The eschatological exposure of the new Jerusalem is not to be moralised into a present legalism, but neither is it, for the Christian, ever to be less than a hope. We yearn not to be secret. This qualifies Peter Harvey's position. The lack of privacy is eschatological, not ethical, and is not legislatively to be dragged into the present. Christians still long for openness, and the persons we will then be shall not be threatened by it, for God will wipe away every tear from their eyes.[12] Privacy exists, then, but its time is qualified. There is a link between our understandings of privacy and person.

Third, I would draw attention to what we tend to call "private opinion." This is speech from the private realm, rather than action within it. This is much more tentative, as it is harder to distinguish from "personal opinion" and the distinction, if it exists, may be little more than emphasis. We are, however, seeing how the private and the personal overlap. The most interesting literary example I know is in Book IX of Homer's *Iliad*. The context is one familiar to any reader of Alasdair MacIntyre, though it is not an example MacIntyre discusses. Achilles is the supreme warrior, a minor king called to defend the honour of the high king, Agamemnon. Agamemnon takes Achilles' maidservant, Briseis, and Achilles retires to brood by his ships. The Trojans advance out of Troy now unchecked and threaten the Achaean camp. Agamemnon, fearing ruin, sends a delegation led by Odysseus, to plead with Achilles to return to the fight. Odysseus, on behalf of Agamemnon, in an elegant speech offers Achilles exaggerated recompense: tripods, cauldrons, gold, horses, women (including Briseis), cities, one of his own daughters. No one could resist such honour and overflowing generosity. But then Achilles makes one of the most extraordinary and moving speeches in ancient literature.[13] Though Briseis was simply the captive of his spear[14] he loved her with all his heart. She was just a slave, but she is irreplaceable, and he hates the proffered gifts.[15] For this passionate outpouring of private feeling, which is sharper and more idiosyncratic than simply personal, Achilles has been called "the one Homeric hero who does not accept the common language."[16] He threatens the link between Homeric language and reality. It is argued that Homer, whose poems are, anyhow, almost entirely made up of formulaic elements, is finally unable to express this depth of discord.[17] What I am trying to point to from this illustration is the human capacity for innovative expression welling out of private belief. Private feeling may be the fuel for change and development of the person. At the end of the speech, Odysseus, who was portrayed as the master of words, is silenced and seems cheapened. Phoenix, the old retainer and upholder of the heroic values, weeps, and Achilles, even in the confusion of his speech, acquires a new grandeur.

Privacy, then, is complex. Let us see what resources John Macmurray offers us.[18] In fact, he hardly mentions the word "private." Instead he discusses what he calls "the personal life." He maintains that within us there is a central core "which is personal in a special sense, and through which all the rest *may* take on a special character that makes it personal."[19] This, of course, anticipates Trudy van Asperen. Macmurray then distinguishes this core of personal life from individual and social life. Personal life is not the life we live in solitude.[20] Somewhat famously, he says: "We are not particularly personal in our baths."[21] Instead, the personal life is "essentially a life of relations between people,"[22] but yet it is not the same as social life. Social life, though also relational is not based on the commitment of the whole of ourselves. To interrelate socially, we have also to hold back, and Macmurray suggests that this tempts us to identify the personal with the individual life. But this is an illusion: "to be ourselves at all, we need other people."[23] He takes this further: personal life "demands a relationship with one another in which we can be our whole selves and have complete freedom to express everything that makes us what we are."[24] Freedom and equality are prerequisites for personal life. It is the life "in which we accept one another freely for what we are."[25] All of this has ethical implications. Macmurray criticises orthodox European morality for being intellectual and external.[26] It reduces goodness to a matter of rule obedience. He suggests that it was the externality of the Pharisees that Jesus condemned, and replaced with an inner emotional basis for behaviour[27]. Thus encouraged, Macmurray suggests that the guide for moral behaviour in sexual matters (the most private area of our lives) is chastity, and that chastity is "emotional sincerity."[28] Emotional sincerity in turn is explained as "an emotional grasp of reality."[29] Reality is emphasised. Love, he tells us, cannot abide deceit, pretence or unreality: it "rests only in the reality of the loved one, demands the integrity of its object, demands that the loved one should be himself,"[30] and sex "must fall within the life of personality and be an expression of love."[31]

There is a great deal here, and all we can do is pick at hints and suggestions. Macmurray's recovery of the notion of person is crucial. He effectively reverses a prevailing assumption that being a person means that one has qualified for a previously defined status, which is understood analogously to a natural kind. It is more that others confront us as person, than that we categorise them, much as we might identify a horse or a rabbit. I suggest that this reversal of the accepted approach is shown in Macmurray's realism. One encounters a person *in their reality*, requiring that they should *be themselves*. Macmurray set this out earlier in *Reason and Emotion:* "Reason is the capacity to behave consciously in terms of what is not ourselves... reason is the capacity to behave in terms of the nature of the object, that is to say, to behave objectively."[32] Thus, to be in personal relation is to allow oneself to hear the other out of his own reality, not to impose our rationality upon him. Person is not an external concept, but something the other gives content to from within. Although Macmurray does not put it like this, I suggest it amounts to a shift from the Latin *persona* to the Greek *hypostasis*,[33] from a static to a dynamic concept.

But so far as privacy goes, what does it offer us? I suggest it provides a different perspective on what is really at stake and to be guarded in what we call privacy. Our usual idea is based in a static Western individualism, which encourages a quasi-legal notion of privacy,[34] illustrated by parallels of property and trespass. Macmurray's suggestion is that the inner core of a person is in its integrity and inexhaustible life in relationship. Achilles' outburst was private, but came from the core of his being and had to be taken account of, embarrassing though it was. Macmurray's aside that we are not very personal in our baths is to the point. Nakedness need not be an ultimate issue, and prurience over the specifics of sexual actions may be a distraction. So I want first to suggest that Macmurray provides an alternative way of gauging what is fundamental and what is peripheral through a dynamic and extended understanding of the personal, in which the private has a real but limited place. An independent, but interestingly similar move was made by Michael Polanyi in the much imitated account he gives of skills.[35] In the performance of a skill, there is an integration of the theoretical and the practical in which the attention of the actor is poured into the task being undertaken. Though there will be unique personal qualifications and gifts, these private elements are dis-attended from and made subsidiary to an external focus. So performance of a skill is a deeply personal act in which that which is private is given a real, but not focal, role. Performance of the skill would break down if we concentrated focally on the private.

Second, Macmurray has been seminal, though often unacknowledged, in the personalist approaches to marital and sexual ethics we see in the work of Jack Dominion, Helen Oppenheimer, Kevin Kelly, Elizabeth Templeton[36] and many others. This approach, invoking the relationality of persons, and then appealing to mutuality and freedom, creativity and integration as quality controls, though undoubtedly scoring many hits against the inflexibility of rule based ethics, has itself been thoroughly criticised by Stanley Hauerwas. Their focus, he maintains, has been "primarily on how persons should deal with their bodies and private actions" and thus they "fail to give adequate attention to the institutional context of sex."[37] This leads to Hauerwas' thesis that sex is a public, not a private, matter for the Christian community. "How we order and form our lives sexually cannot be separated from the necessity of the church to chart an alternative to our culture's dominant assumptions."[38]

This is another challenge to privacy. Can Macmurray's notion of person provide a convincing alternative? Hauerwas' target was not persons or privacy, but the sheer abstraction of the quality controls "freedom," "mutuality" and "integration." He achieved concreteness by re-embedding rules in a narrative, which, as defining story then forms the boundary of a distinctive community. This entailed a shift in the understanding of law. "Law" now becomes those practices which the community encourages, and so righteousness is now not rule-obedience, but a creative entering into the vision of the community, becoming a player in an on-going game. However, Hauerwas has critics of his own, and there is more than one way to skin a cat. Macmurray's notion of person is equally critical of externality, abstraction and rule-obedience, and he can give a better account than can Hauerwas of the speech of

Achilles. Achilles' speech is private in that it is ferociously counter-cultural, but Macmurray's analysis allows us to recognise that it is that kind of speech which is *fundamentally* moral as it is the outpouring of the whole person.

NOTES

1   Her paper was published as 'Professional Confidentiality' in *Studies in Christian Ethics*, 2.1 (1988), 46–60. Sissela Bok's fascinating study *Secrets: On the Ethics of Concealment and Revelation* (New York: New York, 1989) offers an account of secrecy and privacy, confession, gossip, the limits of confidentiality, probing, the right to know and much else. See also: Robert S. Gerstein, 'Intimacy and Privacy' in *Ethics*, 89 (1978), 76–81.

2   van Asperen, ibid., 49.

3   See Bonhoeffer's comment in his *Ethics*, "The fact that he was ashamed when he was discovered praying was for Kant an argument against prayer. He failed to see that prayer by its very nature is a matter for the strictest privacy..." (London: SCM Press, 1955) 7. The sections on "Shame" and on "Telling the Truth" in Bonhoeffer's *Ethics* are among the most profound discussions of covering and uncovering, self-concealment and self-revelation. See also John Zizioulas, *Being as Communion* (London: Darton, Longman & Todd, 1985), chapter 1 'Personhood and Being. From Mask to Person: The Birth of an Ontology of Personhood,' 27–49. What is espcially interesting is Zizioulas' suggestion that it was in the Greek theatre, endowed with a mask, that man could, for a brief time, become free, a "person" (32–3). Subsequently, there occurred an "unforeseen revolution" (36): the identification of the *hypostasis* with the person. I am grateful to Elizabeth Templeton for suggesting that I refer to John Zizioulas.

4   Ibid., 52. For her discussion of anthropological contexts, see 50–51.

5   Peter Harvey's response is printed at in *Studies in Christian Ethics*, 2.1 (1988), 61–65. Peter Harvey is the author of *Death's Gift* (London: Epworth, 1985) and *The Morals of Jesus* (London: Darton, Longman & Todd, 1991).

6   Harvey actually says "moral development" rather than "moral advance" (64). I suggest that he is trying to probe the question of what *genuinely* is moral maturity or advance.

7   Ibid., 64.

8   An impatience with secrecy seems embedded in the Christian hope. The New Jerusalem is described as built of pure gold, "clear as glass" (Rev 21:18). St Paul speaks of the unbeliever, who, when "the secrets of his heart are disclosed," will confess that God is really with the Christian community (1 Cor 14:25), and refers to the ideal of making "every thought captive to obey Christ" (2 Cor 10:5). The same thought is celebrated in the liturgical tradition in the 1662 *Book of Common Prayer's* collect for purity: "Almighty God, unto whom all hearts be open, all

desires known, and from whom no secrets are hid.... ." The linkage between purity and lack of secrecy is interesting.

[9]   Harvey's understanding of Jesus is subtle. Jesus is neither a lawgiver nor an example whom we must imitate. He is the one who opens new possibilities for living. See his *The Morals of Jesus*.

[10]   She has never said this is print, but as she is an old friend, I telephoned her while writing this, and gladly acknowledge her helpful comments, as well as her confirmation of the remark. Some of Elizabeth Templeton's views on sexuality are in the chapter, 'Sexuality in the 90s: thinking theologically' in her book, *The Strangeness of God* (London: Arthur James, 1993). She was also the convener of the report of the Church of Scotland's Panel on Doctrine on The Theology of Marriage, which was presented to the General Assembly of the Church of Scotland in May 1994 (*Reports to the General Assembly*, Edinburgh, 1994) 257–285.

[11]   Interestingly, in the narrative of the fall, it was *the Lord* who made garments for Adam and Eve, thereby clothing them (Gen 3:21).

[12]   Cf. Revelation 21:4.

[13]   It is at lines 308–429 of Book IX of *The Iliad*.

[14]   Line 343.

[15]   Lines 386–7 (the impossibility of recompense) and 378 (hateful gifts).

[16]   Adam Parry, 'The Language of Achilles,' *The Language and Background of Homer*, G.S.Kirk (ed.) (Cambridge: Heffer, 1967), 53.

[17]   Adam Parry writes, "Achilles has no language with which to express his disillusionment. Yet he expresses it, and in a remarkable way. He does it by misusing the language he disposes of." *Ibid.* 53.

[18]   As Macmurray so often covers similar ground, I will look in particular at his essays, 'The Personal Life' and 'The Virtue of Chastity' in *Reason and Emotion* (1935).

[19]   John Macmurray, *Reason and Emotion* , 53.

[20]   Ibid., 55.

[21]   Ibid., 55.

[22]   Ibid., 55.

[23]   Ibid., 55.

[24]   Ibid., 56.

[25]   Ibid., 56. cf. "The personal life is the field of freedom." 61.

[26]   Cf. 71.

[27]   Cf. 73.

[28]   Ibid., 75.

[29]   Ibid., 81.

[30]   Ibid., 81.

[31]   Ibid., 83.

[32]   Ibid., 7. This passage is quoted by Thomas F. Torrance in his work on theological realism, *Theological Science* (Oxford: Oxford University Press, 1969), 11. Though never a pupil of Macmurray's (unlike his brother, James B. Torrance), they were colleagues and acquaintances. Interestingly, Torrance had made a similar point earlier, in dialogue with the work of John Duns Scotus, in explicating the personhood of God. Scotus had drawn a distinction between a voluntary and a

natural object. With a natural object, like a stone, we open our eyes and we *have* to see it. But with a voluntary object (a person, and even more, God), we cannot know him until we come under the compelling claims of his reality. A voluntary object discloses his personhood; personhood is not a category we impose upon him. See Thomas F. Torrance, 'Intuitive and Abstractive Knowledge from Duns Scotus to John Calvin' in *De doctrina Ioannis Duns Scoti*, volume 4. *Congressus Scotistici Internationalis. Studia Scholastico-Scotistica, 4*. (Rome: Societas Internationalis Scotistica, 1968), 291–305.

[33] John McGuckin in his book: *St Cyril of Alexandria: The Christological Controversy* (Leiden: E.J. Brill, 1994) discusses Cyril's understanding of person at 207, 224–5. Cyril steered between the Hellenism of Apollinaris and the Semitic compositeness of the Antiochenes, presenting "a new and hopeful definition of the human person—the one who has the potential to transcend... The divine Lord... who transcended his own fragility and death thus calls out the whole race to become greater than they know themsleves to be, and in this becoming, to become alive" (225).

[34] See the US Supreme Court's 1973 *Roe versus Wade* decision.

[35] See Michael Polanyi, *Personal Knowledge* (London: Routledge and Kegan Paul, second impression with corrections, 1962), chapter 4 (Skills), 49–65.

[36] See Jack Dominian, *Sexual Integrity* (London: Darton, Longman & Todd, 1987); Helen Oppenheimer, *Marriage* (London: Mowbray, 1990); Kevin T. Kelly: *Divorce and Second Marriage* (London: Collins, 1982); Elizabeth Templeton et al., Report on the Theology of Marriage, presented to the General Assembly of the Church of Scotland, May 1994 (*Reports to the General Assembly*, Edinburgh, 1994) op. cit.

[37] Stanley Hauerwas, *A Community of Character* (Notre Dame: University of Notre Dame Press, 1981), 187.

[38] Ibid., 189.

CHAPTER FIFTEEN

Constructing Persons: Macmurray and the Social Construction of Disability

John Swinton

In this essay I shall discuss some of the implications of John Macmurray's conception of personhood for our understanding of and attitudes towards disability and people with disabilities, with particular reference to people with learning disabilities (formerly known as mental handicap) I want to suggest that Macmurray's model of human personhood points towards a radically counter-cultural way of understanding human beings, which has significant implications for our understanding of what disability actually is and the challenge that it presents to the types of the communities we seek to develop.

There are a number of ways in which one can conceptualise the phenomenon of disability, however traditionally the main conceptual model used within Western society is the *medical* model. The medical model defines disability according to discrete physiological, psychological or intellectual pathologies located specifically within individuals. This model views disability in all of its varying forms as a "*personal* tragedy," which primarily affects the *individual*. The medical model suggests that learning disability should be understood in clearly definable terms as:

> a state of arrested or incomplete development of mind that includes significant impairment of intelligence and social functioning. Unlike mental illness, impairment cannot be reversed and therefore cannot be cured because it results from damage to, or malformation of the brain or nervous system before, during, or shortly after birth.[1]

According to this definition, learning disability is looked upon as a *challenge* to be dealt with or an *obstacle* to be overcome. This understanding necessarily prescribes particular solutions, treatments or therapies in this case not to *cure* those individuals but to *correct* their vocational or social functioning. Thus, correction or psychological manipulations aimed at enabling the individual to function within established social structures, has been viewed as the primary means by which people with learning disabilities could achieve cultural acceptance and social assimilation. Those who are not appropriately socialised or corrected find themselves marginalized and relegated to the mystical status of "invalidism." The important thing to draw from the term "invalid," is that it marks a person out as existing in a form which is *invalid*, in that it is not socially accepted as an appropriate form of human existence.   Historically this has meant not just physical dependency or institutionalisation, but more fundamentally, social invalidation. While the medical model claims to be scientific, objective and humane, within its practice has lurked a good deal of ambivalence toward the people it professes to aid. It could be argued that in one respect, the medical model has been the institutionalised expression of societal anxieties about people who look different or function differently. It regards people with disabilities as incapable of managing their own lives, and as such permanently in need of professional, perhaps lifelong, supervision.[2] The important thing to notice within the medical model is that society itself has no need to change to accommodate the individual. The disability is hers, and ways must be found to alter her behaviour or ability in order that she can fit in with the wider social norms. Within the world-view of the medical model we as a society have no responsibility for the person's disability and no necessary responsibility towards those who are disabled. We may *choose* to care; we may *choose* to isolate individuals as in the institutional system, but we have no obligation to do so, and we certainly do not consider ourselves in any way personally responsible for them or their social experience. The idea that we as a community may to a very large degree be responsible for the person's disability and may be fundamental to the process of change and rehabilitation, does not even cross our minds.

It would seem that the medical model assumes a form of abstract knowledge which in Macmurray's words "constructs its object by limitation of attention to what is *known* about other persons without entering into personal relations with them."[3] I would want to suggest that within the medical model's way of perceiving disability, lies precisely the type of destructive Cartesian individualism that John Macmurray speaks so eloquently and convincingly against. To suggest that disabilities are solely located within the individual is to misunderstand the actual experience of disability, and in so doing to discount the vital relational context within which disability is experienced and individuals work out their existence. Such a suggestion also fails to understand the nature and function of personal and communal human relationships in the creation of social identity and the working out of human personhood.

Whilst, to the best of my knowledge, Macmurray does not directly address the topic of disability, the fundamentals of his anthropology bear much relevance to the field of disability studies and to the care of people with disabilities. John Macmurray presents a strong argument for the relational nature of human beings and the communal context for the development of personal identity. In his Gifford lectures he presents strong arguments to support the assertion that human personhood is *not* gained in isolation, but is always the product of some form of action-in-community. Arguing against the Cartesian assertion that knowledge of the essential self can be gained through isolated introspection, Macmurray proposes that it is not possible to understand the Self apart from its *relationships*. Whereas Descartes believed it possible to discover the essential self through a process of inward exploration, Macmurray points towards the absurdity of such a position, and posits the view that all thought is in fact reflection on some form of action (relational activity) and consequently the product of the outworking of some kind of community. To suggest that human personhood can be understood apart from its relationships is, according to Macmurray's analysis, a serious philosophical and practical misunderstanding. In his redefinition of the Self, it is a person's *relationships* that form the essence of who and what they are. Individuality comes to be seen as the product of relationship.

> I exist as an individual only in personal relation to other individuals. Formally stated, "I" am one term in the relation "You and I" which constitutes my existence[4].

Human beings are fundamentally constituted by their relationships with other human beings. We become who and what we are according to the types of relationship that we experience within our lives. The *type* and the *quality* of these relationships determine the nature and character of human persons. In a very real sense we are responsible for the construction of the personhood and life experiences of those whom we relate with directly or indirectly.

The particular form of relationship that Macmurray singles out as necessary for authentic human existence is *personal* relationship. Genuine human existence must always be *personal* existence. Personal existence refers to a particular way of understanding human relationships, and a specific attitude towards other people and the world. Personal relationships share particular characteristics that mark them out from non-personal entities. The absence of such qualities implies *impersonality*, and as such is inequitable with authentic human existence.

> The personal attitude is the attitude we adopt when we enter into personal relations with others and treat them as persons. ...The impersonal attitude is the one in which we do not treat other people as persons in personal relations with ourselves, but as men, that is as members of a determinate class of objects in our environment whose presence and behaviour limits, and so helps or hinders the realization of our own personal ends, and of whom we must take account, since their presence conditions our own actions[5].

To treat someone personally is to treat them as a person to whom one desires to *relate*, as opposed to an *object* that one wishes simply to *use*.[6] If human beings relate *personally* they enable one another to grow and to construct positive identities and a strong sense of being in relationship. If, alternatively, they relate *impersonally*, then the "other" becomes an object upon which numerous negative social identities can be ascribed. Human society then, in its ideal is a community of persons-in-relation, motivated and driven by the desire to enter into truly personal relationships and wholly committed to life in community together. Macmurray therefore offers us a very different way of envisaging the personal Self, which moves away from normal notions of autonomous individual selves. Personhood is not something that is gained in isolation, but is always the product of some form of action/relationship-in-community. The human agent is therefore a person whose identity is inevitably bound up with the material and social world. "I exist as an individual only in relation to other individuals, and rational action is action in which I treat the other as a person rather than an object at my disposal."[7]

Knowledge of both self and world is thus seen to arise out of personal participation in a social world. If this is so, and our social and personal identity is in fact inextricable conjoined with our relationships with others, then it becomes obvious that both individually and collectively each one of us carries a profound *responsibility* for the developing sense of personhood within the other. Not only does this highlight the importance of acknowledging our mutual responsibility towards one another; it also forces us to acknowledge some of the hidden power dynamics that permeate society. Along with responsibility comes an inevitable degree of *power*. Feminist and liberation theologians have shown clearly the ways in which power can be abused by individuals and by societies, and how such abuses of power can profoundly impact upon the self-identity of individuals and groups within society. All of us, whether we realise it or not, individually and collectively have a tremendous, if often unacknowledged, amount of power to decide what a person becomes and how they will be understood by self and others within society. We live in an age when power is considered a virtue. The power to be free to live our lives as individuals; the power to achieve; the power to exclude those we consider unacceptable and different. However, perhaps the greatest power that society has is not to be found in any kind of physical coercion, but in the power each of us has as individuals and as communities, to make a person accept our definition of them.[8]

In his book *The Suffering Presence*, Stanley Hauerwas makes a somewhat startling assertion. He suggests that within a society that had a different moral system that was not dependent on competitiveness, individuality and productivity, the concept of learning disability simply would not exist. In other words, the very term "learning disability" indicates adherence to a particular moral code and system of valuing human beings, which reflects the ideals of individualism, political liberalism and a capitalist economy. Within a society which uses the criteria of independence, productivity, intellectual prowess and social position to judge the value of human beings, people with physical, psychological or intellectual disabilities will inevitably be excluded and downgraded as human beings of lesser worth and value. If this is so, it becomes clear that society is, at least partially, responsible for the disablement of the impaired individual. According to this view, it is not the physical or mental condition of the individual that makes them disabled. Rather it is society that, by placing barriers and developing systems of valuing which exclude, stigmatise or downgrade particular groups of people, transforms physical or mental impairments into disabilities. Whilst not wishing to downgrade the important reality of the disablement brought about by individual impairment, I would want to suggest that it is the imposition by society of a negative social identity brought about by a deeply impersonal system of valuing, which lies at the heart of the social experience of disability. In this sense learning disability is a social construct.

By implication, when barriers are removed, individuals might remain *impaired* but will no longer necessarily be *disabled*. It is the disabling society therefore that needs to be transformed and not the impaired individual that needs to be cured or radically altered. What is required is not a temporary strategy which focuses on the appropriate socialisation of the individual, but a total ideological re-orientation; what Frances Young describes as a "transvaluation,"[9] which will recognise that our individualistically based success oriented values have to be put into a different perspective by other values. What is being suggested here is *not* a concept of "normalisation." The fact that people with disabilities are different has to be acknowledged. Not to acknowledge these differences would be to do the individual a great injustice. The real question is how we are rightfully to characterise these differences, without that very characterisation working to undermine their status as full and contributing members of the community.[10] What is needed is a new way of conceptualising human beings and a new form of human society which will be open to the reality of impairment and difference, but will not allow individuals to be defined or oppressed by that difference.

John Macmurray's propositions concerning the nature of human personhood and relationships provides us with a vital philosophical base, from which we can begin to establish such a transvaluation. Macmurray's conceptualisation of human beings as persons-in-relationship when applied to the lives of people with learning disabilities has a number of critical implications for the way in which we conceptualise disability and ultimately in how those experiencing it will be allowed to function within our communities. Such a re-conceptualisation is not merely an intellectual exercise. To quote the social psychologist W.I. Thomas,

> If men define a situation as real, they are real in their consequences. ...In other words, the subjective "definition of the situation" is just as important as the objective situation in its social effects[11].

The ways in which we conceptualise a situation has a profound impact on the way in which we act within that situation. To think through the implications of Macmurray's re-conceptualisation of the nature of human personhood is to take an important step towards actualising his propositions.

So precisely what can Macmurray contribute to our understanding of people with learning disabilities?

First, Macmurray's philosophical stance draws the focus of human encounter away from the individual and his or her impairment and on to the person and the community. No longer can we justify impersonal banners such as "the mentally handicapped," "the disabled," "cripples" "retards." Not only are these banners highly offensive to the recipients, but also, and more importantly, they are indicative of a society which is functioning at a sub-human level, that is, behaving towards its most vulnerable participants in a way which is profoundly *impersonal*.

Secondly, if we take Macmurray's proposals seriously, we are forced to realise that rather than being a series of isolated individuals thrown together by the whims of fate and time, as human beings we are a community of persons-in-relation, intricately interlinked with one another, and ultimately responsible for what we become as individuals and as a community. Macmurray teaches us that what we are as human beings comes from interconnectedness and not individuality. When we realise that disability is the product of a distortion of this social process wherein a negative, impersonal social construction of personhood is created around an individual or individuals with specific impairments, we can no longer look upon learning disability as simply a "personal tragedy."[12] Instead the person's situation becomes a communal concern, which does not simply need to be eradicated, defeated or overcome through the use of human technology, but has to be understood and cared for through the development of positive personal relationships which embody and reveal the fundamental relationality of human beings.

Finally, Macmurray forces us to re-think our attitudes and values with regard to all people with disabilities. By drawing our focus away from impairment and onto the person, Macmurray offers a powerful corrective to the type of negative social construction that was highlighted previously. No longer can we justify splintering human beings and ascribing worth according to certain isolated attributes, be that their reason, intellect, economic prowess or whatever. Macmurray presents us with a holistic understanding of human beings in which there is no such thing as a pure, essential self that can be extrapolated from the communal life of humanity and said to be *the* essential component of human persons. One cannot understand human beings by looking at discrete parts of them. To understand human beings it is necessary to understand them as *whole-persons-in-relation*. Similarly, to understand disability it is necessary to view whole persons rather than discrete incapacities. Macmurray offers us a holistic picture of human beings in which value is something which is ascribed to another in relationship; it is something that is bestowed on an individual by being loved, wanted, respected, and cherished. Value is thus shown to be inherently a *relational* concept. In this way Macmurray opens the way for the development of attitudes and systems of valuing which respect the personal nature of human existence and enables the individual with a disability to be seen as a person to whom one might wish to relate, rather than a problem which one might like to solve. In pointing towards the inherent relationality of human beings and the necessity of correlating personal relationships with communal responsibility, Macmurray offers us a template for a new community and a new way of seeing and being human which stands as a powerful counterpoint to the disabling society within which people with disabilities work out their lives and within which each one of us participates and, by implication, legitimates.

NOTES

[1] Mental Health Act 1983 cited in The Mental Health Foundation, *Learning Disabilities:The Fundamental Facts* (London: The Mental Health Foundation, 1993), 5.

[2] For an expansion on this critique of the medical model as it is applied to disabilities in general, see Michael Oliver. *The Politics of Disablement (London:* Macmillan and St Martin's Press, 1990). See also, Michael Oliver. *Understanding Disability: From Theory to Practice* (London: Macmillan, 1996).

[3] John Macmurray. *Persons in Relation* (1965) 28–29.

[4] Ibid., 28.

[5] Ibid., 40.

[6] John Swinton & Esther McIntosh, 'Persons-in-Relation: The Philosophy of John Macmurray and the Care of Persons with Profound Learning Disability,' *Theology Today*, 57.2 (2000), 175–184.

[7] David Fergusson, *John Macmurray* (Edinburgh: Handsel, 1992), 16.

[8] For a more comprehensive discussion on this point see Stanley Hauerwas. *Suffering Presence.* (Edinburgh: T & T. Clark, 1988), 159 ff.

[9] Frances Young, *Face to Face: A narrative essay in the theology of suffering* (Edinburgh: T & T Clark, 1990), 144.

10   Stanley Hauerwas *Suffering Presence,* 162.
11   George.M. Furniss.   *The Social Context of Pastoral Care: Defining the Life Situation* (Louisville: Westminster John Knox Press, 1994), 20.
12   Michael Oliver *Understanding Disability*, 31.

CHAPTER SIXTEEN

Macmurray's Understanding of Mysticism

Amy Limpitlaw

In the preface to his 1938 study on the mysticism of St. Augustine entitled *Amor Dei*, the Cambridge theologian John Burnaby describes the philosopher John Macmurray as an "anti-mystic." Burnaby's assessment of Macmurray's alleged "anti-mysticism" is not extensive; he focuses mainly upon Macmurray's call for a Christianity more actively responsive to the practical issues of the day, especially in light of the challenge posed to it by the rise of Communism in the 1930s.[1] Was John Macmurray an anti-mystic? Macmurray never wrote extensively on the subject and specific references in his works to mysticism appear sporadically. In this essay, I will argue first, that a particular understanding of mysticism can be discerned in Macmurray's writings and second, that while Macmurray is indeed to a great extent critical of the part played by mysticism in the history of Christianity, a proper understanding of Macmurray's actual views on mysticism does leave room for a certain role for mysticism in the life of the Christian who is primarily an agent in the world, seeking to advance the divine intention for reality.

To understand how Macmurray viewed mysticism we must first consider his epistemology and the three forms of reflection he identifies as central to human experience. The key epistemological move made by Macmurray was to insist that human thinking or reflection can only be understood if it is related to its purpose within the fullness of life as action. In short, thought or reflection is for the sake of action, and not the reverse. As such, the ways in which we think about reality are determined by the purposes in action for which our reflection arises.[2]

Macmurray identifies three basic modes of reflection, each of which fulfills a specific need in order for effective action to take place. The first to be considered is what Macmurray termed the emotional mode of reflection. This mode of reflection is necessary for action because it is only through emotional valuation that the ends of action can be determined.[3] As Macmurray notes, "the emotional life contains the springs of action."[4] But in order to act, we also need to know *how* to act in order to bring about our ends; specifically, we need to know how to use things. It is this purpose of determining reality as material for use in action for which the second mode of reflection arises, which Macmurray calls the *intellectual* mode of reflection.[5]

In the concrete life of action, both the emotional and the intellectual modes of reflection are operative. The reality of action also entails a further dimension, however, and that is the context of human action within the life of interdependent personal relationship. It is this larger context of human relationship which is the focus of religion as the third specific mode of reflection.[6] Thus, the religious mode of reflection refers to the larger personal context within which action takes place and it includes within itself the two subordinate modes of reflection, that is, the emotional and the intellectual.[7]

Macmurray thus distinguishes three basic modes of reflection, all of which are directly related to and arise from action: the emotional, which attends to value and thus determines the ends of action; the intellectual, which determines the means of action; and the religious, which integrates the emotional and the intellectual by attending to the full context of personal relationship. Separated from their practical reference to the life of action, the emotional mode of reflection becomes the basis for the theoretical activity of art, and the intellectual mode of reflection becomes the basis for the theoretical activity of science.[8]

Religion constitutes the "full reflective activity of the self" according to Macmurray because it integrates the emotional and the intellectual modes of reflection into a unified whole.[9] Because it is inclusive of the two subordinate modes of reflection which are both necessary for action, it is inherently practical. In contrast, art and science, as distinct reflective activities, are necessarily theoretical because they each lack what the other provides for the concrete unity of action. Science can tell us how to use material for action, but not what ends to seek; whereas art may tell us what is of value but not how to achieve it. Science and art are, therefore, limited forms of reflection. When they are undertaken for their own sake, they become, in contrast to religion, primarily *reflective activities*. Macmurray distinguishes reflective activities from practical activities in terms of the governing intention. A practical activity seeks to effect a change in reality. Its theoretical dimension is subordinated to this practical purpose. A reflective activity, in contrast, is theoretical in that it is concerned with achieving a *symbolic representation* of reality. It does not seek to bring about a change in reality itself, but instead takes its object as a determinant given. Science and art, then, are reflective activities governed by a theoretical intention and they are therefore necessarily detached from action. Only when the intellectual and the emotional poles are integrated within the fuller form of religious reflection do they become capable of moving from a merely theoretical to a practical application.[10]

In this admittedly cursory sketch of Macmurray's account of the three basic modes of reflection what is most important to remember is that religion, as the most complete form of reflection, integrates the two subordinate forms, the intellectual and the emotional. At the same time, however, the intellectual and emotional modes, when they are isolated from their function within the concrete unity of practical life, form the basis for the predominantly theoretical activities of science and art, respectively. Science and art as reflective activities are limited. They are limited, first, as we have seen, in that their intentions are theoretical, and thus they are each detached from their practical basis. But they are also limited in that their attention is directed to distinct portions of reality, and not to reality as a whole. This latter limitation is significant because it further differentiates religion from both art and science. Religious reflection is a universal form of reflection in a way that art and science are not. Its object is the wholeness of reality. In contrast there are many sciences but there is no single science which deals with the whole of reality. Similarly, there are many kinds of artistic activity but there is no such thing as "art-in-general." Science and art are fragmentary in a way that religion is not.[11]

Now religion, according to Macmurray is inherently practical in a way in which science and art, as predominantly reflective activities, are not. But for the development of religion there is nonetheless, a necessary and temporary alternation between practical activity and reflection. While for science and art the withdrawal from action is for the sake of achieving a theoretical end, in religion, the withdrawal from action into reflection is for the sake of action, that is, for the sake of extending and deepening the mutual life of persons.[12] Macmurray names the alternating movement of the self from practical activity into reflection and back again into practical activity the *rhythm of withdrawal and return*.[13] In the withdrawal or reflective phase of this alternating rhythm, either one of the two modes of reflection which together form the unity of the religious consciousness, the emotional or the intellectual mode, may take center stage. When the intellectual mode of reflection predominates, what results is the theoretical activity of philosophy or theology. When the emotional mode predominates, the result is mysticism.[14]

Mysticism, then, constitutes for Macmurray the emotional mode or dimension of the religious consciousness. Macmurray identifies mysticism as the emotional pole of religious reflection most explicitly in two works, the 1932 essay, "What is Philosophy?"[15] and *The Structure of Religious Experience* (1936).[16] He does not, however, develop in much detail a theory of mysticism beyond this identification of it as the emotional moment within the unity of religious reflection. However, it is possible to draw a number of conclusions concerning the nature of mysticism based on both what he does say and on what we know of his epistemology as a whole. Since in the concrete unity of action from which all forms of reflection take their rise, the emotional valuation of ends is primary while the intellectual determination of means is secondary, within the unity of religion mysticism as the emotional moment would take precedence over philosophy or theology as the intellectual moment.[17] In form, mysticism would be similar to art. Both are driven by emotion; both are characterized by an emotional contemplation or valuation of their object. They would differ, however, in a number of significant respects. First, the object reflected upon by the artist is necessarily a finite portion of reality. The object of mystical contemplation, in contrast, would be reality in its wholeness.[18] Second, if mysticism finds its proper place within the unity of the religious consciousness, and the object of the religious consciousness is reality apprehended as *personal*, mysticism in its emotional contemplation of the wholeness of reality would contemplate it as a personal wholeness, that is, as the infinite valued or contemplated as a personal reality, or in other words, as God. Third, while mysticism takes precedence over philosophy or theology (which for Macmurray, are basically synonymous),[19] it is still a *subordinate* dimension of the full religious consciousness. And since religious reflection is for the sake of the concrete, active life of mutual personal relationship, mystical contemplation as a dimension of religious reflection itself would only be valid if it took place for the sake of the concrete life of personal mutuality.

Clearly, then, since mysticism constitutes for Macmurray the emotional pole of the religious consciousness, and further, since as the emotional pole it necessarily takes precedence over the intellectual pole within the unity of religious reflection, there is little basis for the accusation that Macmurray was an "anti-mystic." Such an accusation would be valid only if Macmurray dismissed mysticism entirely either as a completely invalid form of reflection or as utterly disconnected from the appropriate concerns of religion. Instead, as we have seen, mysticism for Macmurray constitutes a necessary and essential dimension of religious experience. However, there is a certain critical stance taken by Macmurray which relates to his understanding of the role of mysticism in religion and it is this critique of mysticism to which I would like now to turn our attention.

Mysticism, as we have seen, constitutes for Macmurray the emotional dimension of the religious consciousness. But he did not develop the specifics of how mysticism functions within the religious life at much length, other than by pointing out its formal similarities to art as a reflective activity whose basis is in the emotions. In many of his writings, particularly some of the later ones, Macmurray's references to mysticism seem quite critical. I would argue, however, that his implicit negativity toward mysticism must be understood within the context of his larger critique of the empirical development of religion in the history of humanity.

Macmurray believed that a mature religious consciousness recognizes the inherent connection between reflection and action. But religion, as it has actually developed up to this point in the life of humanity, has not yet attained maturity. Its immaturity is due not so much to the inadequacy of its theoretical concepts, but to the refusal to refer such concepts to the concrete reality of practical experience. Instead, in Macmurray's view, religion as it is generally conceived and practiced is taken to refer to a supernatural, otherworldly realm and is divorced from the actual life of persons as agents living and interacting with one another in the material world.[20]

Now this immaturity of religion, which Macmurray also refers to as a "falsification" of religion,[21] involves the severance of the basic connection between the theoretical and the practical. Rather than the rhythm of withdrawal and return, in which the withdrawal into mystical contemplation and theological reflection are undertaken for the sake of deepening and extending the mutuality of lived personal relationship, the focus of religion remains with its withdrawal phase. Contemplation and theological reflection become ends in themselves. Religion becomes intentionally and exclusively theoretical.[22]

It is this rejection of an exclusively theoretical practice of religion which forms the basis for Macmurray's implicitly critical stance towards mysticism. When the practice of mystical contemplation or the achievement of a mystical consciousness is identified as the purpose of religion,[23] then what has occurred, according to Macmurray, is the falsification of religion. It is, in Macmurray's view, a falsification of religion first because it divorces the reflective side of religion from its necessary reference to the concrete, practical life of persons. This leads in turn to the assumption of a metaphysical dualism. The results of religious reflection are not understood to refer back to the real, concrete world of human action but instead are taken to refer to a "supernatural," idealized spiritual world. God is understood to dwell in a realm above or apart from the world in which we live and so is no longer sought within the realm of everyday experience. This in turn leads to a devaluation of the concrete, material world in favor of the idealized, supernatural world accessed through mystical contemplation. The goal of life becomes one of escaping through contemplation from mundane reality into this other, more perfect spiritual realm.[24]

The identification of religion with mysticism is also a falsification of religion for Macmurray because it confuses religion with art. Since mysticism is, according to Macmurray, the artistic or emotional dimension of the religious consciousness, a reductive identification of religion with mysticism restricts religion to its emotional, artistic side. But art, although it usually involves some kind of active expression, is primarily a theoretical activity in that it does not primarily intend a change in reality. It is disconnected from practical life. Furthermore, Macmurray notes that all reflection by its very nature is inherently individualistic. Thus, in the reflective activity of art the artist stands apart from the object she contemplates; the object is valued but at a distance. As Macmurray puts it, "One must stand aside to contemplate; one must not be personally involved."[25] The artist remains within the isolation of her reflection; she is an observer of reality but not a participant.[26] When religion is reduced to its artistic aspect, it is thus precluded from having any real impact on the lives of persons living in the world. It becomes a solitary activity, disconnected from religion's proper field of personal relationship. Such religion will, in effect, involve contemplation but it will not involve communion.[27]

There is, especially, one aspect of mysticism which seems for Macmurray to make it especially problematic. This is the desire of the mystic to reach a kind of mergence or union with the object contemplated. In *Persons in Relation*, for example, Macmurray defines mysticism in the following way: "self-identification with the whole, with the Other that includes oneself, is mysticism."[28] This characteristic of mysticism seems to be connected to its affinities with the artistic consciousness. Macmurray does not develop this position in much detail, but he does note that one aspect of the artistic consciousness is the desire to possess the beloved object, and especially to attain a possession such that the object no longer exists in time, but is held as an unchanging, timeless reality in the mind.[29] As Macmurray describes it, "the artist isolates his object as an eternal value, and seeks to make it a possession for ever."[30] It may be that such a desire on the part of the artistic consciousness for a timeless possession of the beloved object is related to the mystic's desire for union and the corresponding "self-identification with the whole" which Macmurray describes as characteristic of mystical consciousness. To be sure, Macmurray does not explicitly make such a connection.

However, Macmurray does identify the artistic consciousness as the source for organic conceptions of reality, which he in turn relates to the emergence of totalitarian systems in which persons sacrifice their individual identities in a kind of "mystical" identification with the state. For example, in *The Clue to History*, Macmurray describes Hitler's Germany and fascism generally as grounded in a mystical form of consciousness.[31] What characterizes such mystical consciousness as it works in fascism is a heightened emotional state in which the individual experiences an identification of herself with the collective, that is, with the nation or the state.[32] It involves essentially the willing subordination of human personality to the ideal, collective personality—a kind of mystical mergence or union. This appears to be for Macmurray the major danger of mysticism. It presents as a substitute for the real experience of being a person in which, as he notes, "we must bear our own identities," a false, idealized experience of mergence into a larger whole.[33] One appeal of this is the element of escape. The aim of the artistic consciousness is an escape from time and change, and therefore the mystical identification of the self with the collective whole is really an attempt to escape from reality and from the demands made upon us as agents in the real world where we must act and be responsible for our actions.[34]

As we have seen, Macmurray did take a strongly critical stance toward mysticism but his position must be understood within the context of his larger critique of religion infected by idealism. Certainly, he rejected the position that mysticism is the center of the religious life, and he also pointed to what he saw as a danger in the "mysticism" characteristic of totalitarian, organic societies in which the individual willingly merges his own identity with that of the collective whole. However, within the larger unity of religion which encompasses for Macmurray both an intellectual and an emotional dimension, there may be a place for mysticism. To see Macmurray as an "anti-mystic" is as erroneous as to believe him to be anti-art or anti-emotion.

At this point, I would like to conclude with a few reflections on the adequacy of Macmurray's position on mysticism. What has emerged as a critical stance toward mysticism and the mystical tradition within Christianity arose primarily out of Macmurray's frustration with the idealism he believed had infected Christianity and had made it a religion turned away from the real world where human beings must live together in mutuality. To a great extent, Macmurray's account of Christianity's adoption of idealism is correct. Christianity's mystical tradition has been greatly influenced by the Platonic notion of *theoria* or contemplation as the sole way to gain access to ultimate reality.[35] As we have seen, Macmurray takes an entirely different approach and maintains that reality is not to be attained primarily through reflection but instead through living in mutual relationship with other persons. Reflection's purpose is to enhance our ability to live in mutuality with others, and it is here, in the lived experience of personal communion, that the reality of God is most fully experienced.

In taking this position, Macmurray does indeed run against an assumption which has influenced much of the mystical tradition within Christianity, namely that the goal of the Christian life is to attain access to God through a contemplative practice which typically involves a removal of oneself from society and a detachment from so-called worldly concerns. But if Macmurray's critical comments on mysticism are taken to suggest that *all* mysticism is inevitably world-denying, that *all* mysticism implies a lack of concern for the practical realities of everyday life,[36] then it must be pointed out that there is much in the history of the mystical tradition which belies these assumptions. There have been any number of mystics who have explicitly rejected, as Macmurray has, the notion that it is through separating oneself off from the world that one attains access to the sacred dimension of reality. The thirteenth-century mystic Meister Eckhart, for example, writes that, "...whoever really and truly has God, he has him [sic] everywhere, in the street and in company with everyone, just as much as in church or in solitary places..."[37] In more recent times, the French Jesuit mystic Teilhard de Chardin explicitly argued against the notion that either the material world or the active life are to be avoided or rejected. As Teilhard put it, "God is arrived at not in a negation, but in an extension, of the world."[38] A counter-argument to the view that mysticism is inherently world-denying could also be made by pointing to those mystics whose contemplative practices enhanced their active lives and led them to a very conscious engagement with the political and social issues of their time. Simone Weil's mysticism led her to seek a life not of separation but of solidarity in action with others.[39] Even within the monastic tradition, which ostensibly recommends a separation from the world, we find mystics like the American Trappist Thomas Merton who in the course of his life became increasingly engaged with contemporary social issues and who viewed his contemplative practice as not the antithesis of action, but rather, as a necessary preparation for it.[40] And in recent years there has been increasing attention paid to the mystical element within liberation theology, a movement which can hardly be considered indifferent to the material exigencies of human life.[41] Of course, this is not to suggest that these mystics necessarily embraced of view of reality which is consonant with Macmurray's philosophy; my intention here is simply to point out the fallacy behind the assumption that a religious practice in which mysticism is prominent *inevitably* results in a rejection of the life of action in the material world.

The danger Macmurray points out in a Christianity infected by idealism is a very real one, and it often has resulted in the assumption that the whole point of religion is to achieve certain mystical states of consciousness. Macmurray does us a service by reminding us that reflection, however necessary, is a derivative form of existence, and that its purpose is to enhance our capacities for living in mutuality with one another. Within Macmurray's theory of religion, a place may be found for mysticism as the emotional form of religious reflection which is essential, though not sufficient by itself, to the religious task of extending the range and depth of community throughout the world.

If this practical reference of religious reflection is kept in mind, what might result would be the distinction between healthy and unhealthy forms of mysticism; that is, between the emotional contemplation or mysticism which serves the religious task by deepening our capacities to live in mutual personal relationships with others and the false or dangerous mysticism which promises the dream of an escape from reality into the comfort of an otherworldly, spiritual realm.

NOTES

[1]   John Burnaby, *Amor Dei: A Study on the Religion of St. Augustine* (London: Hodder and Stoughton, 1938) 7-12 passim.

[2]   Macmurray, *Religion, Art, and Science: A Study of the Reflective Activities in Man* , 28–29; *The Structure of Religious Experience*, 38–39; *The Self as Agent*, 21, 165–183 passim, 187–188; *Persons in Relation* , 167.

[3]   Macmurray, *Reason and Emotion*, 11; 'What is Philosophy?' in *Aristotelian Society Proceedings Supplement* 11 (1932) 56; *The Self as Agent*, 193–194; *Religion, Art, and Science*, 42.

[4]   Macmurray, *Idealism Against Religion*, 8.

[5]   Macmurray, *The Self as Agent*, 193; *Religion, Art, and Science*, 15; 'What is Philosophy?,' 57.

[6]   Macmurray, *Persons in Relation*, 157; *Religion, Art, and Science*, 53; *The Structure of Religious Experience*, 23.

[7]   Macmurray, *Religion, Art, and Science*, 70; *The Structure of Religious Experience*, 55–56.

[8]   Macmurray, *The Self as Agent*, 198–199.

[9]   Macmurray, *The Structure of Religious Experience*, 56.

[10]   Macmurray, *The Structure of Religious Experience*, 22–23, 56; *Religion, Art, and Science*, 55; 'What is Philosophy?,' 54, 57–58; *The Self as Agent*, 178–179.

[11]   Macmurray, *Reason and Emotion*, 96-97, 111; *Religion, Art, and Science*, 8.

[12]   Macmurray, *Religion, Art, and Science*, 54; *The Structure of Religious Experience*, 58; *Persons in Relation*, 162–163.

[13]   Macmurray, *The Structure of Religious Experience*, 56–57.

14 Macmurray explicitly makes the point that within the moment of religious reflection, there is a necessary focus on either the emotional or intellectual pole. See, for example, Macmurray, 'What is Philosophy?,' op. cit., 64–65; *The Structure of Religious Experience*, 56–57, 74, 75–76; *Religion, Art, and Science*, 60; *Persons in Relation*, 175.

15 'What is Philosophy?,' op. cit., 64–5.

16 Macmurray, *The Structure of Religious Experience*, 56–57

17 Macmurray, *The Structure of Religious Experience*, 57.

18 Macmurray, 'What is Philosophy?,' op. cit., 64–65.

19 Macmurray, *The Structure of Religious Experience*, 57.

20 Macmurray, *Creative Society: A Study of the Relation of Christianity to Communism* , 13–14, 46, 51; *The Structure of Religious Experience*, 34, 59, 65–66; *Reason and Emotion*, 3–31, 147–148, 150–151.

21 Macmurray, *The Structure of Religious Experience*, 59–67 passim.

22 Macmurray, *The Structure of Religious Experience*, 65–68, *Religion, Art, and Science*, 47, 55; *Idealism Against Religion*, 8–9, 11; *Persons in Relation*, 175.

23 A good example of such an identification of religion with the achievement or experience of a certain kind of consciousness would be found in the work of Rudolf Otto, with his locating religion in feeling of the "numinous" or Friedrich Schleiermacher, with his definition of religion as the "*feeling* of absolute dependence." See Rudolf Otto, *The Idea of the Holy* (London: Penguin, 1959) and Friedrich Schleiermacher, *On Religion: Speeches to its Cultured Despisers*, Introduction, translation and notes by Richard Crouty (Cambridge & New York: Cambridge University Press, 1988).

24 Macmurray, *The Structure of Religious Experience*, 66–71 passim; *Idealism Against Religion*, 8–18 passim; *Creative Society*, 50–51.

25 Macmurray, *Religion, Art, and Science*, 43.

26 Macmurray, 'What is Philosophy?,' op. cit., 57–58; *Persons in Relation*, 179.

27 Macmurray, *Religion, Art and Science*, 43–44; *Reason and Emotion*, 3–34.

28 Macmurray, *Persons in Relation*, 143.

29 Macmurray, *The Self as Agent*, 199.

30 Macmurray, *The Self as Agent*, 211.

31 Macmurray, *The Clue to History*, 215–228 passim.

32 Macmurray, *The Clue to History*, 221.

33 Macmurray, *Persons in Relation*, 143.

34 Macmurray, *Persons in Relation*, 143.

35 For more on the Platonic influence on the Christian mystical tradition, see Bernard McGinn, *The Foundations of Mysticism* (New York: Crossroad, 1991), 23–61.

36 While there is a significant place for mysticism within Macmurray's understanding of religion, he does at times come close to suggesting the identification of mysticism with a world-denying idealism. Cf. *Creative Society*, 131–132.

37 Meister Eckhart, *Counsels on Discernment, in Meister Eckhart: The Essential Sermons, Commentaries, Treatises, and Defense*, trans. and introd. by Edmund Colledge, O.S.A. and Bernard McGinn (New York: Paulist Press, 1981), 251.

38 Pierre Teilhard de Chardin, *Science and Christ*, trans. by René Hague (London: Collins; New York and Evanston, IL: Harper & Row, 1968), 105–106.

39 See Simone Weil, *Waiting for God*, trans. Emma Craufurd (New York: G.P. Putnam's Sons, 1951, reprint, New York: Harper & Row, 1973).

[40] Thomas Merton, *Contemplation in a World of Action* (New York: Doubleday, 1973) 172–179 passim.

[41] See, for example, *The Mystical and Political Dimensions of the Christian Faith*, ed. Claude Geffré and Gustavo Guttiérez (New York: Herder & Herder, 1974); Robert McAffee Brown, *Spirituality and Liberation: Overcoming the Great Fallacy* (Philadelphia: The Westminster Press, 1988).

CHAPTER SEVENTEEN

Friendship as a Moral Norm and the Problem of Boundaries in Clergy Ethics

Christopher Lind

Interview Data

This essay builds on a research project I have been conducting with a colleague for five years. With Dr. Maureen Muldoon[1] I have sought to establish how clergy ethics function in practice. Part of the research involved interviewing clergy on their understanding of clergy ethics, the principles they follow, and the problems they encounter.[2]

For many, friendship is a significant moral concern. For example, ministers[3] and students of ministry frequently debate the possibility and the propriety of making friends with members of the congregations they are serving. Nonetheless, it is clear that friendships are formed. Some of these friendships are strong and durable. Even those who judge that ministers should not make friends in the congregation, admit that they do so in spite of themselves.

Friendships are clearly something people desire and ministers are no different in that regard. The issue of friendship emerges as a significant moral issue because the attraction of friendship can be the cause of certain types of conflict. For example, ministry can be understood as role that one assumes. Retirement signals the end of the role, and poses typical problems where the minister retires in close geographical proximity to his or her former congregation. Others difficulties surround the issue of the exchange of gifts, payment for services, and the question of whether can be oneself with members of one's congregation.

> When I'm a friend to somebody, I'm spilling my guts too with them, and I'm
> saying things from my own personal perspective. When somebody's raising an

issue for me, an issue perhaps of suffering, perhaps an issue of trouble in their lives, or whatever, and they're asking the priest, they're asking for more than just a personal opinion. They're asking me to bring to bear what I know—they may not see that or know that, but I know that that's what I'm to bring to bear. The whole integration of scripture and theology and tradition, our history as a church, everything—our spirituality that integrates us. All of those things come to bear at that moment which is more than me as a person. It's integrated with me as a person, thank God, but it's no longer a personal reflection of who I am.[4]

Perhaps the best known and most sensational conflicts over friendships in ministry involve those that become physically intimate. For many commentators, the problem with friendships that become physically intimate is the problem of an imbalance of power and authority. Ministers have specific forms of authority granted to them (differing in detail depending on denominational polity) and people grant them power because of their spiritual role.[5]

The Carter Heyward Case

Perhaps the first feminist theologian to develop models of friendship as exemplary of the divine human encounter and mutuality as a norm for human behaviour was the American Episcopalian priest, Carter Heyward.[6] In 1993, she published a much more controversial book, *When Boundaries Betray Us: Beyond Illusions of What is Ethical in Therapy and Life*.[7] Though I think Heyward is wrong in her analysis of professional boundaries, she is wrong in interesting ways that will help to clarify the issue of friendship as a moral issue among clergy and other professionals.

Heyward's book tells the story of her relationship with her lesbian psychotherapist, whom she names Elisabeth Farro. (Farro refused to participate in the writing of the book) The therapy began in 1987 after which Heyward began to desire an erotic friendship with her. Farro interpreted this as therapeutic data and refused the repeated invitations. Heyward interpreted the refusal as a kind of deficiency. She claimed that Farro was trapped in the "patriarchal logic" of professionalism while Heyward was desiring the "erotic power of mutual relation." Within the year, Heyward decided she would terminate the therapy and insisted Farro participate in some closing rituals with her. Heyward then changed her mind about ending the therapy. The relationship resumed and Heyward began remembering instances of physical and sexual abuse from her childhood at the hands of her father and a hired hand. The therapy focussed on these memories. Heyward continued to insist on an intimate relationship with Farro although the therapist repeatedly refused.

In 1990, at the end of the therapy, Heyward began to doubt the reliability of her own memories and eventually concluded that they were an unconscious attempt to please her therapist. Heyward continued trying to establish a different kind of relationship with Farro, through almost continuous letter writing, but Farro refused. This refusal continued even after Heyward began sending her drafts of this book.

Although she did not rely on Macmurray in developing her position, Carter Heyward resembles him in her emphasis on friendship as a model of human behaviour and on mutuality as a moral norm. Her conclusion is that the distancing typical of professional therapeutic relationships is wrong insofar as it closes off the possibility of more fully human relations, of a relation between persons as persons, of friendship characterised by mutuality.

Carter Heyward does not stand alone in developing this approach either. Another example would be the American Catholic theologian Mary Hunt. Like Heyward, Hunt seeks the models for true friendship in the lives and friendships of women. This research yields the norms of community, honesty, non-exclusivity, flexibility, other-directedness, and mutuality. Such friendships do exist but they are hard to find. That is because in a heterosexist, patriarchal world women and men can not be equal. This is the nature of patriarchy. Thus a friendship which is characterised by mutuality is possible only when a man and a woman live in contradiction to the prevailing culture. Living in this state of contradiction, conscious of all its pressures, is usually more than most friendships can take.[8]

This is what Heyward was trying to find in her relationship with Farro. She had deliberately sought out a lesbian psychotherapist who, she thought, would understand her desire to live in a state of contradiction with the prevailing ethos of society. The following question naturally arises. Do we need the boundaries characteristic of a professional relationship or should we seek to overcome them?

Some argue for the former. For example, Joretta Marshall, writing in the *Journal of Pastoral Theology*, rejects the expectation for mutuality in every relationship. She suggests that what was ultimately destructive to herself and to the therapist was the denial of the opportunity to claim their sisterhood and mutual relatedness. I would contend that what was ultimately destructive was the lack of recognition that mutuality cannot be idealised in every relationship.[9]

Others are more direct. Marie Fortune argues that "Farro's refusal to join in this public discussion is a fulfilment of her professional responsibility." For Fortune, clear boundaries are a precondition of the safety which is required for real healing to take place.

Boundaries used appropriately create a safe place where an individual can reflect on her own experiences and learn from them without having to deal with the personal needs of the professional. Living without relational boundaries is like driving on the freeway in a snowstorm: very dangerous to all concerned.[10] Heyward interpreted Farro's refusal to move to mutuality as a form of abuse of her personhood. Fortune also rejects this claim. "In any case, the therapist was not cruel and abusive. She appears to have been trying to do her job."[11]

Kathleen Roberts Skerrett, in an impressively wide-ranging critique, goes so far as to reject the whole discourse of mutual relation as a kind of literary sleight of hand. She writes, "Under the guise of a feminist apologetics of mutual relation, Heyward has written an erotic complaint, in which the beloved's no can only incite redoubled assertiveness on the part of the lover."[12]

The Response from John Macmurray

So, while Heyward supports the development of what she calls "good, safe, empowering boundaries," she has presented rigid professional boundaries as a concept that needs to be overcome if we are to achieve real mutuality.

One of the reasons for wanting to overcome them is that they tend to protect the inequality inherent in the professional/client relationship. Would Macmurray say that inequality is an insurmountable barrier to mutuality, to friendship? Not according to Walter Jeffko. In his introduction to the reprint of Macmurray's *Conditions of Freedom*, Jeffko describes equality as being a central, constituent value in

Macmurray's view of friendship. "Equality means that friends treat or intend each other as equals despite whatever social, natural, or other *de facto* inequalities may exist between them."[13]

Perhaps a better distinction to be used here is Macmurray's distinction between a personal and an impersonal relationship. A friendship is an obvious example of a direct personal relationship. In a friendship, persons experience each other as persons. They are motivated not by self-interest but by mutual love. Friends share a common life. They form community together. In their experience of each other as persons, they experience communion.

An impersonal relationship is a relation in which persons are absent. That is, we treat individuals as if they were not persons. In a contract, when we stick to the letter of the contract, we exclude the personal. To the extent that the relationship between Carter Heyward and Elisabeth Farro is a contractual relationship, it is an impersonal one. This is clearly one of the important aspects to which Heyward was objecting. Ministers and congregations also exist in a contractual relationship. Would we be prepared to say that their relationship is then, primarily impersonal? I think not. It would be hard to imagine how anyone could encourage faith in a Gospel of love while operating only out of an impersonal relationship.

Perhaps we need one more Macmurrian concept—the concept of the positive and the negative relation. For Macmurray, a negative relation was not morally negative in the sense of being wrong, it was negative in the sense of being subordinate to the positive. In this sense, society was negative and community was positive because community implied society but society did not necessarily imply community. In this sense, friendship is a positive personal relationship which implies that impersonal relationships are negative. The meaning of this is that a friendship always carries with it some impersonal dimensions, but the reverse is not the case. An impersonal relationship may entail a friendship but not necessarily so. I have an impersonal relationship with the mechanic who fixes my car. The mechanic promises to fix whatever is wrong and I promise to pay. After many years of visiting my mechanic, we may develop a friendship, if we are both open to the possibility. But this is not obligatory. Stanley Harrison calls this "Macmurray's preferred formula for recognizing the essential unity of persons and at the same time doing justice to the complexity of their being."[14]

If we understand friendship as a positive personal relationship which always implies the impersonal dimension, then we have established the possibility for ministers to be friends with members of their congregations since the impersonal dimension must always be there. By constructing it in this way, we have avoided a dualistic separation between personal and impersonal relationships. But we have not yet answered the question as to how we manage the contradictions between the personal and impersonal dimensions.

We are all involved in various roles which shape our interactions. Dorothy Emmett was clear about this.[15] More recently David Fergusson has reminded us that Macmurray's distinction between personal and impersonal relationships is weakly developed. We need to know when it is appropriate to switch between a personal and an impersonal attitude.[16] The clergy interview subject with an earlier career as a nurse, raised these precise concerns in both a medical and a pastoral context.

It seems to me that one criterion we could use is that of "intending the personal well-being of self and other." When friendship is elaborated as a norm, this idea is expressed in the term mutual love. The criterion Thomas Aquinas used was to "do good and avoid evil." In the mixed role relationships such as the priest who is also a friend with the parishioner, the nurse who is a friend of the patient, and the oft-quoted teacher who is friendly with the student, the decision of the person with more power (authority or expertise) to switch roles could be governed by the criterion of "intending the personal well-being of self and other." The priest adopts and switches into role when their friend "drops a bomb" on the kitchen table. She does so because she intends the well-being of her friend.

The therapist may resist attempts to form an intimate relationship with a client either because she intends the well-being of the client or because she sincerely does not desire such an outcome and so intends the personal well-being of self. The teacher may jeopardise a potential friendship with a student by giving the student difficult feedback, but does so because he intends the student's eventual academic success and so, his personal well-being.

What about sexual misconduct and other boundary violations of this sort? Is the criterion useful in this case? I think that it can be. Sexual misconduct typically occurs either where the violation is forced or coerced – obviously not an example of intending the personal well-being of the other – or where one party assumes the intention is personal well-being when it is not. These are cases where we say "I've been taken advantage of." What we mean is, "I thought you were intending my well-being but I was deceived. I was not being treated as a person at all."

Roles carry with them authority and power, but these dimensions are sometimes more easily discerned from the outside than the inside. (The poor are never in doubt about who the rich are. Those who are rich could debate it without end.) For this reason, one more concept we need to consider is accountability. How can people in roles of authority and power, like ministers, tell when they are deceiving themselves about intending the personal well-being of the other? Macmurray talked about our capacity for objectivity in this way. Can we study behaviour as if from the outside? This is possible but also very difficult. It is a very high standard to meet. One of the strategies to assist us in this is the use of public or third party sources of accountability. For example, some ministers deal with the contradictions around money (wedding fees, for example) by insisting that the appropriate Church body develop a policy on how to treat such matters. This makes it a public matter, and by making it a matter of policy, provides a mechanism of accountability.

Conclusion

We have seen in this essay, that the question of friendship is a matter of serious moral concern for some people serving in ordained Christian ministry. We have also encountered one theologian (Carter Heyward) who argues that the moral norm of mutual relation means that no professional boundaries should be so rigid as to preclude the possibility of friendship. Finally we have seen that the thought of John Macmurray remains a fruitful resource for helping to resolve some of these dilemmas. His insistence on the freedom of mutual relation entails that a person does not have to be your friend. On the other hand, his analysis of the difference between positive personal relations and negative impersonal relations elucidates some of the tensions people experience in mixed role relationships. An extension of his thought, using the criteria of "intending the personal well-being of self and other" may provide some guidance in practising friendship.

NOTES

[1] Professor of Religious Ethics, University of Windsor, Windsor, Ontario.

[2] Clergy were selected from the Anglican Church of Canada and the United Church of Canada in Ontario and Sasketchewan. For this paper I reviewed the responses of 18 clergy from the two denominations in Saskatchewan. Of the 18, 9 identified friendship as a significant moral issue for clergy ethics. References are to the archive of data in the possession of the writer.

[3] Throughout this paper I use the terms minister, pastor and priest interchangeably to reflect the ecumenical character of this research.

[4] Chris A5r Text Units 25–121.

[5] Karen Lebacqz is particularly eloquent on this question. See her book written with Ron Barton, *Sex in the Parish*,

[6] See her *The Redemption of God: A Theology of Mutual Relation* (Lanham Md: University Press of America, 1982).

[7] (San Francisco: HarperSan Francisco, 1993).

[8] Mary E. Hunt, 'Lovingly Lesbian: Toward a Feminist Theology of Friendship,' in James B. Nelson & Sandra P. Longfellow (eds.), *Sexuality and the Sacred* (Louisville: Westminster/John Knox Press, 1994), 175.

[9] Joretta Marshall, 'Review of "When Boundaries Betray Us",' *Journal of Pastoral Theology*, 4 (1994), 122.

[10] Marie M. Fortune, 'Therapy and Intimacy: Confused about boundaries,' *Christian Century*, May 18–25 (1994), 525.

[11] Ibid., 524.

[12] Kathleen Roberts Skerrett, 'When No Means Yes: The Passion of Carter Heyward,' *Journal of Feminist Studies in Religion*, 12.1 (1996), 89.

[13] Walter G. Jeffko, Introduction to John Macmurray, *Conditions of Freedom* (Atlantic Highlands, NJ: Humanities Press, 1993) xviii.

[14] Stanley Harrison, Introduction to John Macmurray, *The Self as Agent* (Atlantic Highlands, NJ: Humanities Press, 1991), xviii.

[15] *Rules, Roles and Relations* (London: Macmillan, 1966) 171.

[16] *John Macmurray* (Edinburgh: Handsel Press, 1992), 22.

Compiled by Esther McIntosh

Works by John Macmurray (in chronological order)

Books

Freedom in the Modern World. London: Faber, 1932.
   Reissued with new introduction by Harry Carson, Atlantic Highlands: Humanities Press, 1992.
Interpreting the Universe. London: Faber, 1933. Reissued with new introduction by A.R.C. Duncan, Atlantic Highlands: Humanities Press, 1996
The Philosophy of Communism. London: Faber, 1933.
Creative Society: A Study of the Relation of Christianity to Communism. London: SCM Press, 1935.
Reason and Emotion. London: Faber, 1935.
   Reissued with new introduction by John E. Costello, Atlantic Highlands: Humanities Press, 1992 and London: Faber, 1995.
The Structure of Religious Experience. London: Faber, 1936.
The Clue to History. London: SCM Press, 1938.
The Boundaries of Science: A Study in the Philosophy of Psychology. London: Faber, 1939.
A Challenge to the Churches: Religion and Democracy. London: Kegan Paul, 1941.
Constructive Democracy. London: Faber, 1943.
The Conditions of Freedom. London: Faber, 1950.
   Reissued with new preface, Toronto: John Macmurray Society, 1977 and reissued with new introduction by Walter Jeffko, Atlantic Highlands: Humanities Press, 1993.
The Self as Agent—The Form of the Personal: volume 1. London: Faber, 1957.
   Reissued with new introduction by Stanley M. Harrison, Atlantic Highlands: Humanities Press, 1991 and London: Faber, 1995.
Persons in Relation—The Form of the Personal: volume 2. London: Faber, 1961.
   Reissued with new introduction by Frank G. Kirkpatrick, Atlantic Highlands: Humanities Press, 1991 and London: Faber, 1995.
Religion, Art and Science: A Study of the Reflective Activities in Man. Liverpool: Liverpool University Press, 1961. Reissued, Toronto: John Macmurray Society, 1986.

Search for Reality in Religion. London: Allen and Unwin, 1965. Reissued, London: Quaker Home Service, 1995.

Pamphlets

The Kingdom of Heaven. Oxford: Oxonian Press, 1929.
Today and Tomorrow: A Philosophy of Progress. London: BBC Publications, 1930.
Learning to Live. London: BBC Publications, 1931.
A Philosopher Looks at Psychotherapy. London: C. W. Daniel, Individual Medical Pamphlet 20, 1938.
Britain and Russia: The Future. London: National Peace Council, Peace Aims Pamphlet 12, 1942.
The Foundation of Economic Reconstruction. London: National Peace Council, Peace Aims Pamphlet 15, 1942.
Idealism Against Religion. London: The Lindsey Press, 1944.
Through Chaos to Community. London: National Peace Council, Peace Aims Pamphlet 24, 1944.
A Crisis of Culture: The USSR and the West. London: National Peace Council, Peace Aims Pamphlet 42, 1948.
Mental Health and Personal Relationship. Edinburgh: Scottish Association for Mental Health, 1956.
The Philosophy of Jesus. London: Friends Home Service, 1973.
Ye Are My Friends and *To Save From Fear*. London: Friends Home Service, 1979.

Contributions to Edited Works

'Beyond Knowledge,' in Burnett H. Streeter, ed., *Adventure: The Faith of Science and the Science of Faith*. London: Macmillan, 1927, 21–45.
'Objectivity in Religion,' in Burnett H. Streeter, ed., *Adventure: The Faith of Science and the Science of Faith*. London: Macmillan, 1927. 178–215.
'The Purpose of God in the Life of the World,' E. Shillito, ed., Liverpool: SCM Press, 1929.
'Introductory,' in J. Macmurray, ed., *Some Makers of the Modern Spirit* (London: Methuen, 1933), 37–44.
'The Modern Spirit: An Essay,' in J. Macmurray, ed., *Some Makers of the Modern Spirit*. London: Methuen, 1933, 1–36.
'From Aquinas to Newton,' in J. Macmurray, ed., *Some Makers of the Modern Spirit*. London: Methuen, 1933, 90–97.
'Summary,' in J. Macmurray, ed., *Some Makers of the Modern Spirit*. London: Methuen, 1933, 179–188.
'The Grith Fyrd Idea,' in J. Macmurray, ed., *The Grith Fyrd Idea*. Salisbury: The Order of Woodcraft Chivalry, 1933, 5–10.

'The Challenge of Communism,' in H. G. Wood and J. Macmurray, *Christianity and Communism*. London: The Industrial Christian Fellowship, 1934, 14–32.

'Dialectical Materialism as a Philosophy,' in H. Levy, ed., *Aspects of Dialectical Materialism*. London: Watts, 1934, 31–53.

'Christianity and Communism: Towards a Synthesis,' in J. Lewis, ed., *Christianity and the Social Revolution*. London: Gollancz, 1935, 505–526.

'The Early Development of Marx's Thought,' in J. Lewis, ed., *Christianity and the Social Revolution*. London: Gollancz, 1935, 209–236.

'The Nature and Function of Ideologies,' in J. M. Murry, ed., *Marxism*. London: Chapman and Hall, 1935, 59–75.

'The Nature of Philosophy,' in J. M. Murry, ed., *Marxism*. London: Chapman and Hall, 1935, 27–42.

'The New Materialism,' in J. M. Murry, ed., *Marxism*. London: Chapman and Hall, 1935, 43–58.

'Valuations in Fascist and Communist States,' in T. J. Marshall, ed., *Class Conflict and Social Stratification*. London: Le Play House Press, 1938, 180–191.

'The Christian Movement in Education,' in E. D. Laborde, ed., *Modern Problems in Education*. Cambridge: Cambridge University Press, 1939, 39–48.

'The Nature of Religion,' in J. Macmurray, *The Christian Answer to Fascism*. London: Christian Left, 1939, 5–7.

'The Nature of Christianity,' in J. Macmurray, *The Christian Answer to Fascism*. London: Christian Left, 1939, 7–12.

'Fascism and Christianity,' in J. Macmurray, *The Christian Answer to Fascism* London: Christian Left, 1939, 13–17.

'Gandhi's Faith and Influence,' in S. Radhakrishnan, ed., *Mahatma Gandhi: Essays and Reflections on his Life and Work*. London: Allen and Unwin, 1939, 174–176.

'Freedom in the Personal Nexus,' in R. N. Anshen, ed., *Freedom: Its Meaning*. New York: Harcourt, 1940, 176–193.

'Changes in Philosophy,' in J. R. M. Brumwell, ed., *This Changing World*. London: Routledge, 1944, 236–247.

'Religion in Transformation,' in J. R. M. Brumwell, ed., *This Changing World*. London: Routledge, 1944, 248–262.

'Isn't Christianity 'Played Out'?,' in R. S. Wright, ed., *Asking Them Questions*. Oxford: Oxford University Press, 1950, 204–211.

'Towards World Unity,' in J. Clark, ed., *The Student Seeks an Answer*. Waterville, Maine: Colby College Press, 1960, 309–327.

'What Makes an Experience Religious?,' in K. Barnes, ed., *Quakers Talk to Sixth Formers*. London: Friends Home Service, 1970, 53–58.

'What Religion Is About,' in K. Barnes, ed., *Quakers Talk to Sixth Formers* London: Friends Home Service, 1970, 47–52.

'Science and Objectivity,' in T. E. Wren, ed., *The Personal Universe: Essays in Honor of John Macmurray*. Atlantic Highlands, N.J.: Humanities Press, 1975, 7–23.

Articles

'Is Art a Form of Apprehension or a Form of Expression?,' *Proceedings of the Aristotelian Society*, supplement 5 (1925), 173–189.

'Christianity: Pagan or Scientific?,' *The Hibbert Journal*, 24 (1926), 421–433.

'The Function of Experiment in Knowledge,' *Proceedings of the Aristotelian Society*, 27 (1926), 193–212.

'The Influence of British Philosophy During Those Forty Years,' *British Weekly*, 81 (1926), 164–165.

'Economic Laws and Social Progress—part 1,' *The Auxiliary Movement*, 29 (1927), 117–118.

'Economic Laws and Social Progress—part 2,' *The Auxiliary Movement*, 29 (1927), 141–142.

'Government by the People,' *Journal of Philosophical Studies*, 2 (1927), 532–543.

'Time and Change,' *Proceedings of the Aristotelian Society*, suppl. 8 (1928), 143–161.

'What I Live By?,' *Student Movement*, 30 (1928), 199–200.

'The Principle of Personality in Experience,' *Proceedings of the Aristotelian Society*, 29 (1928–29), 316–320.

'Evangelical Reality,' *British Weekly*, 86 (1929), 315.

'The Limits of Interference Between Sovereign States,' *British Weekly*, 87 (1929), 283

'Our Relations with Russia,' *British Weekly*, 76 (1929), 127.

'The Unity of Modern Problems,' *Journal of Philosophical Studies*, 4 (1929), 162–179.

'Moral Problems of Today,' *The Expository Times*, 8 (1930), 24–26.

'The Conception of Society,' *Proceedings of the Aristotelian Society*, 31 (1930–31), 127–142.

'Can We Trust the Experts?,' *The Listener*, 6 (1931), 911–912.

'The Coming Election,' *British Weekly* (24th October 1931), 1686–1687.

'Coming to Grips with Democracy,' *The Listener*, 6 (1931), 963–964.

'How it Strikes a Contemporary: What are the Real Issues?' *British Weekly,* 91 (1931) 23

'Is a Democratic Culture Possible?,' *The Listener*, 6 (1931), 1064–1065.

'Is Education Necessary?,' *The Listener*, 6 (1931), 581.

'Living in Freedom,' *The Listener*, 6 (1931), 1149–1150.

'Training the Child to Live,' *The Listener*, 6 (1931), 990–992.

'Can Science See Us Through?,' *New Britain Quarterly*, 1 (1932), 6–12.

'What is Philosophy?,' *Proceedings of the Aristotelian Society*, suppl. 11 (1932) 48–67.

'Equality,' *New Britain Weekly*, 1 (1933), 135.

'Fascism?,' *New Britain Weekly*, 1 (1933), 70.

'Invitation to the Young Men and Women of Britain,' *New Britain Weekly*, 1 (1933), 5.

'The Significance of Religion,' *New Britain Weekly*, 1 (1933), 329.

'The Social Unit,' *New Britain Weekly*, 1 (1933), 235.

'Vox Collegii,' *University College Magazine*, 10 (1933), 74–77.

'What About Communism?,' *New Britain Weekly*, 1 (1933), 102.

'What to Do,' *New Britain Weekly*, 1 (1933), 37.

'Art Creates in Imagination, Religion Creates in Reality,' *The Student Movement*, 37 (1934), 28.

'Democracy in the Balance,' *The Listener*, 12 (1934), 692–693.

'Freedom is Power,' *The Listener*, 12 (1934), 650–651.

'Reason in Action,' *The Philosopher*, 12 (1934), 5–10.

'The Nature of Reason,' *Proceedings of the Aristotelian Society*, 35 (1934–35), 137–148.

'The Dualism of Mind and Matter,' *Philosophy*, 10 (1935), 264–278.

'Freedom and Authority in Relation to Power,' *The New Era*, 16 (1935), 18.

'Has Religion a Message for Today?,' *Reynolds Illustrated News* (24 Nov 1935), 2–4.

'Christianity and the Churches,' *News Sheet of the Auxiliary Christian Left*, 3 (1936) 3–4.

'Christianity: What We Mean and Do Not Mean,' *The Auxiliary Movement* (1937).

'The Religious Task of the Christian Left,' *Christian Left*, 7 (1937), 3–5.

'Vox Collegii,' *University College Magazine*, 15 (1937), 10–12.

'Do You Believe in Moral Progress?,' *The Listener*, 19 (1938), 418–419.

'A Philosopher's View of Modern Psychology,' *Lancet*, 234 (1938), 783–784.

'The Provisional Basis of the Christian Left,' *Christian Left*, 10 (1938), 3–6.

'What is Action?,' *Proceedings of the Aristotelian Society*, supplement 17 (1938), 69–85.

'The Philosophic Importance of the Idea of God,' *Plan*, 6 (1939), 3–7.

'Religion in the Modern World,' *Plan*, 6 (1939), 3–11.

'Russia & Finland: Should Soviet Action Be Condemned?' *Christian Left*, 18 (1940) 5–8.

'Socialism and Democracy,' *Christian Left*, 18 (1940), 1–5.

'Beyond Nationality,' *The Listener*, 25 (1941), 471–472

'Persons and Functions' —

    1. 'People and Their Jobs,' *The Listener*, 26 (1941), 759.

    2. 'Fellowship in a Common Life,' *The Listener*, 26 (1941), 787.

    3. 'Two Lives in One,' *The Listener*, 26 (1941), 822.

    4. 'The Community of Mankind,' *The Listener*, 26 (1941), 856.

'Religion in Russia,' *The Left News*, 65 (1941), 1903–1904.

'Socialism and Ethics,' *The Left News*, 59 (1941), 1725–1731.

'Knowledge for Use,' *The New Phineas: The Magazine of University College London* (Spring 1942), 15–16.

'Liberties in a Planned State,' *The Friend* (21 May 1943), 345–347.

'War to Peace,' *Industrial Welfare and Personnel Management* (Sep–Oct 1943), 146–150.

'The Functions of a University,' *The Political Quarterly*, 15 (1944), 277–285.

'The Importance of Voluntary Effort in Adult Education,' *Adult Education*, 20 (1947), 69–70.

'The Pattern of Our Time: A Philosophical Analysis,' *British Export Industrial Magazine for the Future*, 2 (1947), 85–94.

'Science in Religious Education,' *The School Science Review*, 32 (1950), 2–5.

'Concerning the History of Philosophy,' *Proceedings of the Aristotelian Society*, supplement 25 (1951), 1–24.

'Some Reflections on the Analysis of Language,' *Philosophical Quarterly*, 1 (1951), 319–337.

'The Philosopher's Business,' *University of Edinburgh Quarterly*, 15 (1952), 86–92.
'Prolegomena to a Christian Ethic,' *Scottish Journal of Theology*, 9 (1956), 1–13
'What is Religion About?'—
    1. 'The Salvation of the World,' *The Listener*, 56 (1956), 916–917.
    2. 'Friendship and Fear,' *The Listener*, 56 (1956), 984–985.
    3. 'The Celebration of Communion,' *The Listener*, 56 (1956), 1027–1028.
    4. 'The Universal Family,' *The Listener*, 56 (1956), 1073–1074.
'Developing Emotions,' *Saturday Review*, 41 (1958), 22 & 52.
'On Discoveries in Political Philosophy: A Conversation with John Macmurray,' *Northwest Review*, 2 (1958), 5–20.
'The Relation of the University to Its Local Community,' *University of Edinburgh Journal*, 19 (1959), 159–168.
'The Basis of Religious Life Today,' *The Seeker* (April 1961), 3–14.
'Nurses in an Expanded Health Service,' *The Nursing Mirror* (1964), 113–115, 135–137.
'Conditions of Marriage Today,' *Marriage Guidance*, 9 (1965), 379–385.
'The Idea of a University,' *The Times Educational Supplement* (4 December 1970), 2.

Selected Works on John Macmurray

Books

Conford, P., ed., *The Personal World: John Macmurray on Self and Society.* Edinburgh: Floris Books, 1996.
Duncan, A. R. C., *On the Nature of Persons.* New York: Peter Lang, 1990.

Pamphlets

Fergusson, David, *John Macmurray in a Nutshell.* Edinburgh: Handsel Press, 1992.
Warren, J., *Becoming Real: An Introduction to the Thought of John Macmurray.* York: Ebor Press, 1989.

Chapters

Aves, J., 'Persons in Relation: John Macmurray,' in C. Schwöbel, ed., *Persons, Divine and Human.* London: T&T Clark, 1992, pp. 120–137.
Daly, R. W., 'The Physician as Moral Agent,' in Engehardt and Spicker, eds., *Philosophical Medical Ethics: Its Nature and Significance.* Boston: D. Reidel, 1977, pp. 234–240.
Emmet, D., *Philosopher's and Friends.* London: Macmillan, 1996, pp. 50–61.

Fergusson, D. A. S., 'Towards a Theology of the Personal,' in P. McEnhill & G. B. Hall, eds., *The Presumption of Presence: Festschrift for D. W. D. Shaw*. Edinburgh: Scottish Academic Press, 1997, 105–118.

Guntrip, H., *Psychology for Ministers and Social Workers*. London: Allen and Unwin, 1971, 137–157.

Johann, R. O., 'Freedom and Morality from the Standpoint of Communication,' in R.O.Johann, ed., *Freedom and Value*. New York: Fordham University Press, 1970, 45–60.

Jones, J. W., *Religion and Psychology in Transition: Psychoanalysis, Feminism and Theology*. New Haven: Yale University Press, 1996, 24–94.

Kirkpatrick, F. G., *Community: A Trinity of Models*. Washington D.C.: Georgetown University, 1986, 137–220.

Rutenber, C. G., 'Macmurray's Metaphysics of Action: An Alternative,' in D.Y. Hadidian, ed., *From Faith to Faith: Essays in Honor of Donald G. Miller on his Seventieth Birthday*. Pittsburgh: The Pickwick Press, 1979, 403–417.

Articles

Barnes, K., 'Experience and Philosophy: My Friendship with John Macmurray,' *Appraisal*, 1 (1996), 55–56.

Blaikie, R. J., 'Being, Process and Action in Modern Philosophy and Theology,' *Scottish Journal of Theology*, 25 (1972), 129–154.

Bozzo, E. G., 'Mutuality and Normative Ethics,' *Thought*, 45 (1970), 521–541.

Brittan, S., 'Tony Blair's Real Guru,' *New Statesman* (7 February 1997), 18–20.

Calder, R., 'Macmurray – Man and Mind,' *Chapman*, 73 (1993), 72–80.

Cizewki, W., 'Friendship with God? Variations on a Theme in Aristotle, Aquinas and Macmurray,' *Philosophy and Theology*, 6 (1992), 369–381.

Conford, P., 'John Macmurray: A Neglected Philosopher,' *Radical Philosophy*, 16 (1977), 16–20.

Duncan, A.R.C., 'Macmurray's Religious Philosophy,' *Chapman*, 73 (1993), 82–89.

Duncan, A.R.C., 'The Metaphysics of the Personal,' *ITA Humanidades*, 9 (1973) 133–143

Ewens, T., 'Vocation of the Artist,' *Philosophy and Theology*, 6 (1992), 329–352.

Fergusson, David., 'Macmurray's Philosophy of the Family,' *Appraisal*, 1 (1996) 68–74.

Fink, P., 'The Challenge of God's Koinonia,' *Worship*, 59 (1985), 386–403.

Fink. P., 'Theoretical Structures for Liturgical Symbols,' *Liturgical Ministry*, 2 (1993), 125–137.

Florival, G., 'Affective Comprehension in the Philosophy of John Macmurray,' *Philosophy and Theology*, 6 (1992), 313–327.

Fox, D., 'Personal Logic and Christian Affirmation,' *The Journal of Bible and Religion*, 32 (1964), 326–333.

Fox, D. A., 'The Principle of Contra–Action,' *Faith and Philosophy*, 2 (1985), 168–174.

Gee, P., 'Beyond Buber: A Reassessment of Buber's Contribution to Psycho–therapeutic Thinking and an Introduction to the Thought of John Macmurray,' *Appraisal*, 1 (1996), 85–91.

Harrison, S. M., 'John Macmurray Centennial Conference,' *Philosophy and Theology*, 6 (1992), 297–403.

Harrison, S. M., 'The John Macmurray Centenary,' *Chapman*, 73 (1993), 69–71.

Higgs, P., 'John Macmurray's Philosophy of the Personal and the Resurrection of Theism,' *South African Journal of Philosophy*, 1 (1982), 147–153.

Hodgkin, R. A., 'Making Space for Meaning,' *Oxford Review of Education*, 23 (1997), 385–399.

Hoffman, J. C., 'Religion and Religious Experience in the Thought of John Macmurray: A Critique,' *Studies in Religion*, 4 (1974–75), 1–7.

Johann, R. O., 'The Return to Experience,' *Review of Metaphysics*, 17 (1964), 319–339.

Jung, H. Y., 'The Logic of the Personal: John Macmurray and the Ancient Hebrew View of Life,' *The Personalist*, 47 (1966), 532–546.

Kerr, W. O., 'Persons and the University: Confusion About Ends and Means,' *Religious Education*, 63 (1968), 283–286.

Kirkpatrick, F. G., 'The Logic of Mutual Heterocentrism: The Self as Gift,' *Philosophy and Theology*, 6 (1992), 353–368.

Kirkpatrick, F. G., 'Love and Power: What Does Macmurray's Notion of Community Have to Say to the 'Devices of Politics' in the Contemporary Political Order,' *Appraisal*, 1 (1996), 75–84.

Kirkpatrick, F. G., 'Toward a Metaphysic of Community,' *Scottish Journal of Theology*, 38 (1985), 565–581.

Kjaergaard, A., 'Action and the Person: Macmurray's Form of the Personal,' *Inquiry*, 13 (1970), 160–198.

Lam, E., 'Does Macmurray Understand Marx?,' *The Journal of Religion*, 20 (1940), 47–65.

Langford, T. A., 'The Natural Theology of John Macmurray,' *Canadian Journal of Theology*, 12 (1966), 9–20.

Largo, G. A., 'Two Prophetic Voices: Macmurray and Buber,' *America* (1973), 83–286.

Lauder, R. E., 'Macmurray's World Community as Antidote to Kant's Theism,' *Sophia*, 31 (1992), 28–38.

Lind, C., 'John Macmurray and Contextual Theology,' *Philosophy and Theology*, 6 (1992), 383–400.

Long, E. T., 'Persons, Law and Society,' *Proceedings of the American Catholic Philosophical Association*, 49 (1975), 125–137.

Mooney, P., 'Macmurray's Notion of Love for Personal Knowing,' *Appraisal*, 1 (1996), 57–67.

Morrissey, M. P., 'Reason and Emotion: Modern and Classical Views on Religious Knowing,' *Horizons*, 16 (1989), 275–291.

Muir, K., 'Makers of Modern Thought,' *Student Movement*, 40 (1937), 61–62.

O'Connor, D. D., 'John Macmurray: Primacy of the Personal,' *International Philosophical Quarterly*, 4 (1964), 464–484.

Roy, L., 'Interpersonal Knowledge According to John Macmurray,' *Modern Theology*, 5 (1989), 349–365.

Schutte, A., 'Indwelling, Intersubjectivity and God,' *Scottish Journal of Theology*, 32 (1979), 201–216.

Schutte, A., 'What Makes Us Persons?,' *Modern Theology*, 1 (1984), 67–79.

Shinn, R., 'The Relation of Religion to Democracy and Communism in the Writings of John Macmurray,' *Review of Religion*, 12 (1947–48), 204–215.

White, L. J., 'John Macmurray: Theology as Philosophy,' *Scottish Journal of Theology*, 26 (1973), 449–465.

NOTES ON CONTRIBUTORS

Brenda Almond is Professor of Moral and Social Philosophy at the University of Hull and the author of a number of books including *Exploring Philosophy: the Philosophical Quest*, and *Exploring Ethics: a Traveller's Tale*. As Brenda Cohen, she also wrote several books on education, including *Education and the Individual* and *Means and Ends in Education*. She holds an Honorary Doctorate from the University of Utrecht and was elected to the Austrian Academy of Sciences.

Andrew Collier is Professor of Philosophy at Southampton University. His most recent book is *Being and Worth* (2000). His current research interests include critical realism and its use in the philosophical understanding of Christianity and Marxism.

Jack Costello SJ is a faculty member at Regis College, the Jesuit college in the Toronto School of Theology at the University of Toronto. He is Director of the Jesuit Centre for Faith and Justice in Toronto. His biography of John Macmurray is due for publication in 2001. He is currently editing for publication two volumes of previously unpublished essays by John Macmurray.

Nigel Dower is Senior Lecturer in Philosophy and Director of the Centre for Philosophy, Technology and Society at the University of Aberdeen. He is the author of *World Poverty: Challenge and Response* (1983), *World Ethics: The New Agenda* (1998) and numerous papers on the ethics of international relations, the environment and development. He also serves as vice-chair of the International Development Ethics Association and is currently writing a book on global citizenship.

Robin Downie is Professor of Moral Philosophy at the University of Glasgow. He has published books in areas of interest to Macmurray scholars, such as (jointly) *Respect for Persons*, which was actually reviewed by Macmurray, and *Roles and Values*. More recently he has published extensively on the philosophy of medicine and the Scottish Enlightenment (Francis Hutcheson, *Philosophical Writings*, 1994).

David Fergusson is Professor of Divinity at the University of Edinburgh. He formerly held the Chair of Systematic Theology in the University of Aberdeen. His publications include *John Macmurray* (1992) and *Community, Liberalism and Christian Ethics* (1998). He delivered the Bampton lectures at the University of Oxford in 2001.

Michael Fielding is Reader in Education at the University of Sussex Institute of Education. He has recently guest edited a special issue of the Journal of Education Policy in which the editorial article 'Education Policy & the Challenge of Living Philosophy' and his own contribution 'Community, Philosophy & Education Policy' rest substantially on an articulation and extension of Macmurray's work on the nature of community.

Stanley Harrison is Associate Professor of Philosophy at Marquette University in Milwaukee, Wisconsin. He wrote the Introduction to the *Self as Agent* (Humanities Press, 1991) and edited a special edition of *Philosophy and Theology* devoted to John Macmurray (Vol.VI, No. 4, Summer, 1992). He has been introducing the thought of Macmurray to undergraduates for over twenty years.

Hwa Yol Jung teaches political theory at Moravian College, Bethlehem, Pennsylvannia. References to Macmurray are found in his subsequent publications: *The Crisis of Political Understanding* (1979) and *Rethinking Political Theory* (1993). He is currently writing *Mikhail Bakhtin and the Making of Body Politics* for Rowman and Littlefield's series on 'Twentieth Century Political Thinkers.'

Frank G. Kirkpatrick is Ellsworth Morton Tracy Lecturer and Professor of Religion in the Religion Department of Trinity College, Hartford, Connecticut, where he has taught since 1969. He is the author of numerous articles on religious epistemology, the philosophy of religion, and religion in American society. His published books include *Community: A Trinity of Models* (Georgetown, 1986), *Together Bound: God, History, and the Religious Community* (Oxford, 1994), and *The Ethics of Community* (Oxford, 2001). He did a doctoral dissertation on John Macmurray's concept of God at Brown University in 1970 and has been involved in various associations and scholarly projects dealing with the thought of Macmurray since that time.

Amy Limpitlaw recently received her Ph.D. from the University of Chicago's Divinity School. Her thesis was entitled 'The Kingdom of God as a Unity of Persons: Teilhard de Chardin's Organic Model and John Macmurray's Form of the Personal'. She is currently employed as an academic librarian by the Boston Athenaeum, and continues her scholarly interests in philosophical theology, mystical theology and the relationship between religion and science.

Christopher Lind currently serves as President of St. Andrew's College, Saskatoon and St. Stephen's College, Edmonton, Canada. He earned his Doctorate in Theology from the University of St. Michael's College, Toronto, specializing in Ethics and Economics. His most recent book is *Something's Wrong Somewhere: Globalization, Community and the Moral Economy of the Farm Crisis*, (Halifax, 1995)

Esther McIntosh is a lecturer in the Department of Theology and Religious Studies at the University of Leeds. She completed her doctoral thesis on Macmurray at the University of Aberdeen. Her continued research is mainly on the nature of the person and the ethics of personal relations, within philosophical theology.

Susan Parsons is Director of Pastoral Studies at the Margaret Beaufort Institute of Theology in Cambridge. She is the author of *Feminism and Christian Ethics* (1996) and of *The Ethics of Gender* (forthcoming), and the editor of *Challenging Women's Orthodoxies in the Context of Faith* (Ashgate, 2000) and of the *Cambridge Companion to Feminist Theology* (forthcoming).

Iain Torrance is Professor in Patristics and Christian Ethics and Dean of the Faculty of Arts & Divinity at the University of Aberdeen. He is working on a new translation and introduction to the *Didaskalia Apostolorum*. He previously taught at the University of Birmingham, and was a minister of the Church of Scotland in the Shetland Islands. He has been editor of Scottish Journal of Theology since 1982.

Colwyn Trevarthen is Professor (Emeritus) of Child Psychology and Psychobiology at the University of Edinburgh. He has published in brain science and intersubjectivity in infancy, and is interested in the scientific and philosophical implications of innate human motives and interpersonal sympathy, especially ways in which the rhythms and emotions of children's play and imagination support cultural learning and furnish the interpersonal foundations of language. He holds an honorary doctorate in psychology from the University of Crete and he is a Fellow of the Royal Society of Edinburgh and a Member of the Norwegian Academy of Sciences and Letters.

John Swinton is currently a senior lecturer in Practical Theology at the University of Aberdeen. Prior to entering academia he worked as a nurse and a hospital chaplain, specializing within the areas of psychiatry and learning disability. He is currently the editor of the UK's leading journal of pastoral theology: *Contact: the interdisciplinary journal of pastoral studies*. Recent publications include *From Bedlam to Shalom: Towards a Practical Theology of Human Nature, Interpersonal Relationships and Mental Health Care* (2000) and *Resurrecting the Person: A New Model of Care for People With Severe Mental Health Problems* (2000).

INDEX

A

Adorno, Theodore, 18
Agency, 36ff., 44ff., 141ff., 242ff.
Alexander, Samuel, 11, 27
Aquinas, Thomas, 14, 54, 61, 62–67
Arendt, Hannah, 177, 180f.
Aristotle, 13, 54, 63, 64f., 67, 71, 122,
    125, 137, 146, 155, 210f., 224
Asperen, Trudy van, 229f., 232
Augustine, 150f., 249
Ayer, A. J., 49, 159, 218

B

Bacon, Francis, 18
Baillie, J. B., 14
Barnes, Kenneth, 17, 24, 25, 29, 30, 32,
    33
Bateson, Mary Catherine, 82, 99
BBC, 18, 21
Bedford, Errol, 25
Bentham, Jeremy, 12
Blackston, William, 184
Blair, Tony, 109f., 164, 212
Block, Martin, 18
Bok, Sissela, 235
Born, Max, 27, 81
Bosanquet, Bernard, 12, 14
Bowlby, J., 100
Bradley, F. H., 14
Bråten, S., 91
Brazelton, T. Berry, 82
Broadie, Frederick, 25, 29
Brunner, Jerome, 82
Buber, Martin, 27, 101, 128ff., 150,
    174
Buddhism, 39
Bullowa, Margaret, 83

Burnaby, John, 249

C

Caird, Edward, 14
Cairns, David S., 9
Cairns, David, 15
Campbell, Duncan and Jocelyn, 32
Christian Left, 17, 20, 30
Christianity, 16, 38, 73, 160, 256ff.
Clausewitz, Karl von, 172
Coates, Joseph, 17
Cole, G. D. H., 17
Comenius, 97f.
Communism, 32, 38, 72ff., 160
Communitarianism, 193ff., 210
Community, 38, 46–48, 122f., 128,
    162, 190, 209ff., 223ff.,
Confucian ethics, 179
Copernicus, N., 176
Costello, Jack, 145
Crick, Bernard, 220
Cripps, Stafford, 21
Crossman, Richard, 15, 18
Cyril of Alexandria, 237

D

Downie, Robin, 224
Dominion, Jack, 234
Durkheim, E., 12
Dawes-Hicks, 13
Descartes, R., 13, 43, 52, 54, 82, 133,
    141, 174f., 184, 241
Durbin, Evans, 15
Duncan, A. R. C., 25
Davie, George, 25f., 50
Dewey, John, 27